HENRY MILLER

HAPPY ROCK

BRASSAÏ

HENRY MILLER
HAPPY ROCK

TRANSLATED BY JANE MARIE TODD

University of Chicago Press / Chicago / London

Brassaï (born Gyula Halász, 1899–1984) was a photographer, journalist, and author of many photographic monographs and literary works, including *Brassaï: Letters to My Parents, Conversations with Picasso,* and *Proust in the Power of Photography.* Jane Marie Todd has translated a number of books, including *Conversations with Picasso* by Brassaï, *Largesse* by Jean Starobinski, and *The Forbidden Image* by Alain Besançon.

The University of Chicago Press, Chicago 60637
The University of Chicago Press, Ltd., London
© 2002 by The University of Chicago
Originally published as *Henry Miller, rocher heureux,* by Brassaï, © Éditions Gallimard, 1978
All rights reserved. Published 2002
Printed in the United States of America

11 10 09 08 07 06 05 04 03 02   1 2 3 4 5

ISBN: 0-226-07139-1 (cloth)

Library of Congress Cataloging-in-Publication Data

Brassaï, 1899–
    [Henry Miller, rocher heureux. English]
    Henry Miller, happy rock / by Brassaï; translated by Jane Marie Todd.
        p.   cm.
Includes index.
    ISBN 0-226-07139-1 (cloth : alk. paper)
    1. Miller, Henry, 1891–   2. Miller, Henry, 1891– ——Friends and associates.   3. Authors, American—20th century—Biography.   4. Brassaï, 1899– ——Friends and associates.
    I. Title.
    PS3525.I5454 Z65813 2002
    818′.5209—dc21
                                                                    2002004770

CONTENTS

Author's Note: In summer 1969, Henry Miller read this manuscript and returned it to me with numerous annotations, which I added to this book. Since then, however, several chapters have been expanded, and I also added the chapter on our last meeting in Los Angeles, which Miller did not read. His annotations, therefore, do not cover the entire volume.

Editor's Note: The present work is the sequel to *Henry Miller grandeur nature* by the same author, published by Editions Gallimard in November 1975.

CHAPTER 1

Spring 1953

Immediate and profound disappointment on Miller's part upon his return from Greece. The American coast seemed gloomy, inhospitable to him; Boston, his first stop, was "ugly in a sinister way." From the very beginning, the happiness he had felt in Greece evaporated. After the marvelous apogee, he was now plunged once more into the dark depression of his youth. "I returned to New York the way Rimbaud returned to Marseilles from Abyssinia, exhausted and ill."

He began to write *The Colossus of Maroussi*, probably his best book. But he met with rejection from publishers. Three years earlier, Durrell had prophesied, a bit naively, that once Miller's books were published in the United States, they "would shake the national psyche to the roots with a thousand-volt shock." But no one was interested in him, and the public at large did not know his name. Even six years later, he would bitterly observe that no American publisher had the courage to publish him. It was then that, to get to know America better, he undertook a cross-country trip. Nevertheless, after Doubleday and Co., which had given him a small advance for his travel narrative, read the manuscript, it decided not to publish it. It was not the joyful book expected, but *The Air-conditioned Nightmare*, a violent diatribe against the American way of life.

After two years of disappointments in New York, Miller moved to Los Angeles. He was taken in by friends and would spend two years at the "Green House" in Beverly Glen, near Hollywood. "Everyone comes here to sell his soul. It's terrible. Young and old, Americans and foreigners. No one thinks of resisting. Get dough, that's all." He too would have liked to "sell his soul" to get by, but no one was interested. All the articles and screenplays he proposed were rejected. More penniless than ever, he often had to *walk* from Beverly Glen to Hollywood, about six miles. "I have never seen anybody walking along the road. It looks like an expedition to Alaska." Despair and poverty. Beverly Glen would be one of his most humiliating "hells." His letters became increasingly heartrending. "I am sick and disgusted with being a burden." He dreamed of his solitude in Greece: "To live at the most rudimentary level, without thinking about earning money. . . . I will go straight to the bled, where there are nothing but ignorant and admirable people. If I had a cabin on a hill, I think I'd become a hermit."

In Los Angeles in 1943, he met Jean Varda, a Greek painter living in Monterey, who one day took him to the most wild, uninhabited place on the California coast: Big Sur. And it was love at first sight! In 1944, Henry moved there. The influence of Jean Giono's books undoubtedly played a role in that decision. The author of *Le poids du ciel* (The weight of the sky) taught him to live between earth and sky, to observe the stars. Had it not been for Giono, would that child of Brooklyn, that city boy, have dreamed of the seasons, of wild animals, winds, forests, the ocean, the "song of the world"? In Big Sur, Henry was reminded of both Tibet and of Manosque, France, "two places that abolish space and time."

In fact, his life as a "hermit" was entirely relative: he shared his solitude with a very young Polish woman, Janina M. Lepska, whom he had just married. And, like Robinson Crusoe, he wanted to transform the jungle into a paradise. The old dream of the American pioneers of yore: clear vast areas of land, plant fruit trees, a vegetable garden, raise cattle, chickens, rabbits, peacocks. Henry rises at dawn, works the land with his callused hands. After escaping the poverty of Los Angeles, he becomes the slave of his cabin, his land, his garden, then of the two children who are born there.

During his stay in Greece in 1939, where he was starting a new life for himself as Europe was burning, Miller thought: "And far from France! As for me I am so far from France in heart and soul, that it seems almost as if the ten years I spent there were lived on another planet, in another incarnation. I seem to be through with it for good" (letter to Anaïs Nin, 1939).[1] But he had hardly set foot back in America when he was again struck by homesickness for France, with even greater force now that France lay crushed, occupied, defeated. And, as in earlier times, when Paris was as yet only a magical name for him, he spread the metro map out on the floor and began to mutter the litany of streets: rue de la Gaîté, rue Mouffetard, Vavin, Raspail, Denfert-Rochereau, Montparnasse . . .

No one writes about France with so much love, warmth, and understanding as Miller in his tender moments. It's all there: good food, good wine, good conversation, good artists and writers, good spots to visit, and also Frenchwomen, admirable for their innate goodness, their easy virtue, their heroism, their wit, their charm, their keen intelligence, the French soul in its entirety. Nowhere else in the Western world, thinks Miller, has the *spiritual* aspect of man been so totally acknowledged and generously developed. At a time when the American public considered France virtually erased from the world map, he wrote: "What is French is imperishable. France has transcended her physical being. . . . As long as one Frenchman survives all France will remain visible and recognizable. It does not matter what her position, as a world power, may be" (*Remember to Remember*).[2] And, in a chapter of *The Air-conditioned Nightmare* titled "Vive la France," he added: "France . . . dead? What an abominable lie! France prostrate and defeated is more alive than we have ever been" (p. 50).[3]

During his long trip through the monotony and uniformity of America, what is he seeking to discover? That "something" that reminds him of France: a little life, a little leisure, a little real conversation, a little decent food, a glass of good wine, the time to forget. But also: a road lined with trees, a street where you can stroll, as in Charleston or the French Quarter in New Orleans; a place where you can relax, as in New Iberia, under the Spanish moss. Some landscapes remind him of Dordogne: "But," he asks, "where was . . . the marriage of heaven and earth, the superstructure which man rears in order to make of natural beauty something profound and lasting?" (*The Air-conditioned Nightmare*, p. 68).

When France was liberated, he felt a certain desire to return there. But "with the prospect of imminent war," he wrote me, "I doubt I can come this year. In addition, my wife is expecting a baby" (letter to Brassaï, April 4, 1948). "I still hope to come to Paris with the family. But, to do so, I have to increase my royalties. Next year perhaps. It's been *ten years* this month since I left Paris. Incredible!" (letter to Brassaï, June 17, 1949). And, three years later: "Greetings to you and all my friends there. I'll be back some day" (letter to Brassaï, March 12, 1952). Despite his yearning, Miller would for twelve years resist every temptation to return to France; the other reason was that he wanted to complete his autobiographical novel in the solitude of Big Sur. But in 1952, three things weakened his resistance. In the first place, a young and beautiful woman had recently come into his life and he was always proud and eager to show off a new conquest to the world. Second, a fantastic check fell from the sky. Third, a mysterious record arrived from London. When the record player began to play, the voices of Lawrence Durrell and Fred Perlès came out. "What a message!" he wrote to Fred. "I laughed and I cried! Never had I felt so happy, nor so alone and melancholy. When you started speaking French, the robust and vulgar street slang of old pals and even of the one-legged whore of Montmartre, I almost had an attack. The effect it had on me was like champagne and caviar, and was diabolical on top of everything! Never had Paris been at once so close and so far away" (*Aller Retour New York*).[4] Overwhelmed, Miller decided to return to France.

In the meantime, his married life had been through some profound changes. In the grandiose setting and solitude of Big Sur, arguments and fights between Miller and his young wife had become a daily affair. It was truly the war between the sexes, Strindberg's *Dance of Death*, as June had predicted. "This has been a year of total accomplishment," Henry announced in May 1944. "Everything succeeded—*except love*. I'll be damned if I'm telling a lie. I have worse luck in that area than I could ever have imagined. I am, so to speak, *out of action* at the moment. *Everything ends in disaster!*" Seven years later, the mutual destruction between the two spouses reached its paroxysm: one or the other of them would have to flee that conjugal hell. It was Lepska. After a final violent scene, she abruptly left home, leaving her husband alone with his two small children, Valentine and Tony. Henry was in despair: "Haven't been able to write you because I've just been through another crisis—Lepska has decamped. I am to keep the children. . . . I pray every day now that Providence will send me the woman I need for my children" (letter to Lawrence Durrell, October 22, 1951).[5]

Five months later, Henry's prayers were answered. A young woman, the sister-in-law of a painter friend living in the area, on learning of his distress, came of her own accord to deliver him from household chores. That is how Eve McClure entered his life. She was a seductive creature, as intelligent as she was beautiful—the stature of a queen, a pearly complexion, green eyes—and he would soon marry her. From one day to the next, Henry's letters changed in tone: "I went through seven painful years because of my wife. All that is really over now. Everything is starting to look good for me in every way. And miracle of miracles! I have just found a young woman—twenty-eight years old—beautiful, sweet, full of understanding, and—another miracle!—she adores me. So I'm coming back to life at a feverish pace! And it's entirely possible I'll soon come to Paris with her. I'll have the means, a choice of houses, castles, lodgings of every kind at my disposal—everywhere in Europe" (letter to Brassaï, April 7, 1952). Two weeks later, he wrote: "I am seriously beginning to think of going abroad next September, to visit or travel for a few months. My life has suddenly changed—for the better. For the moment, everything is going like 'clockwork.' I have found an adorable woman. I will have my children home with me the whole summer. I am happy—completely happy" (letter to Brassaï, April 15, 1952). He also informed Durrell of his unexpected happiness: "Every day I congratulate myself on my great good fortune. . . . It's just unbelievable what a change she has wrought in me. It's like living on velour, to be with her. . . . I haven't lost my temper once, nor been grouchy or irritated or depressed" (letter to Durrell, April 27, 1952).[6] And when Larry announced that his wife had ditched him, leaving him with an infant on his hands, Miller responded as an "expert" in the matter: "Know how you must feel. It's all a frightful ordeal!" And he advised him to live by himself for awhile, as he had done: "You will soon find that you are better off. . . . Take your time about finding another mate. Let her find you. Don't get frantic!" (letter to Durrell, May 1, 1956).[7]

At sixty-two years old, free from material cares for the first time in his life, Miller would give in to the euphoria of success and of his belated renown, happy to see his old and new friends again. As for Eve, who was a gifted painter and had never been to Europe, this trip would be a delight. But would Henry rediscover the world he had known and loved? "I steeled myself against the most terrible disappointments. How can you rescue from oblivion an image when you know in your heart it does not really exist?"

After arriving in a snowstorm on December 31, 1953, the Millers would stay in Europe for eight months. At first, they were the guests of Maurice Nadeau, the literary critic, and his wife, Marthe; in 1946 Maurice had created a committee to defend Miller's books from censorship. The Millers would then spend two weeks in Le Vésinet, at the home of Edmond Buchet, the publisher of *The World of Sex* and *Sexus*, which was banned. *Plexus*, the second book in the trilogy, was supposed to come out on January 15. But during that harsh winter Henry caught a bad flu. He had to stay in bed for a week. "I had never known such a cold winter in Paris. I thought I'd never see the sun again." His host complained of his recalcitrant patient, who turned away doctors, thermometers, medication. The book signing for *Plexus*, delayed by a week, was tumultuous: it was Miller's first public appearance in Paris.

After a short stay in Monte Carlo with Eve, whose simplicity and kindness won over all Henry's friends from the start, he was eager to get in touch with Michel Simon, his "incomparable brother," who had invited them to his property, "La Ciotat," near Marseilles. What Henry liked was not so much the great actor who had left the mark of his genius in several theatrical and film roles, but rather the odd fellow, a regular at the brothels and in the shady world located around Porte Saint-Martin, and also the collector who, over the space of half a century, had assembled the richest museum of erotica in the world, more than thirteen thousand pictures and objects: Chinese, Japanese, Persian, Hindu; miniatures, fans, snuffboxes.

In late March, Eve and Henry again find themselves in Le Vésinet. Their host takes them to see the painter Vlaminck. But Miller's great desire is to meet Utrillo, who lives in the neighborhood. One day, he remembers, when he was completely broke, he sat on a public bench and read Francis Carco's book on the painter of Paris streets. "It was raining and I was crying." But Utrillo's physical deterioration is such that no one can see him. Henry is content to stand in front of the gate to the painter's bungalow and meditate.

After a reception in his honor at the home of Blaise Cendrars and a visit to Chambord and the châteaux of the Loire Valley, the Millers leave for Languedoc to spend a few days with Joseph Delteil and his wife, Caroline, an American originally from Chicago, one of the four Dudley sisters, part of a curious family devoted to the arts and letters. One of them, Mrs. Harvey, was a literary critic, another the partner of Bertrand Russell, and the fourth, Katherine, an old friend of Picasso's. Caroline had come to Paris as the manager of the Revue Nègre de Harlem starring Josephine Baker. It was her great wish to get to know Joseph Delteil. "If you want to earn his trust, madam," her publisher told her, "order a cask of his 'sparkling wine.' That will flatter him more than if you asked him to autograph a book. He's more proud of producing a good wine than of producing a good book." "That's just what I did," Caroline told us with a laugh, "and I earned his trust so completely that we never parted ways again." In fact, she became Mme Delteil. Henry admired Delteil, a former surrealist, famous at twenty-five—his *Joan of Arc* won the Prix Femina in 1925—who preferred retirement in the countryside to a literary career. Far from the noise of the world, he wrote some thirty vehement, heated books, filled with torrents of images. From the start, Miller felt a great affinity for him: did not he too have the desire to "regress, regress," back to the innocence of childhood? A few years later, noticing Gilberte holding *Saint Francis of Assisi* in her hands, he exclaimed: "That little book is a pure masterpiece! Delteil writes the richest, the most delicious French. What a vocabulary! His *Saint Francis* moved me deeply. Everything his saint says and thinks about poverty is an expression of my own thoughts: get rid of every encumbrance that limits and chains our freedom. Like the great Buddha:

when he understood the role that had fallen to him, he stripped himself of all his possessions, left his wife, his son, and then he too went out on the road with a beggar's bowl in his hand." In the same way, Delteil saw Miller not as a "man of letters" but as a primitive or even "Paleolithic" man, lost in our civilization.

On the terrace of the Tuilerie de Massan near Montpellier, on the Delteil property, where the author of *Cholera* had lived in seclusion since 1936, Delteil opened many bottles of his "sparkling wine," treating all his Languedoc friends, who had flocked there to hail Miller. Oddly, the infatuation of young people in France for the author of the two *Tropics* manifested itself in Languedoc particularly. One of the younger writers, F.-J. Temple of Montpellier, was carrying on a correspondence with Miller and had written an essay on his *Black Spring*. Henry welcomed him with open arms: "My uncle from America stood there," Temple recounts, "tanned, with blue, inquisitive eyes, his pants held up with a magnificent Hopi or Navaho belt, telling me that one day the Indians would again rule America."

But Henry was anxious to question Dr. Fontbrune, a brilliant exegete of Nostradamus in Sarlat, on the famous *Centuries*. Curiously, it was in that very city that, in 1939, a bookseller had given him a book on Nostradamus. In 1961, when Henry again passed through Montpellier, F.-J. Temple would have a surprise for him: at the medical school, in the "book of records," he would show him the signature of Nostradamus and also that of an author revered for his humor: François Rabelais! It was in Montpellier that he had studied medicine. The red gown Rabelais had worn would also be brought out for Henry, and he would put it on with "childish emotion and grave happiness." Ten years later, he told me: "I am writing something on Nostradamus. When I went to Salon to see his house, it looked abandoned, in ruins. Is that possible? What's the reason behind that neglect? The most illustrious person in all of France! In Saint-Rémy-de-Provence, the door was locked—on two occasions—when I tried to visit his house" (letter to Brassaï, November 25, 1964).

In the summer of 1950, Jean-Michel Hornus, the Protestant minister of a small parish in Le Gard and another fan in the Languedoc cult of Miller, crossed the ocean and all of North America to meet his god. After a great deal of hitchhiking with a pack on his back, and of walking in the California sun, he took the cornice road from Los Angeles to San Francisco, climbed the paths that twisted alongside the cliffs of Big Sur. He finally arrived on June 5. The Millers welcomed him with open arms. Although Americans had to "turn tail," the French were always welcome. "Every time a French visitor arrives," wrote Henry, "something starts to sing deep within me. He's like a living specimen of everything I learned to appreciate about the French way of life. It's as if he had waved a magic wand and brought back to life everything I cherished for the ten years I spent in France" (*Big Sur*).[8]

Hornus would recount this journey and this encounter in a Christian student review under the title "J'ai rencontré un coeur pur" (I met a pure heart). Praise of the devil in a religious publication caused a real storm. Hornus was attacked for his "scandalous and immoral sympathies for Miller." He defended himself: he believes that, for the author of *Tropics*, the way of the flesh is only a roundabout way to the great mystic road, which he wants to free from sexuality. He believes the writer is a prophet preaching for a "gradual conversion of *material* Eros into *spiritual* Eros, of carnal lust into spiritual lust." And he quotes a Protestant writer: "We are penetrating where hell itself is depicted, where evil celebrates its black masses, and we do not substitute critical examination for prudish silence or anathema. For everything belongs to God, even his servant, Satan." Henry thanks Hornus, but protests: he has no intention of liberating himself from his sexual pursuits. And he rebels against the idea that, in "evolving," he has taken a "moral" turn: "Morality is not in my line of sight. . . . I think that, unconsciously, my chief model was Goethe. . . . Don't take me for a good Christian or a moralist or a repentant sinner, but for a man like any other, who seeks the truth and possesses an unshakable and inexhaustible, but indefinable faith."

After a visit to the prehistoric caves in Dordogne on May 10, in the company of the Delteils, Eve and Henry leave for Catalonia. As early as 1930, Henry had thought: "To go to Spain, what a dream!" Another attraction of the trip: in Barcelona, he is to meet Fred Perlès, whom he has not seen in fifteen years! And, as I have already said, that meeting unleashed contagious laughter, which shook the Millers and the Delteils throughout the Spain trip. Henry and Eve would then spend a month in Vienne, in the department of Isère, at the home of another Miller fan, André Maillet, "one of the most faithful and interesting of them." To meet his idol, in August 1950—two months after Hornus—Maillet too made a pilgrimage to Big Sur, where he arrived after many adventures. That young writer also saw him as a new Christ and, in his youthful ardor, wrote a book titled *Henry Miller surhomme et poète* (Henry Miller, superman and poet). Maillet, who was also attacked for praising the author of *Sexus*, made amends. "Afterward, I was a little sorry about the term 'superman,' which also bothered Miller and prompted him to say, 'You make me blush.' I have gotten past the stage where, having discovered him, I was almost bewitched."

In Vienne, Henry met the erudite subprefect Fernand Rude, who owned a remarkable collection of utopian books and was the author of *Voyage to Icaria*, the adventure of two workers from Vienne who, in the middle of the nineteenth century, left for America to join Etienne Cabet's experimental colony in Nauvoo, Illinois. Henry also met another curious character, a friend and former secretary of Anatole France, Dr. P.-L. Couchoud, author of a Life of Jesus and of *The Mystery of Jesus*. But he would especially remember the Pantagruelian banquet offered in his honor by M. and Mme Point at the famous Pyramid restaurant in Vienne, an obligatory gastronomic stop on any tour of the Midi. He would always speak with emotion of that "feast for body and spirit."

Late June found the Millers in a suburb of Brussels, Woluwe-Saint-Lambert, where they were the guests of Hélène and Pierre Lesdain, a Belgian writer with whom he kept up a regular correspondence. They visited Bruges-la-Morte—"a memorable event"—and the cathedral of Gent and its famous triptych, *The Mystic Lambs*, by the Van Eyck brothers. And the most intense memory: a visit to the abbey of Groenendaal, near Waterloo, where the admirable Ruysbroeck, the great fourteenth-century mystic, had once lived. Miller also went to England, to Corwen, Wales, to visit his old teacher John Cowper Powys. Still young and alert at eighty, "Priest John," as he liked to call himself, had lived in New York for thirty years, close to the common people: he gave his lectures at the trade union offices, at Cooper Union or Labor Temple. The price of admission was only ten cents. Henry was twenty years old at the time and was literally under that man's spell. "[Powys's] words, even today, have the power of bewitching me. . . . His book is full of life wisdom. . . . I had an unholy veneration for the man. Every word he uttered seemed to go straight to the mark . . . He was like an oracle to me" (*The Books in My Life*, p. 135).[9] After one of his lectures, Henry waited for him at the exit so he could shake his hand. Warmly welcomed by the old man forty years after their first meeting, he learned with surprise and joy that Powys not only knew his writings but liked and respected them. It was this pilgrimage to the home of his venerated teacher that ended the memorable journey of 1953—his first postwar visit to Europe.

During the Millers' stealthy stays in Paris, we rarely saw them, since we ourselves were traveling in Austria, Turkey, and Spain. But in late March we found ourselves in Paris. "A dinner at your house would be perfect," he wrote me. "Excuse my audacity. But it's better to dine in private than out at a restaurant." The dinner took place on April 15. We had assembled about ten friends. But I have searched my memory in vain and cannot recall even the subjects of our conversation. It is probably impossible to be both a dinner host and a memoirist at the same time. Among the guests were Hans Reichel and his wife, Lucie. That evening, we dined for the last time with our dear Reichel. A year later, Miller recalled "that regal feast" and, even five years later, wrote: "And that memorable evening in 1953! My wife, Eve, still talks about it. She likes you a great deal, you and your charming wife. She loves her!" (letters to Brassaï, December 10, 1954, and December 2, 1958).

CHAPTER 2

Sunday, April 19, 1959

Six years have gone by. Miller and his family have just arrived in Paris. And this morning, I am going to see them again at their home on rue Campagne-Première. A flurry of letters preceded this journey. All his friends were alerted. A month ago, Henry told me: "Yes, everything is arranged: passports, visas, tickets. All I need to do now is relax. Working feverishly to finish re-reading *Nexus* before I go!"

As for Eve, she announced their return with this exclamation of joy, in capital letters: "WE ARE COMING BACK TO FRANCE!" And she added: "I say COME BACK because that's what this journey means to me. In Henry's mind, it's just one more trip. So there you have it!" And she ended her letter: "I want my children to have a real sense for what it is to *live in France*, and not only to be *passing through*" (letter to Brassaï, January 28, 1959).

When I arrive at the studio in Montparnasse, Henry exclaims: "What a pleasure to see you again. Most of the friends and acquaintances I saw in Paris are faring well. But just think if you lived in the United States! There, at forty you're prematurely old, used up."

BRASSAÏ   How was your trip?

HENRY MILLER   It's the first time I've flown in a jet. San Francisco–New York: five hours and forty-five minutes. It's fantastic! Nine thousand meters up and not a bump. I felt like I was living in the future, the future that is becoming our present.

BRASSAÏ   What do you think of Paris? Has it changed in six years?

MILLER   So many cars in the street! It's astounding! People think New York's a frenetic city. But it's really Paris! The traffic is even heavier here and the police wave their arms to get people to go even faster. When I have to cross a street, I start to shake. I fear for me and my children. Fortunately, French cuisine hasn't changed, it still lives up to its reputation. But the odd thing is, I've lost my passion for Paris. I've changed. I don't like big cities anymore and I'm looking forward to being in the country. It's different for Eve! She loves Paris and wants to know it better. She'll stay here while I visit the Scandinavian countries with my children.

From the kitchen where she's been making breakfast, Eve appears, still as beautiful as ever. And Henry introduces me to his children: Valentine, called Val, a tall blonde girl the same age as Juliet, sparkling with life, and Tony, who reminds me of James Dean: straw-colored hair, rebellious locks sweeping across his transparent blue eyes, his grave voice breaking as he curses with adolescent grace. He has the seductiveness of the hero of *Rebel without a Cause*, and also the arrogance. When Henry calls him over to introduce him, he turns his back and walks away.

MILLER   Regular savages. Ill-mannered, stubborn, unruly, undisciplined. I love them! Apart from Big Sur, they don't know very much of the world. Oh, that's not true! Once I took them to San Francisco. Sometimes I try to put myself in their place, to imagine their childhood memories. They're important your whole life! What could a kid from Williamsburg, that seedy Brooklyn neighborhood, dream about? The only images filling my childhood were gloomy vacant lots, smoking chimneys, mounds of garbage and trash being incinerated. But marvelous memories nonetheless. Other kids remember a beautiful garden, a forest, a trip to the seashore, a loving and tender mother. What will Tony and Val dream about, I wonder. Probably about cliffs, eagles, vultures, sea elephants warming themselves in the sun, whales passing off the coast, those terrible storms that come crashing down on the Pacific. For a long time I was hesitant to take them to Europe. Larry advised strongly against it: "Travel is already tiring in itself," he wrote me, "one must be free and without a care to take advantage of it." Obviously, without the kids it would have been less bother. But I adore them. And they like it in France. I'm looking forward to having them in the Midi. In the country we won't have to keep them on a leash. Larry has rented a house for us in Saintes-Maries-de-la-Mer, I think. But I dread La Camargue. "You're going to see medieval France again, unchanged, intact," he wrote me. "The notaries are straight out of a Balzac novel and everyone shits outdoors." Well, no thank you! I can't adjust to medieval life again, to houses without the modern conveniences. America has spoiled me, corrupted me. Why live like idiots in the atomic age, without a minimum of comfort, of hygiene? I'm also afraid of mosquitoes. It seems La Camargue is infested with them."

Mosquitoes! Along with ants, flies, and drafts, mosquitoes are for Henry the "poison apples that spoil paradise." He wrote of Big Sur: "The flies wake me up at six o'clock in the morning." And when he was camping in Corfu: "The camping is fine, but why add ants, flies, etc.? I hate flies! I don't think there would have been so many if I'd been alone. I would have camped under the olive trees, not on the sand." He remembered Far Rockaway beach as a nightmare. Invited to the home of June's friends, they were eaten alive. "The instant I saw the mosquito net above the bed, I knew what we were in for. It started right away, that first night. Neither of us could sleep a wink."

BRASSAÏ Are you thinking of leaving Big Sur to settle in France?

MILLER Eve would like to and Larry has strongly advised us to go looking in Provence for a good spot to settle permanently. But I don't agree. I can't leave Big Sur just yet.

BRASSAÏ But you complain of being invaded there.

MILLER My wonderful solitude, my peace and quiet, haven't existed for a long time now. Success comes at a high price. They think I'm the Dalai Lama. And I'm too weak to resist. It's hell. As soon as I sit down in front of the typewriter, my work is interrupted. It drives you crazy. Impossible to collect your thoughts. And yet, despite its inconveniences, I'm attached to Big Sur. It's my haven. And the sea, the wind, the cliffs, the sky, the stars are irreplaceable! I'd never find a promontory like that in France.

BRASSAÏ How long are you thinking of staying in Europe?

MILLER Four months. We've reserved our return seats for August 20. I'll be delighted to see the Durrells and to meet Claude and the children. I look at the map, I measure the distance from Saintes-Maries-de-la-Mer to Nîmes and other places. There's a lot I'd like to visit: Le Puy, for example. Have you been?

BRASSAÏ An odd city, dominated by two volcanic cones. One bears a colossal statue of the Virgin at the summit—quite ugly in fact; the other has an adorable little eleventh-century chapel—Saint-Michel—a real Romanesque jewel.

This morning—a Thursday—he wants to take his children to the Eiffel Tower, and asks me to go with them. He's red with anger, fed up. Valentine played a practical joke in the building: she trapped the tenants in the elevator between two floors. Yelling, calls, complaints. The life of the building is disrupted. And now, out of breath, streaming sweat, Tony appears. Against his father's orders, he crossed the dangerous boulevard Raspail to go roller-skating the length of Montparnasse cemetery. Still an unfamiliar sight for me: Henry Miller, who could be their grandfather, in the role of father, grappling with these little devils. He bellows, explodes, scolds them. Tempers rise. He responds to Eve tit for tat, and she constantly criticizes him: "Just look at the result of how you raised them. They do what they like, naturally! Refuse to obey their father. You can shout all you like, you have no authority anymore." A fierce enemy of submission of any sort, deep down Henry undoubtedly approves of his children's escapades, even applauds them. And he's annoyed at himself for giving in to anger. He is about to explain himself when the doorbell rings. It's the telegraph boy. Henry reads a long dispatch from Stockholm.

"A few months ago, *Sexus* was seized as pornography in Sweden. My lawyer appealed. He found a good argument: a Swedish book, also banned for obscenity, was cleared recently and could be published again. So why not *Sexus*?"

BRASSAÏ And you won?

MILLER Wait, I don't know yet. [He reads the dispatch, shakes his head, grunts, and bursts out laughing.] No, we've lost for good! The argument was rejected by the appeals court, and do you know on what grounds? The judges did a sort of chemical analysis of the pornographic ingredients of the two books. According to that expertise, the Swedish book, which is really filthy by the way, contained only 10.3 percent obscenities, and *Sexus* 15.7 percent. My book was thus 5.4 percent filthier. Therefore, the appeal was rejected and the ban continues. It's really high comedy! Imagine all those grave magistrates, those high priests of justice, poking their noses into my novel, rifling through it, analyzing every page, every sentence to extract such and such a percentage of obscenities from it. Incredible, don't you think?

That bad news does not trouble Henry's serenity, however. He's seen enough already! With the slanted eyes of a Chinese sage, he laughs until he sheds bitter tears: "You'll see, one day I'll win the Nobel Prize all the same! And other grave magistrates will praise my books." He's joking. Yet I detect a glimmer of hope in his words. Five months ago, he wrote me: "We may see each other again when I receive the Nobel Prize (what a joke!)" (letter to Brassaï, December 2, 1958). After all, couldn't he get the award in Stockholm? Obscenity is no impediment. The winds can change. Wasn't André Gide among the elect despite—or because of—his defense of homosexuality? Wasn't he honored precisely for his courageous struggle against hypocrisy? The same arguments may one day work in Henry's favor.

MILLER   The battle is now joined in earnest. My books had the same misadventure in Japan. They were all banned. My Japanese publisher held an exhibition of my watercolors and sold a lot of them. Now he wants to keep my money and even my watercolors, as "compensation." The ban has completely ruined him, he wrote. That's what I've come to.

Young Claire, the daughter of Maurice Nadeau, arrives. We set out to conquer the Eiffel Tower. Thursdays are the tower's big days! Hundreds of schoolboys and schoolgirls, flanked by men and women teachers, nuns, stand in line to go up. Finally they herd us into the elevator. Then we have to change cars because the kids want to go all the way to the top, to the sky, 320 meters up. The sight of Paris from bird's-eye view, the glistening ribbon of the Seine traversed by its bridges, the gilded Prussian helmet that tops the emperor's tomb at Les Invalides, its white replica at the Panthéon, the Arc de Triomphe with its twelve-pointed star, Sacré-Coeur perched on its Montmartre pedestal: all these monuments on the left and right banks, a pleasure for the eye to pick out on every side, interest them very little. For them, that ascent is only an amusement park ride and they're having a great time: they drink and eat everything offered—hot dogs, ice cream, lemonade, Coca-Cola—and buy out the gift shop: postcards, globes, miniature Eiffel Towers.

BRASSAÏ   Do you know the Eiffel Tower was the result of a competition: design an iron tower three hundred meters high? At the Sainte-Geneviève library one day, I looked over all the plans. There were some astounding ones. An elephant, among other things, a hundred meters high, holding a sort of two-hundred-meter-tall pagoda on its back. Even Eiffel's original plan was rather different from the present tower. When they calculated the resistance, it produced purer forms, more beautiful curves. And do you know that, up above us, there's a little private apartment with several rooms, traversed by iron girders? I was able to visit it one time. Eiffel lived there for several weeks. It was his office. Now it's reserved for heads of state.

MILLER   How old is it?

BRASSAÏ   Just seventy years old, two years older than you.

MILLER   And it hasn't been eaten away by rust?

BRASSAÏ   No. It can survive another two centuries. It seems that steel lasts longer than concrete and the longevity of a steel tower is greater than that of a skyscraper. But only if it's repainted every seven years. A rather extraordinary acrobatic sight!

Miller exclaims: "The children, where the hell are the children?"

While we were talking, they wouldn't hold still and were running around the platform knocking into lovebirds and people contemplating suicide.

Could they have ventured into the stairwells? We finally find them. Val and Tony beg their father to let them take the metal stairs down to the third floor, on foot. After a categorical no, Miller caves in and gives them the green light. We take the elevator and wait for them on the second platform.

MILLER You don't have children. So you don't have these problems.

BRASSAÏ Have you read *Emile*?

MILLER A few passages, and I found them very appealing. A fundamental book. I also read the books by Ferrer, Montessori, and Pestalozzi. The question of education interests me passionately. I agree with Rousseau. He was against pedagogues, against schooling, and, like me, he recommended the return to primitive virtue. I didn't see the usefulness of stuffing my head with school learning. I only wanted to learn what seemed of vital interest to me. I had to discover everything on my own. There's only one good pedagogue: life. I wanted to raise my children in the greatest freedom. That's what my wives always criticized me for: I thwart their efforts, I'm not ruthless enough, I take a malicious pleasure in seeing them misbehave. That horrible *discipline* I should have inculcated in them was really always the main reason for our quarrels. But I rejected such a cruel, stultifying upbringing.

BRASSAÏ So you took your own lack of upbringing as a model for upbringing?

MILLER Yes, my own experience. I grew up on the streets, that's where I learned what it means to be truly human. Until the age of nine, we were little rascals, budding young gangsters, but our own masters. None of us idolized our parents. We were hungry for knowledge, we discussed burning questions. Around a campfire in a vacant lot we were able to talk about serious things: love, death, life, birth, sex, God. I had the good luck never to have been spoiled by my parents! They gave me a free hand. I could wander, return any time of night without reporting to anyone.

BRASSAÏ Céline also claimed that high school is the root of all evil. And so did Nietzsche! As a young philologist in Basel, in five lectures he denounced the major defects of "modern" education, from elementary school to the university, the "gray and useless" erudition "of an impenitent barbarism."

MILLER School plunges us into a fog of words and abstractions. It debilitates us, and right at the age when people are burning with curiosity. Now, along with Rimbaud, I think that "everything taught at school is wrong," that everything of vital importance to the child is taboo both at school and at home. Yes, I went astray. How right I was!

BRASSAÏ And you became a writer. But you might have also become a gangster. Most of the young people in prison are there because the only school they had was the streets.

MILLER None of us became jailbirds that I know of. But, if given the choice, I prefer emancipated adults, strong men, even those on the fringes of society, to those who have become morons, braying asses, because of book learning.

BRASSAÏ You reject what you call "book" learning. Yet you always speak of certain books as *vital* experiences. You even said that reading Dostoyevsky was a more important event for you than falling in love for the first time. After all, you learned more from Dostoyevsky, Nietzsche, Rabelais, and Knut Hamsun than from the little rascals on vacant lots.

MILLER Of course. But who propelled me toward those authors? It was the education of the streets, my revolt against society.

BRASSAÏ So you're for a rebellious childhood—unbridled, unfettered.

MILLER Normal, healthy children are *naturally* turbulent, *naturally* reckless, *naturally* disobedient. Yes, they're "rebels." They're not made for the egoistic discipline we require of them or for the cushy life we offer them. What would be the point of repeating: "Don't do this, don't do that"?

BRASSAÏ And yet this morning you were very annoyed that you couldn't make them obey. Val had the whole house up in arms and Tony almost got run over by a car.

MILLER That's true. My nerves were frayed and I let myself lose my temper. It happens sometimes, I too lose patience with my kids and, when I get fed up, I even spank them. But I've always felt ashamed afterward and have sworn to myself that I'd never do it again.

In front of the stairwell where the children are supposed to come out, Henry anxiously examines the forest of iron girders.

MILLER It's a difficult thing, bringing up children. Especially if you have a strong personality. There are so many sad examples of children born to men of genius! My biggest concern is not to dwarf them. They'd be ill-suited for life. So, instead of training them as a father, I have instead tried to be their pal. I've remained childlike myself and my books do battle with the adults who massacred the child living inside them. I try to join my kids in their own world. And I've succeeded fairly well. Obviously, I have no authority over them. They don't respect me. They often call me an idiot, an imbecile, a moron. I prefer that! Wouldn't it be disastrous for them to take me for a serious man, or worse, for a man of genius? I prefer to suffer on account of my lack of authority. Durrell wrote me one day: "You're going to make a rather crazy father." That's right. I act like a clown, a crackpot, and, as much as I can, I hide my "celebrity" from them. But since they aren't stupid or blind, they see that their moron father receives many signs of respect and consideration. And then there are all those people who make appeals to me, wine and dine me, flatter me. Television, interviews, photos. That must be a problem for them. And their suspicions bother me.

This problem of the "genius's son" has preoccupied Henry. He often asked me what had become of Picasso's son Paolo: "What's he doing with his life? What a tragedy for a son to have such an illustrious father!" (letter to Brassaï, November 13, 1964).

When I get home, I'm still thinking about Henry's relationship with his children. He abandoned his daughter Barbara, born during his first marriage, even though he adored her. Abandoned her not to a convent, as Rousseau did, but to her fate, without concerning himself about her anymore. Even in Paris, he still thought about that daughter he didn't really even know. And, in Big Sur, when he was exhausted by those unruly little savages and had to let their mother take them back, he suffered so much that he burst out sobbing: "I was . . . heartbroken. And with the dull ache came exhaustion and loss of spirits. The place now seemed like a morgue to me. A dozen times a night I would wake with a start, thinking that they were calling me. There is no emptiness like the emptiness of a home which your children have flown. It was worse than death. . . . I wept like a madman. I wept and sobbed and screamed and cursed. I carried on like that until there wasn't another drop of anguish left in me. Until I was like a crumpled, empty sack" (*Big Sur and the Oranges of Hieronymus Bosch*, pp. 190, 191).[1]

CHAPTER 3

Thursday, April 30, 1959

This evening the Millers dine at our home. It is muggy. A storm breaks. They arrive drenched, like four wet cats. The heat of the wood fire in the fireplace and the alcohol will warm them up. I look at Henry, whose face is drawn. He has lost weight since he arrived in Paris. I tell him, laughing, "Fame is exhausting."

MILLER Almost as much as poverty! I was harassed all week. And I think back almost nostalgically to the time when no one knew me.

BRASSAÏ Were you happier then?

MILLER Maybe. Certainly freer, in any case. I would have liked to see again certain neighborhoods in Paris that I used to enjoy. There was no way to find the time. Oh, but all the same, the other day I went to Belleville and Ménilmontant, which are still almost unchanged.

BRASSAÏ But you must also like that long-awaited success. Or don't you?

MILLER It baffles me, disorients me. And I can't believe it's being directed at me. Obviously, it's an event in an artist's life to finally be accepted. But you still have to know by *whom* and for *what reason*. "My peers," the only ones whose judgment counts for me, already recognized me ages ago. And I'm afraid that the mob of readers now flocking to my books are doing so for the wrong reasons. No, this rather noisy, scandalous success does not give me much pleasure. And what a disruption it's been in my life! I've never had so many intrusions, so much trouble, so many absurd things going on.

BRASSAÏ A few years ago—in 1955, I think—I went to Kilchberg, on Lake of Zurich, to do a portrait of Thomas Mann, and I heard the same complaints from Erika Mann.

MILLER Success is a bitter fruit: sooner or later, what you have created turns against you, becomes your torment.

BRASSAÏ The writer's wife told me: "We would never have imagined that my husband's eightieth birthday would be such a cruel ordeal. He's exhausted, ill. We were literally invaded: journalists, photographers, filmmakers from every country. Just yesterday an American reporter took some 150 photos of him. My husband lives with the dread that he won't be able to finish his last book before he dies. Every minute devoted to posing and interviews comes at the expense of his work." A fine preamble, don't you think, for a photographer who is also about to bother the great man!

MILLER And what did you do? Did you give up on the idea?

BRASSAÏ I couldn't. The portrait was being done for an American magazine. But I took upon myself the risk of taking only two or three photographs: Thomas Mann alone, then with his wife. He in the garden with Lake of Zurich in the background, then the couple in front of the library. I took only a few minutes of his life. He was flabbergasted. He died a few months later.

MILLER I've returned from Blaise Cendrars's place. Do you know him?

BRASSAÏ I've often run into him on boulevard Arago walking his dog. He's almost my neighbor and we go to the same bank. One day the teller called out a strange German name, something like "Sauser," and I was surprised to see Cendrars go to the window wearing his Basque beret, with the inevitable cigarette butt between his lips. That's when I made his acquaintance.

MILLER Yes, he's Swiss. "Blaise Cendrars" is his nom de guerre.

BRASSAÏ He has the mug of an old Legionnaire. He looks like Victor McLaglen in *The Informer*. I'm sorry I didn't know him sooner and better.

MILLER After he read *Tropic of Cancer*, he came of his own accord to pay me a visit at the Villa Seurat. I'll never forget it. That's how he was, always the first to greet a stranger, to offer his help. Not only did he pay me that unforgettable visit, he also wrote the first enthusiastic article on my book. No French writer paid me a more distinguished honor.

BRASSAÏ Fred was at your place during his visit, wasn't he?

MILLER Yes, fortunately, because I was intimidated. Cendrars arrived at three o'clock in the afternoon and left us late at night. We were broke, starving that day. He took us to place des Abbesses in Montmartre to a friend of his, a wine merchant. He offered us a tasty meal with plenty of wine. We laughed a great deal that night.

BRASSAÏ Did you know his writings before you met him?

MILLER I knew some of them already in the United States: his *Anthologie nègre, L'Or, Moravagine.* I read others in Paris, especially *L'homme foudroyé,* undoubtedly one of his masterpieces. I also read his nostalgic book: *Banlieue de Paris.*

BRASSAÏ With the beautiful photographs done by my friend Robert Doisneau. Did Cendrars have a great influence on you?

MILLER With the exception of John Cowper Powys and Céline, no contemporary writer made as great an impression on me. I was fascinated by the man and also by his works. Cendrars is a scrupulous reporter of life and, at the same time, a sensitive poet. He has found—and how rare it is!—a common denominator between language and life, literature and action. He's always on the lookout for the unknown, the unexpected. He can truly say: "I have lived!" How dull, sad, devoid of events my own life seemed next to his! I envied him.

BRASSAÏ You wrote very warmly about him. But you also spoke of his detours, his parentheses that go on for several pages, his digressions, his squandering of words. Weren't you indirectly defending yourself? You too have often been criticized for being prolix and verbose, for lacking a sense of form.

MILLER We have some affinities, to be sure! From him I learned to follow my nose, to glorify the present, to defend the truth of life against its slanderers. I also admire how prolific he is. He has only one arm, his left, never uses a secretary, goes all over the world, and, since he hates to write—he works for only two hours before dawn—the rest of the day is devoted to living. Yet that man will leave a considerable opus behind him.

BRASSAÏ And now he's paralyzed.

MILLER You cannot imagine how painful my visit was, how sad it was to see him bedridden, helpless! He had twenty books in the works when the paralysis struck. Now he truly is *l'homme foudroyé,* the man struck by lightning! I can still see him full of vitality on the terrace of a café near Porte d'Orléans in May 1939. It's odd, don't you think? Cendrars was the last person I happened upon in the final moments of my farewell to Paris. My "Homage to Cendrars" had just come out in Chinese in a Shanghai literary review. He'd seen it: "You blew me away!" he said.

During the meal, I am seated next to Eve.

"Henry and the children absolutely must remain in France," she tells me. "If he returns to Big Sur, he'll be a goner! You cannot imagine what it's like to live there."

BRASSAÏ   You surprise me. It's a marvelous place. Everyone says so.

EVE   Marvelous, of course! The setting is magnificent, stirring! The natural beauty is grandiose! The landscape spellbinding! You go into raptures at the sight of the Pacific, the distant horizon, so sharp, so clear. Eden! Paradise! But to live there is something else altogether! Cut off from the world, without human contact, away from all civilized life. Never seeing a movie, visiting an exhibition or a museum, never listening to a concert or a lecture. We live without electricity, without the conveniences. The supermarket is in Carmel. Monterey, the closest city, is seventy kilometers away. And the telephone! That may be what we miss the most. All my life I've been accustomed to it. Sometimes we have hallucinations: we hear it ring. And Henry's the one who has to do all the chores, like a slave: collect dead branches, saw, cut the wood. Sometimes, but rarely, a friend helps us. You have to struggle with the smoking stove, the kerosene lamps, the leaky roofs. Isn't it demoralizing to see Henry waste the better part of his time at such futile, such degrading tasks?

BRASSAÏ   Nevertheless, he'd like to work more with his hands, to practice several trades.

In fact, in his initial enthusiasm, he wrote me from Big Sur: "I live in an isolated place. Not even a town here—out in the wild: sea, forest, and brush everywhere. But sublime! That's why I'm not eager to take a world tour. I'd like to have a good idea of what it is to be a carpenter, a mason, to work even more with my hands. Life is so simple and good when you live away from the city" (letter to Brassaï, April 4, 1948).

EVE   But it's killing him! He's not used to such arduous work. When he starts writing, he's already exhausted. And the wind! It blows over those cliffs twenty-four hours a day, three quarters of the year. You cannot imagine how nerve-racking that unleashed fury is. Its moaning can last several days running without a moment's rest. It's Wuthering Heights. And the rainy season! Torrential rains! They seep into the house through the roof. The air is saturated with humidity, the thick black fog blots out the horizon and envelops you like a shroud. It drives you crazy! During storms, we're housebound, wading in a sea of mud. Or else it's the ice, the ice pack surrounding the house that you have to break with picks to get out. And the road! It's dangerous, often blocked by landslides. It zigzags at the edge of the precipice. When the storm blows in, to get through you have to push aside the rocks that have fallen from the cliffs. There are signs everywhere warning: "Caution! Dangerous Curves, Falling Rock!" Our old Cadillac convertible is a '41, it's falling to pieces. And the incessant money worries. We live from hand to mouth. I can't go on. Henry is an impenitent optimist, but he's exhausted with the life we've been leading for six years. It's only his pride that makes him cling to the idea of staying in Big Sur. Talk him out of it, I beg you. He doesn't listen to me. He may listen to you. I can't go back there again. We absolutely must stay in France.

That unexpected outburst baffles me. But, upon reflection, did not Henry himself sometimes depict Big Sur in very somber colors? After "the preliminary bout of intoxication . . . follows the trouble period," he wrote in *Big Sur and the Oranges of Hieronymus Bosch*. "Inner doubts pave the way for domestic squabbles, and the whole horizon grows dark with conflict" (p. 37). In that isolated place, the slightest problem takes a dramatic turn: "If the soul were to choose an arena in which to stage its agonies, this would be *the* place for it" (p. 145) And he acknowledges: "I have had here some of the most bitter experiences of my life" (p. 30). He has probably also had moments of exaltation. One does not rule out the other. He likes that wild promontory—his Tibet, his Lhasa—even for its fog and storms, grandiose spectacles that give him the delicious feeling of smallness and powerlessness. A bittersweet experience no doubt, but, he thinks, "all experience is enriching and rewarding" (p. 30).

I was able to follow that "experience" through the many letters he sent me. A year after he settled there, in 1948, his enthusiasm had already been dampened: "I'm planting vegetables and fruit trees, in anticipation of a famine when war breaks out," he wrote naively. "For me, it's difficult to find two hours a day for work; there is so much to do in the country. In addition, I am invaded!" In 1951: "Winter arrived with its parade of rains. I have never seen it rain like it did this winter. For days and days, like punishment from heaven, the deluge beat down on us. Val couldn't go to school because the road was partly flooded." Nine years later, in 1960, he wrote: "Upon returning to Big Sur, I find a jungle around the house—but I don't have the strength to clear it." Four years later, after I myself had purchased a piece of property in the Midi, I asked him for some advice. His response sums up his troubles, his disenchantment with Big Sur and the idyllic wild life:

> Now let's talk about your country house. In Big Sur, I went through the whole mess you told me about and *I will never do it again. It's an illusion, this life in the country.* Yes, I like the country, but only with the assistance of servants, peasants, to do the chores. For a whole year in Big Sur, I dug ditches (as during the Balkan War) everywhere in my yard—an acre and a half, about six thousand square meters—to root out the pest called "poison oak." I planted all sorts of fruit trees. I killed rattlesnakes by the dozens. I went up and down the hill to get the mail—four miles. Every trip took a good hour, and sometimes I had to

do it twice in a day. I had only old cars that often broke down. Visitors invaded me almost every day, sometimes twenty in one day. No thank you! *Never again for me!* (letter to Brassaï, September 4, 1964)

So Eve was right! There really *was* a hell hiding behind that paradise! And, in an irony of fate—I'm anticipating—it was Henry, not Eve, who left Big Sur in 1962. Eve died in Big Sur four years later.

Although Miller, a sexagenarian sick of city life, left the city behind him without regrets (like those Chinese artists who, when they got old, retired to a wild region to meditate in peace), could such young women as Lepska and Eve find the same attraction he did in that solitude, that life of an anchorite? Those young creatures were burning with the desire to throw themselves into life, to know the world and its pleasures. At twenty-two, while on a tobacco plantation in North Carolina, did not Miller have the same yearning for the civilized and social world as his young wives in Big Sur? He wrote: "I realize . . . the need I have for people, conversation, books, theater, music, cafés, drinks, and so forth. It's terrible to be civilized, because when you come to the end of the world you have nothing to support the terror of loneliness" (*Tropic of Capricorn*, p. 308).[1] This was the same complaint I heard that evening from Eve. After she had emptied her third glass of whiskey, she continued: "You cannot imagine what this trip to Europe means to me. *The happiness of being in Paris!* I have never been so happy in my life! I'm brimming over with joy! I roam the streets, look at the store windows, visit the museums, the theaters, the gardens, the quays of the Seine. I don't know which way to turn anymore. So why would I go to Denmark? Paris is the *only* chance I have in life! I won't join Henry and the children until they get to the Midi."

Henry has brought us his latest book. I ask him where its strange title came from: *Big Sur and the Oranges of Hieronymus Bosch.* Are there oranges in Big Sur?

MILLER I have just one orange tree in my yard and it has never borne fruit. I don't know why. But one day a visitor, seeing my sterile tree, told me: "Your orange tree reminds me of the painting by Hieronymus Bosch, in which there's an orange tree loaded down with fruit. For me, that's the epitome of Paradise!" Because I had the supreme bliss of nature in Big Sur, which is rare in America, I called my book *Big Sur and the Oranges of Hieronymus Bosch.*

And in his handwriting, so clear, so legible, he writes in the copy he intends for us:

A little dedication to Brassaï and Gilberte, in memory of the reunion in Paris after so many years, during which nothing has changed except the photographer's eye, which is becoming more and more cosmological. So it's the Virgin Lighthouse. Therefore, everything is for the best here below and on high, don't you think? Hail, dear Friends—and farewell! Henry Miller, April 30, 1959. P.S. And now a gracious word just for Gilberte, who offered us a wonderful meal in an intimate setting. H. M.

CHAPTER 4

May 1959

Henry's Danish publisher, who had just published *Quiet Days in Clichy* illustrated by my photographs, invited Miller and his family to Copenhagen. Henry went there with Val and Tony, but without Eve. This evening we find him at the home of the Rattners with his wife, but without his children. I ask Eve if they stayed home.

EVE They can't be left together. They're so violent, so irritable! They might kill each other. It's always been that way. Arguments, fights. And when their father intervenes, it's worse. Only Tony stayed home, Valentine was sent to stay with friends.

Henry is about to leave for Sommières, but Eve refuses to go with him.

MILLER I'll be delighted to see Durrell again. I haven't seen him in fourteen years. And Fred will soon join us.

BRASSAÏ The reunion of the three musketeers.

MILLER I hope it'll be like it was at the Villa Seurat. When we get back together, it's not just the sum of the three of us. Each of us is changed and we form a burlesque trinity. In real life, Larry is rather reserved, as diplomats are; Fred is bitter and melancholic; as for me, deep down I'm serious. But when we're together, we give off a charge of extraordinary merriment. We burst out laughing and can't stop.

Three weeks later, Eve left Paris only grudgingly, in the company of Fred on his way from London, to join Henry and the children in Gard. As for us, we left for the Midi. The postcard we received from Henry was postmarked Die and showed a panoramic view of the Vercors, headquarters of the Resistance. "Dear Friends, this is a very beautiful country that somewhat resembles our paradise in Big Sur. My friends offered me a Ping-Pong table.

There are wonderful players here, but I'm still unbeatable!" Ping-Pong! That's his great passion. He excels at it and nothing gives him so much pleasure as to win a game. We had hoped to see them again in August, but Eve's mother had a serious illness and they were obliged to return. And I myself had to leave for Brazil in August.

In a letter to Henry, I described my trip and spoke of the "planetary, cosmological view the airplane offers us today." He answered me: "What a surprise to learn you were in Brazil! What a marvelous trip! I envy you! We took the New York–San Francisco jetliner. For me as well, it was a revelation. I saw the 'future' as in a mirror. Now I'm planning a trip of a few months to the East: Siam, Cambodia, Japan. After January 1. And *alone* this time" (letter to Brassaï, October 15, 1959).

A little later, he wrote me: "I recently saw two plays by Ionesco—performed by amateurs—*The Chairs* and *The Bald Soprano*. I was overwhelmed. Now I'd like to try a drama myself. Something fairly 'loony.' But I'm a little like Ionesco, I don't know how to distinguish between comedy and tragedy" (letter to Brassaï, November 16, 1959). And, in another letter, he returned again to his great desire: to know Picasso! "One day I'll have to meet Picasso. With you it would be a great pleasure. Perhaps you'll see me next summer in Paris or Eze" (letter to Brassaï, November 22, 1959).

I read in my response: "Since November 12, the day I opened the box titled *Conversations with Picasso*, I have written 240 typed pages, and I am not too unhappy with them. In a few days, I'll send you excerpts. Your opinion counts a great deal to me. It will be the *Story of Marie,* but on the scale of Picasso! He will come to life before the reader's eyes, as he is, I hope: sometimes demiurge, sometimes juggler." And, as a postscript, I add: "Picasso has just acquired the château of Vauvenargues, near Aix-en-Provence, a historic château. Do you know about the marquis de Vauvenargues—Luc de Clapiers is his real name—one of the great French moralists, who died very young, at thirty-two? Perhaps you've read his *Maxims*? In them he defended—before Henry Miller—the human passions. It would be wonderful if we could go together to Picasso's home some day. I'm sure he'd be happy to make your acquaintance" (letter from Brassaï to Miller, November 28, 1959).

After the Millers left, the news of their separation started to circulate. Nothing was working out between Eve and Henry anymore. Of course, Eve's refusal to accompany her husband to Denmark and Holland, her reluctance to join him in the Midi, Henry's announcement that he would leave *alone* for Asia, were troubling signs. But Eve never said a word against him, did not talk of separation or divorce. And we had the impression that it was only out of fondness that she was trying to drag him away from the harsh life in Big Sur and that she wanted him to settle in France. But Edmond Buchet, who put them up in Le Vésinet, was undoubtedly better situated to observe the deterioration in their relationship: "Eve is proving to be unbearable. Right now, you feel she's exasperated," he wrote in his *Journal*. "She doesn't miss an opportunity to say that she married an old man and we have the impression that, once again, poor Henry is going to find himself without a wife." The publisher pitied him, but was consoled by the idea that this "new sad adventure" would lead to an increase in vitality (Edmond Buchet, *Les auteurs de ma vie*). From Big Sur, Henry also announced the news to us: "Eve now lives in a house nearby, whereas I am here. She's talking about divorce. We are good friends all the same" (letter to Brassaï, July 27, 1960).

That news saddened us. It also upset the Durrells and all Henry's friends. Eve had gained their sympathy. In reflecting on the fated and inevitable breakups between Miller and his women—wives or girlfriends—I was obliged to make this curious observation: all Henry's love affairs lasted exactly *seven years,* not a year less or more. Beatrice Wickes, 1917–24; June Mansfield, 1923–30; Anaïs Nin, 1930–37; Janina Lepska, 1945–52; Eve, 1952–59; Hoki, 1966–73.

CHAPTER 5

April 9, 1960

At half past noon, Gilberte and I are waiting for Henry at Orly. A month ago, he wrote me: "Good news! I'll be in Paris on April 8 for three days only. I was chosen as a member of the jury at the Cannes Film Festival—from May 4 to 21. Must go to Germany, Denmark, Belgium, and various places in France before I arrive in Cannes. . . . In haste. Don't tell anyone, will you, about this 'business' in Cannes. Warm greetings to Gilberte. Henry. P.S. I am coming *all alone* this time!" (letter to Brassaï, Big Sur, March 5, 1960). I answered him: "From what you wrote me and what I learned from musketeer Larry, you've earned many millions of dollars. I therefore thought (even as I was cutting the pages of the third volume of your *Crucifixion*, which has caused a great stir here) that you were already somewhere in Asia, perhaps in Japan. And now you're a member of the jury! You'll have a good time, I'm sure of it, though three weeks is rather a long time. I have good memories of the Cannes festival—three years ago—when they presented my short film, selected by France: *Tant qu'il y aura des bêtes* even won a prize!" (letter from Brassaï to Miller, March 1960).

In a second letter, Henry gave me his arrival time, again asking us to keep it an "absolute secret." And he added: "Durrell was wrong. I rejected the millions offered by Grove Press. I think I'll go to Japan in September! Will meet Perlès in Rome on April 16—for five or six days. Then Hamburg and so on. Don't forget to introduce me to your friend Picasso! I'm coming all alone. Henry" (letter to Brassaï, March 31, 1960).

We pick him up at Orly. Lunch at the house. I am surprised that he agreed to be a member of the jury at Cannes.

MILLER That surprises you? I've always liked the movies and I've seen almost all the silent films. The first—I remember it well—in a Protestant church: a Chinese man was crossing the Brooklyn Bridge in the rain, a braid down his back, his hands hidden in his sleeves. It was phenomenal! Unforgettable! Later, I liked the Frankenstein films, the embodiment of the monster that slumbers within us—whether it's called the subconscious, the unconscious, whatever you like, what propels man to behave in unexpected ways. I also liked *Port of Shadows, The Baker's Wife, Lost Horizon,* and so on. I even wrote several articles on films, on Buñuel and his *Golden Age,* and on Machaty's *Ecstasy,* on Raimu as well, I think. I'm an old film buff.

In Paris, in fact, Miller regularly frequented the movie theaters of our neighborhood, which were more within range of his wallet than those on the boulevards. And he preferred dubbed American films: "Those beautiful American actresses," he told me at the time, "have such disagreeable voices that it's to their advantage to express themselves with the pretty voices of Frenchwomen."

BRASSAÏ But that's the past! A distant past. For ages now film hasn't interested you.

MILLER That's true. And because of that I'm a rather dubious choice for member of the jury. But did the French choose me for my competence? I don't think so. No, it's a tribute to my writing. I'll be frank with the journalists, I'll confess to them that for the last fifteen years I've seen hardly any films. But I'm excited by film. It's one of the freest, most effective means of expression. Especially in the realm of dream and fantasy! What wonders, what joys it may hold in store for us! Some day film may replace literature.

BRASSAÏ And you're going to meet Georges Simenon.

MILLER I'm delighted about that. I often heard about that literary "phenomenon" when I was in Big Sur. One of the rare authors who shuts himself away to execute a novel in three weeks of continuous and relentless labor. Alas, that's not true for me! And I've often told myself: "How marvelous it would be to be like him, to withdraw completely from life, to neglect one's correspondence, one's family, one's friends, one's visitors, to not be there for anyone."

BRASSAÏ Have you ever met him?

MILLER Never. But we've corresponded for many years. [*Miller's marginal note:* "But it's not a very extensive correspondence. H. M."] I'm happy to finally make his acquaintance. In fact, it was at his insistence that I gave in. I'm also secretly nursing the hope of meeting your friend Picasso. To know Picasso! If you're in the Midi at the time, could you perhaps introduce me to him?

BRASSAÏ Don't you have the feeling that spending three weeks in Cannes looking at films morning till night, films without any great interest for the most part, will be a waste of time for you?

MILLER Ten years ago, even five years ago, that is, in fact, what I would have thought: a tremendous waste of my time. But not anymore. A new era in my life is beginning. I feel it. Having said what I had to say one way or another, I'll now be able to take a well-deserved vacation and travel the world. *Nexus I* will be followed by *Nexus II*, then there won't be anything else.

BRASSAÏ How can you make that assertion? Many subjects will still appeal to you, subjects you're not even thinking about right now.

MILLER I don't think so. As you know, one day in 1927—I remember it well, it was the day Lindbergh crossed the Atlantic—in the blackest despair, on a few sheets I composed in telegraphic style the years of love spent with June, the draft of my "autobiography." Everything I've written since—except *Tropic of Cancer, The Colossus of Maroussi,* and a few other texts—is built on that schema, traced in a few hours in the shed of the Park Department in Queens. It's that telegraphic text that I'm stretching out to the dimensions of several books. And I follow it scrupulously. The five hundred pages of *Tropic of Capricorn,* for example, take up only two and a half pages in it.

BRASSAÏ Did you know that all of *The Divine Comedy* was virtually contained within two stanzas of *La vita nuova?* And not only the chief characters: the poet, his master Virgil, and his beloved, the immortal Beatrice, but also their ascent from earth to heaven. Dante was twenty-five years old at the time and it took him thirty years to develop his idea.

MILLER I didn't know that. But it hardly surprises me. If you took a survey of the great writers, you'd find that the original idea for their works already existed when they were between twenty and twenty-five.

BRASSAÏ André Gide claimed that as well.

MILLER Me, I'm a bad example, an exception. It was only at thirty-five that I sketched out my autobiographical novel. And, after ten years of gestation, it took me twenty years to write.

BRASSAÏ Your *Remembrance of Things Past.*

MILLER No, my *Remembrance of a Lost Love.* I didn't want to relive my *whole* life, like Proust, only the four years of my love affair with June, from our meeting in that dance hall on Broadway until the moment she betrayed me and left.

BRASSAÏ And why that strange title: *The Rosy Crucifixion?*

MILLER That betrayed love was my "calvary," my "crucifixion." I wanted to tell of the almost unbearable sufferings of a man. But, after I got back together with June after she ran away, the original plan was modified. The next year, 1928, we spent in Europe together. That's what I'll recount in *Nexus II*, the end of my trilogy. Now do you understand why my *Crucifixion* became a *Rosy Crucifixion?* Even though my love story took a bad turn, it was not a true tragedy. Since that night June left me, I've carried the matter of my books inside me. But once the final volume is finished, it won't matter to me if I ever publish another book. I will have fulfilled my literary obligations. So I don't have the slightest plan. I'll finally be able to breathe, to whistle! And to allow myself to live. I'll be empty. On December 26, I'll be sixty-nine years old. But I don't really feel my age so much. Obviously, I can't jump or run the way I could when I was thirty, though I'm still good at Ping-Pong. But as far as writing is concerned, I don't feel any difference. Naturally, death can come at any moment. It doesn't frighten me. Death is the completion, the crowning of a life, of a body of work. I will await it without fear. From now on, I want to travel. Cannes is only the first milestone. Next fall, it'll be Japan, then Asia. You know how much the countries of the Orient appeal to me. Alas! I no longer have any hope of seeing Tibet, Lhasa, my great dream.

His great dream! That fabulous journey! Mecca, Lhasa, Delhi, Tombouctou, the quartet of holy cities, forbidden, inaccessible cities—ever since I have known him, they have represented the most ardently desired regions for him. Like Proust, Miller is spellbound by the magic of names, especially when their aura of mystery comes from the Orient. They were inscribed on large sheets of packing paper affixed to his wall, and he also listed them in his letters in an incantatory litany: "Easter Island, the Papuan Wonderland, Yap, Johore, the Caroline Islands, Borneo, Patagonia—Tibet, China, India, Persia, Arabia—and Mongolia" (*The Air-conditioned Nightmare*, p. 188). A single one of these names was enough to put him in a trance for the rest of the day. He admired René Caillié, the first white person to reach Tombouctou and to have come out alive. And Marco Polo! To cross Asia in the thirteenth century, spend twenty-four years at the home of the Great Kublai Khan of Mongolia, return safe and sound to Venice: what a fantastic adventure! One day, in a book relating that memorable journey, Miller read: *"When Marco Polo went to the East, the whole of Central Asia, so full of splendour and magnificence, so noisy with nations and kings, was like a dream in men's minds"* (*The Air-conditioned Nightmare*, p. 180). Miller reread this sentence several times. He would have liked to have written it: "The fullness of the earth opens up," he wrote. "The imagination is drowned before the sentence is finished. Asia. Just Asia, and the mind trembles" (*The Air-conditioned Nightmare*, p. 182). He dreams of everything that has come from Asia: prophets, sages, mystics, conquerors, dreamers, madmen, fanatics, drugs, incense, spices, cloves, pepper, cinnamon, vanilla, coffee, tea, carpets, the plague, cholera, demigods, gods. He also thinks of the dusty trails of the caravans, of the smells, the landscapes of the Far East, the camels, the green waters of the Nile, the Mosque of Omar, the outlandish languages, the bled, the beggars, the monks, the dervishes, the fakirs. "My brain was in such a whirl," he wrote, "that if someone didn't appear soon I would go mad" (*Plexus*, p. 48).[1]

Of all the countries and cities of the East, it was Tibet that brought together the marvels and mysteries of the universe for him. Disguised as a Buddhist monk, his robe and its colors already getting him worked up, he would have liked to go all the way to the "Roof of the World," and to the city of Lhasa. Magical names, said Miller, which, in diametrical opposition to the high priests of logic and science, attract everyone driven by the passion for secrets and the occult. "The ancestral spirits are calling me; I can't put them off much longer. '*When Henry Miller left for Tibet . . .*' I can see my future biographer writing that a hundred years from now. What ever happened to Henry Miller? He disappeared. He said he was going to Tibet. Did he get there? Nobody knows. . . . That's how it will be. Vanished mysteriously" (*The Air-conditioned Nightmare*, pp. 188–89).

As soon as Miller met Lawrence Durrell, who was born at the foot of the Himalayas, the latter acquired a halo of inestimable prestige in his eyes. "You should thank your lucky stars," he wrote him, "you were born there at the gateway to Tibet" (March 1937).[2] And when Durrell described for him his wonderful childhood memories of the Himalayas—the mountain passes leading to Lhasa, covered with ice, which melts a little on the outskirts of the forbidden city—and expressed his desire, never satisfied as a matter of fact, to cross the icy passes, Miller pressed him for more details about his life in India. "If I go anywhere from here [Paris]," he wrote, "it will be there. Maybe I shall be the next Dalai Lama—from America sent" (letter to Durrell, 1937).[3] And, very seriously, he tried to find out whether he might have Mongolian or Tibetan blood somewhere in his ancestry.

During the war, the Ramakrishna-Vivekananda Center, a monastery on the border of Nepal, offered him hospitality if he ever managed to get there. An unhoped-for opportunity! For lack of money he stayed in Big Sur and wrote with resignation: "This place will have to be my Tibet, pro tem. It's got everything but—the essential. I have to supply that" (letter to Durrell, October 7, 1946).[4]

BRASSAÏ So, for you, the time of great journeys is beginning. Oddly, I'm becoming more and more of a homebody. I haven't stopped traveling since 1945. But the more I traveled, the more I found that countries and manners are all alike. Whether I was in Turkey, Africa, America, Ireland, or Brazil, after a few days of culture shock, the strangeness, the exoticism vanished, and the life of men remained.

MILLER I understand you. For a long time I shared your state of mind. I didn't even think of taking vacations. To work well, one must not deviate from one's habits. When I travel, I am empty and my mind is numb. I also had the impression that I was not missing a great deal by not budging. I was happy wherever I happened to be: at the Villa Seurat, in Clichy, in Big Sur, as if I carried the whole universe inside me. But now, as a writer, I have reached the "age limit." Have you noticed? Writers have completed most of their body of work *before* age sixty, seventy at most, unlike painters and sculptors, most of whom have produced their most important works only *beginning* at sixty and with no age limit. So with *Nexus II*, my work as a writer will be done. But I'll still be able to do watercolors.

BRASSAÏ Come on, I'm skeptical. You'll unearth another "Colossus" in Lhasa, other "Maxes" in Mexico, other "Devils in Paradise" in Japan or China. Didn't you tell me that it is your fate to describe forever and that death will strike you while you're writing?

CHAPTER 6

May 7, 1960

Henry wanted us to spend a little time together, and this morning, via the blue train, I join him in Cannes. I arrive early at the Hôtel Montfleury on the hill of Californie, not far from Picasso's villa. "Mr. Miller is very tired and has ordered no visits, no telephone calls, until breakfast," I am told at the reception desk. But since I am expected, they tell him I am here. Near me a stranger is arguing with the concierge. "No, not an ironing board and not a bread-board. . . . Just a simple board made of whitewood, just wide enough so I can sleep on it. I've never been able to sleep in a bed. . . . That's right, you'll put the board at the foot of the bed."

I prick up my ears. The man is speaking with a rough Castilian accent and is swallowing his words. The concierge has difficulty understanding. But I, knowing that this peculiar client always slept on a wooden board at the Hôtel de l'Aiglon in Paris, on boulevard Raspail where he usually stays, I discern that he is the director Luis Buñuel. The man of about thirty next to him is his son Juan-Luis. At the Parisian hotel, Buñuel, instead of going out to eat in a restaurant, preferred to cook in his room, and odors strongly scented with garlic invaded the corridors and bothered the other guests.

In the center of a large room in the shape of a boat prow and streaming with light, Henry is in the middle of his breakfast. The bay windows look out on a stand of tall palm trees that remind me of Rio.

MILLER I'm touched that you've come.

BRASSAÏ How was your trip to Rome?

MILLER I was not very happy there. It may have been the bad weather, the cold, the wet.

BRASSAÏ Oddly, every time I stayed in Rome I shivered with cold. I had to pinch myself: was I really in ancient Rome? I had trouble imagining the Romans in that cold city, where rain and even snow were coming down in torrents. We see them in togas made of carefully draped white wool, their shoulders, arms, and feet bare.

MILLER And what did they wear under their togas?

BRASSAÏ Almost nothing. A linen tunic, I think. The athletes walked around naked, a linen loincloth around the middle.

MILLER What about the women?

BRASSAÏ They too often wore tunics made of cotton or silk. I have trouble imagining them in February in the rain or snow. I thought that the Roman world existed in a very hot, almost African climate. But I read somewhere that Emperor Augustus, who was very sensitive to the cold, wore three tunics one on top of another under his toga. Perhaps the climate has changed. Did you see Fred?

MILLER Always the same: comical, clownish. We spent a few days together. But he was not alone: his new wife, Anne, was with him.

Someone brings Miller his mail, about twenty letters. A small collection of postage stamps. Embarrassed, Henry makes a face.

BRASSAÏ You ought to have a secretary.

MILLER I know. But then I'd have to concern myself with him as well. One more worry. I sometimes had one in Big Sur. The experiment was inconclusive. Will you help me?

I unseal the letters. The first is a long-winded missive from a very conceited young novelist. He has not published anything yet, but he asks Miller to read his novel, to write a screenplay based on it, to get it accepted and produced by a great director. Only after "the world success that the film will not fail to have" will he let his novel be published.

MILLER I was stupid enough to respond. And now he's making another try! They're all the same! The nicer you are, the more they take advantage of you. Rip it up, throw it in the trash! I find four or five such requests in my mail every day.

BRASSAÏ And here's a letter from Mme Fernand Léger. Invitation to the inauguration of the Léger Museum in Biot, Friday night. Attended and officiated by Picasso, Braque, Chagall, André Malraux, and all the rest.

MILLER Hmm, hmm. Should I go? I don't want to at all. In any case, I have to reply.

BRASSAÏ Did you know Léger?

MILLER I met him in the United States during the war. He asked me for a piece on the circus, which he wanted to illustrate. I then wrote, specially for him, *The Smile at the Foot of the Ladder,* the story of a clown. But Léger was very disappointed with it. He wrote me that he would have preferred something more "spicy," more "Milleresque," in the style of the *Tropics.* [*Miller's marginal note:* "In the end, he did not illustrate my book, but wrote and illustrated his own, titled *The Circus.* H. M."]

BRASSAÏ And what's that money order?

MILLER Must be my literary agent sending me funds. Where can I cash it? Which post office? What should I do with all that money?

I tell him and ask: "So, what do you think of the Cannes Film Festival?"

MILLER At first, it was terrible! In fact, I almost handed in my resignation. Oh, the films were all right. Four hours a day of viewing doesn't exhaust me. But everything around it! They wanted to put me up at the Carlton. But not for a million dollars did I want to stay in that palace besieged by journalists and photographers. So they offered me the Hôtel Montfleury, away from all the hubbub. But even here I'm harassed. How can I get away from it?

BRASSAÏ How's the jury?

MILLER With Georges Simenon, there was a direct, warm, friendly connection from our first meeting. He protects me. He has even excused me from wearing a tuxedo at the opening gala. At seventy years old, I'm not about to start wearing one. But that didn't happen on its own. I had to give the authorities an ultimatum: "Miller without a tuxedo, or no Miller." Since "evening dress" is required at the late showings, I'll never attend them. So we can spend the time together.

BRASSAÏ Who are the members of the jury?

MILLER There's Diego Fabbri of Italy, Konzunstef of Russia, a Japanese judge, a German, an Argentine, and four French people, including Marc Allégret. He's handsome, distinguished, attractive, but he baffles me a little. I would have taken him for a South American. Do you know him?

BRASSAÏ Yes, fairly well. He was a good friend of André Gide's. His best film, I think, will always be *Ladies Lake,* filmed in Austria, a film awash in sensuality, with the young Simone Simon, who does a marvelous job with her part.

MILLER I remember that actress—she moved to Hollywood.

BRASSAÏ Yes, and even in life she continued to play the role of an amorous she-cat. She caused a lot of talk by handing out the gold key to her villa. Do you remember?

I hand Henry my book *Graffiti,* which has just been published in Germany.

MILLER (*leafing through it*) Hmm, hmm. It's very beautiful, very exciting. As interesting as a book on the primitive arts. Will you sign it for me?

So I write: "To Henry Miller, the male member of the jury of the Cannes Film Festival."

Henry takes two vitamin capsules: "It's thanks to these capsules that I can stick it out."

At one o'clock, on the steps of the festival palace, he introduces me to Georges Simenon, who takes a pull on the long pipe belonging to Superintendent Maigret.

Change of location. A fish and shellfish bistro in the old harbor. Gilberte has joined us with a Japanese friend. Henry is delighted to have lunch with a Japanese woman and to get tips about Tokyo, which he wants to visit soon. Another reason to like Japan: alongside France, it is the country where his books have had the greatest success.

"Do you know what I like most about the Chinese and Japanese? It's their *impassiveness.* Even when they're in the grip of a violent emotion, they never reveal their feelings. We Westerners show our anger, our joy, our sadness, we open up. Not the Japanese. Is that impassiveness congenital, a characteristic of the race, or is it the result of upbringing, of training?

JAPANESE WOMAN More of upbringing. We are inculcated at a very early age in the art of controlling ourselves in all circumstances of life, the art of not showing our feelings. It's sort of a strength, don't you think?

MILLER But doesn't that make them suffer?

JAPANESE WOMAN Yes, of course, it even makes them fairly unhappy.

MILLER I love Nipponese films. I place some of them above our best productions. When someone asks me what my favorite films are, I always answer, without a trace of hesitation: *Rashomon.* Did you see the Japanese film that was shown last night? *Odd Obsession?* [*Miller's marginal note:* "The title of this film is also *The Key*, I believe, or, in Japanese, *Kagi.* H. M."]

BRASSAÏ No, but Gilberte went to see it.

MILLER I can't say anything about it, I'm a member of the jury! [He puts two fingers to his lips.] Hush, hush. But I can certainly listen to what other people think of it. Gilberte, did you like the film?

GILBERTE It baffled me. One of the strangest films I've seen.

MILLER Why was it so poorly received?

GILBERTE I think people were expecting a film with the whole panoply of geishas, samurai, cherry trees in blossom, hara-kiris. And since the subject was scabrous and dealt with the tragedy of impotence, people had some hope of getting to see erotic scenes, suggestive images. So the public was disappointed by that morbid film, handled with discretion and delicacy. It made me think of Buñuel's obsessions, but expressed in the Japanese manner: shameful desires, latent hatred, concealed jealousy, sexual awkwardness. In my opinion, the scene between the mother and the daughter, who has a brutal frankness that clashes with her parents' hypocrisy, is a great moment in film.

MILLER You're right! The violence of that scene is unprecedented, I see no equivalent to it. [Miller catches himself and puts two fingers to his mouth.] Good heavens! I'm giving myself away! Let's not talk about it anymore. It would be reckless of me.

GILBERTE If only you'd seen those poor Japanese! Even being the good Orientals they are, the actors and authors of *Kagi* could barely conceal their confusion after that defeat. The most tragic scenes in the film caused hilarity in the auditorium. And no one applauded. The audience didn't understand a thing.

MILLER Japan intrigues me more than any country in the world except China. We were still back at Pearl Harbor, the kamikaze planes, Hiroshima, the unconditional surrender. And now here it is on its feet, stronger then ever. How do you explain that resurrection?

JAPANESE WOMAN We are a disciplined people, military in our souls. The factory workers have the same fanaticism, the same submission, the same spirit of sacrifice as our soldiers.

MILLER But that doesn't explain everything! Your capacity for adapting, your exceptional talent for the modern age—because you've equaled us, you're already surpassing us in many areas, even in art. Your cinema proves it.

JAPANESE WOMAN We are not creators or inventors, but we have the gift, I think, of assimilating and then improving every technology.

MILLER I always see two Japans. The traditionalist one and the one oriented toward technological progress. How can you reconcile the kimono with overalls? Is your incredible drive to modernize yourselves really a love for the West?

JAPANESE WOMAN I don't think so! But we had no choice. It was either let in the West or perish.

MILLER Under the veneer of modern technology, your old way of thinking and living, the virtues of your ancestors, continue to exist. How can the Japanese reconcile the past and the present so well? That's what astonishes me, what's still a riddle for me. I have a keen desire to visit your country.

JAPANESE WOMAN When would you like to come?

MILLER This fall. I'd like to spend six months there. I'll go with a young woman from Big Sur whom I love, and with a young poet who's very gifted, enthusiastic, and rich. To live in one of those partitioned wood houses with the beds on the floor—that's my dream. In Big Sur, when I had my studio built, I was thinking of those houses. But can you have a maid or a servant over there?

JAPANESE WOMAN Yes, you can have a boy.

MILLER But I'm afraid I'll catch cold. Can those wood houses be heated?

JAPANESE WOMAN Very poorly. And if you haven't been toughened up since childhood, you suffer from the cold. You'll be much better off in a modern house with central heating.

BRASSAÏ Do the teahouses still exist, and the geishas?

JAPANESE WOMAN Of course! All that exists on the fringes of modern life.

MILLER I've always dreamed of living with a geisha.

JAPANESE WOMAN When I was young, I wanted to become a geisha myself. But I had no vocation for it. You have to be gifted, you see. It's a long hard apprenticeship. At age eight, you have to leave your family and all the joys of childhood. The geishas are cloistered like novices.

MILLER And yet what a difference! They learn everything that can make them agreeable to *man* on earth and not to *a god* in heaven.

JAPANESE WOMAN Westerners often confuse geishas with prostitutes! But that's not it at all! A geisha is a person cultivated in all areas, even in the arts.

MILLER I share Keyserling's admiration for the Japanese woman. He says that no Western woman can rival a geisha in elegance of body and mind. He considers her the most perfect thing ever created. It must be delicious to live with a woman full of grace who has no pretensions other than to be what she is.

JAPANESE WOMAN They hold a privileged place in our society. In our country, wives are not allowed at parties. But the geishas go to them. Sometimes they even become famous. A geisha named Teruko is a doctor of letters.

BRASSAÏ Somewhere I read a terrible story about something that supposedly happened at a school for geishas. The master is said to have gone crazy and to have decapitated his pupils. Is that a legend or a true story?

JAPANESE WOMAN A true story! The master, on returning home one evening from the theater, perhaps under the influence of the play he'd just seen, grabbed a heavy saber and began to decapitate the sleeping geishas. Only one managed to escape the massacre: her name was Tsumakishi. The madman cut off both her arms but not her head, and she managed to run away. In fact, she became one of the most famous geishas.

Miller is beaming. Geishas excite him. We are on our third bottle of *côtes-de-provence* and he orders a fourth.

Maliciously, I wonder what cruel disappointments await him in Japan. The idea he has formed of it is such that the reality can only disappoint him. Won't he find a Japan that is more Americanized, more "air-conditioned nightmarized," than the United States itself? A Tokyo that has grown haphazardly, with no center and no sewer service in a large part of the city? A monstrous proliferation of urban cancer, which is already disfiguring the most beautiful landscapes? And many signs of sadism and perversion openly displayed—women with tortured, bound, martyred bodies—the counterpart, no doubt, of the repression and impassiveness so admired by Henry. Will not Japan, gradually transformed into a phalanstery, efface the beautiful image he's dreamed up?

BRASSAÏ And how did your trip to Germany go?

MILLER I liked that country a great deal. And what a pleasure to have Ledig-Rowohlt as my guide! He's the one now in charge of the Hamburg publishing house. In his Mercedes-Benz, he had me visit the cities of the "Hansa." I had taken a trip with him to Sète, to see where Paul Valéry is buried in the "graveyard by the sea." It was there he invited me to Germany.

BRASSAÏ The reconstructed Hamburg is very interesting, I'm told. And its "red-light district" is teeming with people.

MILLER I preferred Bremen with its enormous rathskeller, but with a very familial atmosphere. And especially Lübeck. I naturally thought of Thomas Mann there, and of his novels: *Buddenbrooks* and *Tonio Kröger*. I used to admire him and would have been over the moon to meet him. I looked at Lübeck through the eyes of Tonio, a young writer returning from Florence, his native city, to the misty north—which he had left contemptuously thirteen years earlier. Torn between middle-class life and adventure, the seriousness of his German father and the imaginativeness of his Italian mother, he roams that city, which has become almost foreign to him, in search of his past, in quest as well of the women he loved in his youth. His house has been sold, he doesn't know anyone anymore, and no one knows him. Yes, that was a book that mattered, that moved me deeply at the time.

BRASSAÏ I think the story Thomas Mann told was a little bit his own. His family was part of the Hanseatic middle class and they lived in an eighteenth-century patrician house. His father was a businessman and a ship owner. At his death, his business was liquidated, his house sold, and Frau Mann had to leave Lübeck for Munich with her five children.

MILLER I don't have the heart to reread *Tonio Kröger* again. And I don't have the same admiration for Thomas Mann anymore. I ranked him with the greatest writers. I thought at the time that, for me to write well, I had only to dissect their texts to get at the secret of their style. And it was him I most wanted to imitate. But a few years ago, rereading aloud *Death in Venice,* which is taken for his masterpiece, I realized he was only a good craftsman, not a genius.

BRASSAÏ And what do you think of the new generation of Germans?

MILLER Sympathetic and promising. The spirit of the young has been sensitized so to speak by everything that's going on in the world. Almost all my books have been translated into German. In Lübeck we were put up in a sort of inn, set up in a patrician house full of beautiful things, almost a museum. And all the time I was thinking of Heinrich and Thomas Mann. When the innkeeper learned who I was, he let out a cry of joy: "I know you well, Mr. Miller, I own all your books. Let me show them to you in my library." Of course, I was surprised and moved. Many writers see their readers only as buyers. Me, I write for my friends. I need their moral support, their warmth. I feel as if I'm protected. I have hundreds, thousands of unknown friends in the world. Durrell, Cendrars, etc., are readers who have become friends. I could cite dozens of others. Once, a reader from Sacramento wrote me to ask me for a signed photo. We exchanged a few letters. Then, one day, the stranger arrived in Big Sur. His name was John Kidis, Mestakidis was his real name. A Greek. He showered me with gifts: an armload of books, sweaters, socks, pants, caps, Greek pastries, jars of honey, children's toys, paints, tires, records, and so many other things! He even left his job to devote himself to selling my books. It's very moving to discover, somewhere in the vast world, the face of one of your anonymous readers!

BRASSAÏ Nietzsche also met one of his rare readers one day, on the terrace of San Miniato in Florence: a German astronomer, who had read all his books and could even quote many long passages from memory. He was naturally as surprised as he was moved. To hear back about one's books and to discover a friendship one knew nothing about! And he was so frustrated about them!

MILLER What about you, Brassaï, has that ever happened to you?

BRASSAÏ Yes, from time to time. The most surprising of those encounters was one I had in Marrakech in an Arab nightclub, where the dancers and the orchestra of Glaoui, the pasha of Marrakech, were showing off. I wanted to take a few photographs, so I went to ask the club manager, who was rather reserved. But when he saw my card, he exclaimed: "You are—Brassaï? I love your photographs and I own several of your books. Will you sign them for me?"

MILLER My first reader was June, naturally. And it was the excitement I saw on her face while she was reading my books that sustained me for a long time. Even later, when I reread freshly written pages, struggling to imagine the effect on my future readers, it was always June's delight I thought of.

Sunday, May 8, 1960

This morning at the Hôtel Montfleury, Henry is arguing with a French television producer about the twenty-seven questions for the broadcast that
will take place tomorrow morning. At noon, he must attend Eden-Roc,
Cap d'Antibes, the luncheon offered by the mayor of Cannes to the members
of the jury. And since he has an appointment with Simenon at the festival
palace, we go on foot from Californie to La Croisette, passing by the Hôtel
Gallia, a strange art nouveau jewel with its theater, its twisted gates, and its
ecstatic statues. Converted into an apartment complex, it is vanishing behind
a horrible cement building.

MILLER There's a question I've wanted to ask you for a long time. Is it true
that Hans Reichel was confined to a psychiatric hospital for awhile?

BRASSAÏ A strange story! One night around midnight, somebody rings
my doorbell. I had already gone to bed, I was sleeping. "Who is it?" "It's
me, Reichel!" I open the door. With a packet under his arm, he's giving off
a strong odor of eau de cologne. What could have brought him to my house
at such a late hour? "Can you lend me twenty francs? I have to rent a hotel room," he tells me. "Yes. But what's going on? Were you kicked out of
your studio?" "I had to flee impasse du Rouet, I'm being pursued." "Pursued? But by whom?" "A band of assassins! I was at home, the door was
locked. Suddenly I heard: 'Reichel, open up! Open up or we'll shoot!' I
looked through the keyhole. There were three of them, two men and a
woman. 'Open up, open up, or we'll shoot.' What would you have done in
my place? I didn't dare open the door. They would have killed me. I was
trembling all over. I put out the light. I hid in a corner. They kept on for an
hour. Then they left, or so I thought. Quickly, I collected my toothbrush,

a bar of soap, a towel, my pajamas, and I crept out like a mouse, just like a mouse."

The story seemed implausible to me. "But who are these people who are threatening you? Do you know them?" "I know the woman. It's possible the men want to get their revenge out of jealousy." "You should alert the police." "Me, the police? My dear Brassaï, you know my relationship with the police. If I file a complaint, I'll be the one put away before anything else. I know that!" "And where did you go?" "I walked up and down the little streets behind avenue du Maine for an hour, two hours. Then I see a little hotel, I rent a room. I go upstairs, lock the door. I get ready for bed and what do I hear? The voices of my assassins! They were already in the room next door! How could they have tracked me down? I wonder. I didn't know myself what street I was on, what hotel I was at. They're very strong! I heard their voices: 'No, no, we mustn't use a revolver to kill Reichel! We have to tie him to his bed and beat him with chains till he croaks.' I was sweating. Quickly, I dressed again, opened the door, and tiptoed downstairs. Once outside, I ran over to the Villa Seurat as fast as my legs could carry me."

MILLER The Villa Seurat?

BRASSAÏ Yes. In his confusion, Reichel thought that only Betty Ryan could save him.

MILLER Oh, Betty Ryan! What an adorable creature!

BRASSAÏ Reichel was madly in love with her.

MILLER Who wasn't in love with her? She was so beautiful, so attractive. She had such a sweet voice. And since I also loved her, Reichel became madly jealous. He started to hate me. One day he even tried to kill me. Poor Reichel! That was the only subject of discord between us. Go on.

BRASSAÏ Betty Ryan was an ethereal, unreal creature, lost in her dreams. Touched by Reichel's devotion, she sometimes bought him a canvas, but her feelings for him went no further.

Betty was already in bed and didn't want to let Reichel in. "I begged her," he told me, "'Open up, open up! I'm in the street. I'm being pursued. I have to spend the night outdoors.' Finally, Betty took pity on me. She let me in, comforted me, offered me a piece of cheese and some wine. And she gave me a bottle of cologne as a gift. But I was so upset, so agitated, that on my way downstairs, I slipped and took a tumble, and I broke the bottle in my pants pocket. All the cologne spilled onto my clothes. Can you lend me twenty francs?" "Yes," I replied, barely awake and exasperated, "but you don't have to tell me some detective story!" "So you don't believe me? It's all true, I swear it! Save me! Give me the money and a glass of red wine. That's all I'm asking from you. And I'll go away, I'll let you sleep. Pardon me for waking you up." He emptied the glass and disappeared. With him, you were always in the midst of some Dostoyevsky drama.

MILLER What a story!

BRASSAÏ It's not over. The next morning, his nocturnal visit seemed like a bad dream to me, but the empty glasses were on the table and the twenty francs were missing. Then I felt bad that I'd let him leave in that condition. But in what condition? He wasn't drunk. When he'd been drinking, his gestures, his voice were entirely different. I'd seen him drunk many times. To clear things up, I went to impasse du Rouet. His studio—which looked out on the courtyard—was locked. I questioned the concierge. "Mr. Reichel?" she said, "Poor man, he's just been taken away to the prefecture." "What happened to him?" "Well, he came in early this morning. He had thrown the door of his studio wide open and had begun to drag his bed into the middle of the courtyard. I ran over and asked him: 'What are you doing, Mr. Reichel?' 'You don't see?' he said. 'I'm moving.' 'I can see very well that you're "moving," Mr. Reichel.' I was frantic, I started to cry. Then I called police emergency. The van came, they put him inside. I don't know what's become of him!"

MILLER Is that when he was taken to Sainte-Anne?

BRASSAÏ Yes, I learned about it the next day, at the infirmary of the police prefecture. A few weeks later, he came to see me. Gay, jovial, well-rested. He was fit as a fiddle. He found it amusing to tell me everything that had happened. "When I left your place, I took a room in a little hotel across the way. I had so much anxiety that I couldn't go to bed. I didn't dare leave the hotel. I spent the whole night on my feet, trembling, in the middle of the room. It was horrible! A cold sweat broke out on my forehead. At dawn, I left the hotel and went home. But I didn't dare stay by myself in my studio. To see that the concierge and the tenants would protect me from my 'assassins,' I dragged my bed into the middle of the courtyard. That's when the Chinese intervened!"

MILLER (*very intrigued*) The Chinese?

BRASSAÏ Does that surprise you? At the time, you were fascinated by China. You talked about it to everyone. And you wrote in your *Walk through China* that Paris is France and France is China, that it's the only place in the world where you could lead your Chinese life. You felt you were speaking Chinese and going up the Yangtze in a *dhaw*. And curiously, Reichel had the same sensation. Crossing the Seine in the police van, he told me, he felt like he was crossing the Yellow River, and the prefecture yard seemed to be filled with helmeted Chinese.

MILLER   How odd! As for me, I wrote *Walk through China* in a sort of delirium. But did Reichel remember his stay at Sainte-Anne?

BRASSAÏ   Down to the smallest detail! And he recounted every one with humor and detachment, as if they had happened to someone else. It's as if there was an internal split in him. Two beings who barely got along inhabited him. The well-behaved, sensible Reichel always gleefully reported the misadventures of the other one. At the prefecture infirmary, the psychiatrist questioned him: "Where are your pants, sir?" "My pants?" Reichel replied. "I have no idea. All I know is that the potatoes are on the night table." "That's enough for me!" said the psychiatrist. And in a padded van our friend was transported to Sainte-Anne hospital. There he fell into a deep, cataleptic sleep. "Did I sleep for twenty-four hours? Forty-eight? I have no idea. When I woke up, I found myself among crazy people. It was awful! Seated around a long table, we ate with our fingers, like Arabs. No spoon, no knife, no fork. At the end of the meal, we had to stay seated without moving a muscle. Digestion is the critical moment of agitation, it appears. And, in fact, my fellow diners didn't sit still. They bombarded one another with little wads of bread. I often walked the grounds, and sometimes I even forgot I was among crazy people. It was spring. A Japanese cherry tree was blossoming. A blackbird was singing. It was marvelous. Next to me, there was a little man in a beard. I cried out, to communicate my enthusiasm to him: 'Isn't it magnificent?' The man grabbed his beard with both hands, began to whirl like a dervish, and his voice got shriller and shriller as he repeated: 'It's magnificent! It's magnificent! It's magnificent!' It gave me chills up and down my spine. Obviously, I was among the mentally ill. In vain I begged the doctors to free me. They wouldn't hear of it. 'Even if you're cured, the law obliges us to keep you under observation. We have too great a responsibility.' I tried again: 'Doctor, I beg of you, let me go free! You see very well I'm not crazy.' Then, one day, point-blank, he asked me this question: 'Sir, do you have relatives or friends?' I replied: 'Yes, Doctor, I have friends. Why?' 'They must answer for you, must guarantee in writing that you won't go back to drinking. If you do, you hear me, it'll be delirium tremens and the mental institution forever!' 'I have many friends, dear Doctor,' I replied, 'but none of them can guarantee that I won't drink again.' The doctor gave me a slap on the shoulder: 'That's the response of a man who is sound of mind,' he told me. 'I'm going to let you go this very day.'"

MILLER   What happened to him in Dieppe?

BRASSAÏ   Reichel was stuck in Paris, broke, and he always dreamed of the sea. "Oh, if only I could go take a look at the sea!" he'd sigh. One day, when he'd gotten hold of a little money, he bought a round trip ticket from Paris to Dieppe. He actually took the train, actually arrived in Dieppe, but he never saw the sea.

MILLER Why's that?

BRASSAÏ He woke up in the dark. He began to grope around and his hands knocked against four walls. "Gradually," he told me, "my memory came back: the Gare Saint-Lazare, the train, a bar in Dieppe filled with whores and sailors. And then, nothing. A thick fog. With all my might, I began to knock on the door and to yell at the top of my lungs. No reply. Suddenly, a window opened and a grave voice shouted at me: 'Will you stop that racket? Shut up!' 'All the same, I would like to know where I am!' 'You'll find out!' And the individual closed the peephole on me. I understood: I was in prison. But why? I only learned when I went before the judge. I must have gotten into a fight with some sailors. The police intervened and had put me away. But the judge, when he learned I was an 'artist,' proved to be rather indulgent. I got off with a fine. But what misfortune! I had to leave Dieppe on the spot, without even looking at the sea. What bad luck, don't you think?"

MILLER I didn't know that story. Reichel had spoken to me of another prison in Germany, though he was not very talkative about his past. The revolutionary writer Ernst Toller was his friend, and Reichel was supposedly arrested with him. What you say about his "split" is very true. Like some of Dostoyevsky's characters, he was a man *possessed*. There was the jovial, affectionate Reichel, full of consideration for his friends. The watercolor lessons he gave me were more or less therapy. Life therapy. After he left me, I saw, heard, and tasted things better. But a drop too much and the demon took the place of the angel. He would fall into the hands of a terrifying power. Filled with anxiety, he thought everyone was making fun of him. In his rages, he insulted his best friends, accused them of all sorts of crimes. I remember dreadful scenes at the Villa Seurat.

BRASSAÏ But Reichel hated his demon! He fought against it. He wanted to keep it from spending his hard-earned money while on a binge. He would have preferred to buy paints, canvases, paintbrushes, pay his arrears at the hotel. So he used all sorts of ruses to foil the plans of the Dr. Jekyll who lived inside him. If he received a thousand-franc note, he immediately changed it into ten hundreds and hid them with his eyes shut under the mattress, in a book, a pocket, a drawer, so that the "other" wouldn't find them. Curiously, Balzac had the hero of *The Wild Ass's Skin* perform the same operation: in order not to spend his thirty francs, to put "a barbed barrier between him and his money," he scattered the coins with eyes shut in his drawers, in his old clothes, in his straw mattress, among his papers. And, like Reichel, he turned the whole room upside down in a fit of nerves to find them. With the first hundred-franc bill, Reichel's demon took a taxi to Montparnasse. At the counter of Le Dôme, he bought a round for everybody, whores, bums, strangers. A half-hour later, broke, he returned in a taxi to the hotel in search of the second bill. He then rifled through his room while the taxi waited to take him back to Le Dôme. That feverish shuttling back and forth often lasted till dawn, until the last hundred-franc bill was found and spent.

MILLER What flabbergasts me is that, in such a state of drunkenness, nothing untoward ever happened to him.

BRASSAÏ It's as if a guardian angel protected him. One winter day—Christmas Eve—in the snow, he fell down in front of the train station on place Denfert-Rochereau. In spite of his desperate efforts, he could not manage to get up. "Don't fall asleep! Don't fall asleep! Identity card," a remnant of consciousness whispered to him. You see, his papers were not in order. Suddenly, he's being shaken, someone puts him on his feet, an authoritarian voice asks him for his name, his address, his papers. Reichel thought it was the police. Who else would concern himself with a drunk spread out on the sidewalk on Christmas Eve? But it wasn't the police, it really was an angel! Without leaving his name, the stranger led Reichel back to his hotel. What a difficult chore! Because he fought with you, insulted you. I took him back any number of times, I know what I'm talking about.

MILLER I wonder if alcohol was beneficial to his painting?

BRASSAÏ Beneficial, without a doubt! He needed to grind down his consciousness from time to time, to plunge into the chaos of his inner life. The alcoholic fits rose up in him abruptly like cyclones, it must have happened the same way for Modigliani or Utrillo. After every crisis, he was calm, he recovered his serenity, and for some time he had what he needed to feed his painting. I'm sure of it: his capacity for creation was bound up with alcohol. In a state of inebriation, Reichel could achieve an extreme lucidity, a sort of clairvoyance. He could uncover your most secret thoughts. I don't know if you had the same experience. He told me one day: "Get rid of your thoughts of suicide." And I had to admit that such thoughts had come into my head. "Your gaze has changed," he told me one night in his drunkenness, "it has become supreme. Nothing can escape you now!" And that sounded to my ears like the prophecy of an oracle in a trance. I'm sorry I didn't note down all his luminous ideas on music, in which he was steeped body and soul, like his friend and teacher, Paul Klee. His lecture, interspersed with shouts and exclamations, on the influence of the *names* of musicians on their music, has become deeply rooted in my mmory. I can still hear him telling me: "*Zart, zart, zart,* the second syllable of Mo-*zart*—which means: tender, delicate, frail—isn't that the quintessence of his music?" In the same way, he explained to me once that the *name* "Bach" means "stream" in German. For Bach, music was only a *stream* that flows and sings. And Reichel was persuaded that Bach was aware of the repercussions of his family name on his music. Later, I was able to verify that his intuition was altogether correct: Bach was indeed influenced by his *name*.

CHAPTER 8

Sunday evening, May 8, 1960

La Croisette is decked out in flags. Gawkers, coming from eighty kilometers in all directions, watch, crowded behind the white barriers, for the stars. When the showing is over, we fish Henry out of the crowd surging from the palace stairwell and head for Juan-les-Pins.

MILLER Finally, a happy, amusing film! Everything I've seen until now has been dreary, depressing, or tragic, as if a joyful spectacle were necessarily vulgar or stupid! I prefer the audience's laughter to weepy sadness. *Never on Sunday* is a Greek farce, carefree, sunny, with excellent actors.

BRASSAÏ Did you see any starlets?

MILLER I only saw a few appetizing thighs from afar, a few butts wiggling under rustling skirts. But at the Japanese reception I ran into a few beautiful Nipponese girls and also a black girl of breathtaking beauty! A black panther! A goddess! Is she French or American? I would really like to know.

GILBERTE She's probably one of the two black models who are posing for *Vogue*. A minor revolution! Never before has an American fashion magazine—except the one for blacks—dared present dresses worn by black women.

Night falls. Now we are under the immense pine parasols of Juan-les-Pins.

MILLER I like this place. I'm a man of instinct and habit. When I enter the suburbs of a city, I nose out whether I'll like it or not, whether I'll be happy or unhappy there. I have the feeling Juan-les-Pins will do me good.

BRASSAÏ Picasso had the same sensation. In Paris one day, he painted this city without ever having seen it. And, in 1920, arriving here for the first time, he saw he had anticipated Juan-les-Pins as it was. Overcome, he cried out: "There is no doubt, this city belongs to me!"

GILBERTE At this time in the spring, Juan-les-Pins is marvelous. But in the summer! It's the noisiest place on the coast! A hundred jazz groups compete here under the pine forest—Juan-les-Pins has become the French Newport.

We have dinner at the home of Mme P. B., a Russian.

MME P.B. I like the Americans for their generosity. We often criticize them, forgetting that France is free only thanks to their intervention.

MILLER Let me stop you there. You forget that, when France succumbed, we were, to be sure, very sad, but we didn't lift a finger to help. In the same way, we abandoned England to its fate. Without the traitorous attack of the Japanese on Pearl Harbor, we would never have intervened to fight Hitler. We entered the war—we claimed—"to make the world free." Fine slogan! In reality, it was ourselves we were defending. Don't be fooled! Only propaganda makes the American people believe they are the *rescuers,* the *liberators,* that they are fighting for *justice.* Therefore, our soldiers can kill in a rage with the clearest conscience in the world.

MME P.B. Granted. All the same, you can't question the Americans' generosity. They're the ones who gave life and hope back to us.

MILLER Even though I've criticized America very harshly, it warms my heart to hear my compatriots praised. You're right, we are generous. There's a spirit in us that can inspire a man to offer you everything he owns without expecting any gratitude at all. But careful! The degree of generosity depends on the degree of *sacrifice* it entails. Giving away extras is not the same thing as depriving oneself of the necessities. America is enormously rich, and when it helps a poor country, what it offers is only crumbs. And yet, there is so much poverty in the world! I'm thinking of the Greeks and their indescribable penury. Durrell sent me heartbreaking letters from Rhodes. And Katsimbalis—the model for my *Colossus of Maroussi*—painted a picture for me of the dying lined up on the sidewalks of Athens, screaming in the snowstorm: "I'm hungry! I'm hungry!" I send clothes and food to my Greek friends. And I often hit up my friends and acquaintances: "You've got so many dresses collecting mold in your closet. Give me half or even three quarters of them, that won't be a hardship for you." The United States could be the finest example on the globe, could radiate peace, joy, goodwill, generosity.

BRASSAÏ You're being a little unfair in praising the immense wealth of the United States without mentioning the *immense effort* it took to develop. Wheat, corn, and petroleum do not rise up out of the ground miraculously.

MILLER I agree. But the great tragedy of our time is precisely that the United States, like Russia, can't even take advantage of what nature offers. With the two of them pitted against each other, the better part of their resources goes to rockets and bombs; whereas, if they were united, they could improve the fate of the whole world's population. Even so, those two vast, rich continents resemble each other. There's no paradox in that! There are so many affinities between the two! Secretly, and sometimes even openly, they respect each other, even admire each other. And both are very *humane*. Back when I was in Paris, almost reduced to beggary, it wasn't the French who helped me out, it was the Russians.

MME P.B. So did the French disappoint you?

MILLER They're reserved, they're slow to make friends. I like that, in fact. You have to seduce them into it. And they're not free with their money. Of course, now they throw open their doors and their purses for me, but only since I've become well-known and recognized. I don't hold it against them! They have so many other good qualities.

MME P.B. You judge the French by the Parisians. You don't know the peasants. You can't imagine their self-sacrifice, their generosity during the Occupation. I know what I'm talking about.

MILLER That's very possible. Durrell feels the same way. The selfishness and hardness of the French may apply only to certain city-dwellers. He also lauds the generosity of country people. In any case, in Paris I understood fairly quickly and at great cost that you couldn't ask anyone to give you credit. Bakeries, grocery stores, and butcher shops post "No credit given" all over the place. And too bad if you're short a penny or two. They'll grab the bread or croissant right out of your mouth. That happened to me several times. One day, on place d'Alesia—it's strange, you can never forget these things—I wanted to go to the movies. But beforehand, I wanted to have a cup of coffee. And I was short a few cents. "Tough," I thought, "They know me in that café. For once, they'll give me credit." I go up to the cashier. Coldly, cruelly, she repeats the well-known phrase: *"No credit given!"* And she says that to me, an old regular! I was so overcome with anger that, once I'd shown her the pennies owed for the coffee, I threw them down on the ground. They were still rolling around when I left the café, swearing never to set foot in there again.

BRASSAÏ It seems to me, though, that the owner of a little restaurant gave you credit.

MILLER You're right. It was the Restaurant des Gourmets, on rue des Canettes. An exception. The New York restaurateurs would never be more generous, in fact. They'd feed you, of course, but, in exchange, they'd force you to wash the dishes all day long.

MME P.B. Do you think people in the United States are more trusting of you?

MILLER Definitely! At the beginning of my stay in Big Sur, I lived with my wife Lepska and the children almost in poverty. What I was earning was not even enough to feed us. And do you know who gave us credit? And sometimes as much as three hundred dollars? Jack, the mailman! He was the one who provided us with the basic necessities. And with no hope of being reimbursed one day. In Big Sur I met a marvelous woman: Jean Wharton. Seeing how poorly we were housed in our shack, she offered me her beautiful house. "I would gladly accept," I told her, "but I can't even give you a partial payment." "Move into my house," she replied, "You'll pay me when you have money." She didn't ask for my signature or for a security deposit or anything. "Do you know my books?" I asked her. "If you'd read them, you'd have a completely different opinion of me." She replied: "I accept you as you are, as I know you. What you write is completely indifferent to me." Do you have many examples in France of that kind of trust, that generosity?

BRASSAÏ And you never paid for the house?

MILLER Oh yes, with the little money that remained from my royalties in France. Imagine! I had lived almost in poverty in Big Sur, up to my neck in debt, not owning even a car, when one day a letter from my Parisian publisher, the young Maurice Girodias, informed me that I had at my disposal *forty thousand dollars!* I threw the letter on the table and, nervously, I started laughing like crazy. It's not true, I thought. But it was true! After the Liberation, an enormous quantity of the *Tropics* books were sold to American soldiers. And they were the ones who peddled my books in the United States and introduced them under the counter.

MME P.B. And you finally got your hands on that fortune?

MILLER No, nothing. Or almost nothing! It wasn't permitted to transfer the money to me. I could have come to France, bought an apartment in Paris, a château in the country, or even a yacht. But I didn't want to leave Big Sur before finishing my books. And the runaway inflation and devaluation made my nest egg completely melt away.

MME P.B. You spoke of the generosity of the Russians.

MILLER Yes, based on my own experiences in Paris. It was always the Russians who shared their meals with me, who put me up, who paid for a room for me.

BRASSAÏ You're probably thinking of "Pachou."

MILLER   Yes, among many others. I saw him again a few days ago, since we've remained good friends. He's now seventy. I ran into him on rue de Vanves one summer day. I hadn't eaten a thing in thirty-six hours. Attracted by a large poster of Olga Chekhova, I stopped in front of a movie theater. It was playing a silent film, *Le Moulin Rouge,* I think. Chekhova was the niece of the great Chekhov, whom I admired. And I had an insane desire to see that film. My attitude probably seemed bizarre to the man on a ladder putting up the posters, and he called out to me. "I'd like to see that film," I told him, "but I don't have a cent in my pocket." "What nationality are you?" "American," I answered. "American? You're joking!" He was probably thinking of my superrich compatriots who were lounging on the terrace of the Café de la Paix. It's true that penniless Americans like me were rather rare in Paris. The stranger immediately invited me to eat and drink at the corner café. We lit cigarettes.

BRASSAÏ   And he offered to play a game of chess with you.

MILLER   No, I offered. I was immediately attracted to that simple and generous man. We played three games. I asked his name. "Alekhine!" he replied, with a malicious smile. Because he was playing like a champion and checkmated me three times. His name was Eugene Pashutinsky, "Pachou," a Russian émigré who had deserted the Red Army. And he told me about his life in Paris after 1923.

BRASSAÏ   You were working on *Tropic of Cancer* at the time.

MILLER   Yes. I took out my notebook and began to take notes. "What does that mean?" he asked me haughtily. "Are you taking notes? Are you from the police?" I reassured him: "I'm writing a novel and maybe I'll put you in it as well." "So," he remarked with a smile, "don't speak too spitefully of me." That man helped me, gave me money. I'll never forget it. And I rewarded him as I could. One day, "Pachou" took the train without a ticket. Inspection. Police report. A few weeks later, summons to appear at the offices of the railroad company. A nasty affair! But, to his great surprise, he was received with deference and was asked to sit down. He was called in not to pay a fine but to receive a fairly large sum of money. Here's what had happened. One day I had written an advertisement about some region of France, for a tourism magazine that was published by the railroad company. So, to repay my debt to my benefactor, I asked that the fee be paid to him. Hence the summons.

MME P.B.   Have you written many tourism texts?

MILLER   Fred was commissioned to do them, but sometimes he passed them on to me. They could bring in about fifty francs: five good meals at the time! Back then, I consulted old issues on tourism, a guide, or an encyclopedia to compose my texts.

MME P.B. Have you seen Griegori Chukhrai's *Ballad of a Soldier?* I would have so liked to see that film. What do you think of it?

MILLER Shh . . . Shhh. My lips are sealed. But I can tell you it was warmly received. Two minutes of ovation! It really excited the audience. A film steeped in humanity and free of the usual propaganda slogans. Let me just mention one scene. It struck me deeply. A seriously disabled soldier, who had lost a leg in the war, hesitates to return home to his wife. She didn't love him very much, she'd even cheated on him. Finally, he gives up the idea of going home. "What are you going to do?" a comrade asks him, "where will you go?" Then the invalid flings open his arms and cries: "Russia is vast!" That's what struck me. *"Russia is vast"* is the exact rejoinder of the American *"The West is big."* To go West was—still is—an obsession with us. That's what led me to the great cliffs of the Pacific. [Henry drinks a glass of *côtes-de-provence* and continues.] You know that one of my gods is Walt Whitman. The cosmological scope of his vision no doubt owes a great deal to the "vastness" of the American continent. Whitman was dreaming of a new race on the scale of that land, an earthly paradise. Despite everything about American life that's been spoiled, that potentiality still exists, I'm convinced of it.

BRASSAÏ Deep down, you've remained profoundly American.

MILLER I realize that. Everything that's found around the Mediterranean is too civilized for me, the landscapes, the sea, even the climate. Nature under man's sway oppresses me. I don't like vineyards, olive trees, cultivated fields, domesticated animals. I prefer rocks, sand, uninhabited deserts, vultures, eagles. I would have liked to live in Asia, in Tibet. Big Sur doesn't take their place, but it's a haven for me.

MME P.B. Yet you often come back to France, to Europe. What draws you here?

MILLER Everything I don't have in the United States, especially *wit!* I'm divided. One part of me is happy only in America, the other, only in Europe. Without Americans, I would be very much at home in my country.

MME P.B. But how did you come to hate them to that extent? You never miss an opportunity to beat up on your compatriots.

MILLER That hatred grew gradually in me and exploded one night in New York. We were hungry, June and I. And without enough to buy a piece of bread. So I had begun begging.

MME P.B. BEGGING? Not possible!

MILLER I had no other solution. I was begging near my residence or else on Times Square, outside the theaters. With my collar turned up, my hand out, I sometimes spent hours without collecting a cent. But sometimes—rarely—

someone stuffed a big bill into my hand before I even opened my mouth. Other times I stole. Or let us say, rather, pilfered. Yes, a few cents from the newspaper vendors to at least get a cup of coffee. On the night that triggered my hatred, a man passed by me in a suit and top hat. Seeing my hand out, he rifled through his pocket, and, without stopping, without even deigning to look at me, he threw a fistful of dimes and pennies on the pavement and into the gutter. What an odious pleasure he found in seeing a poor hungry devil get down on his belly to collect his offering. As if I was not humiliated enough already to be reduced to beggary! It was that evening, and because of the sadistic cruelty of that individual, that I became forever disgusted with Americans and that the idea came to me to seek my salvation in Europe. [*Miller's marginal note:* "Brassaï! I'm not so sure it was that incident that made me hate my compatriots. I think rather it was that incident that made me decide never to be a beggar again. H. M."]

In his famous synopsis of *The Rosy Crucifixion*, Miller evokes in a few words this scene of beggary: "At dawn I go out to steal bottles of milk and rolls from the hallways. I beg along Broadway at the theater exits and the strip joints. Incident in Borough Hall: a guy threw money for me into the gutter."[1] He would also evoke that incident in *Tropic of Cancer*, in his novella *The Old Soldier*, and in *Max and the White Phagocytes*. But curiously, the epilogue to that last version is joyful. After the man in cape and top hat had thrown the fistful of small change in his face, Miller hesitates: should he catch up to the lout and "vomit all his bile on him" or rather gather up the coins? He prefers the few cents, which he triumphantly brings back to June. "I'm hungry, aren't you? Let's go eat." And he writes: "And so it was that at six o'clock in the morning one Easter, we went out in force from our secret dungeon to order two hamburgers and two coffees in the greasy cafeteria at the corner of Myrtle Avenue and Fulton Street. I felt strong and purified, as after a thrashing I had deserved. Never in my life had I felt my mind so refreshed and in good spirits."[2] Always feeling both extremes, the struggle between contradictory feelings. The insolence of the man in top hat, far from spurring his hatred toward America, in this case stimulates his mind and his joie de vivre.

MME P.B. Frankly, I don't understand. How could you, a strong, healthy man, have become a beggar?

MILLER I grant you it's difficult to understand. At thirty-three, I was almost on the brink of madness. Without being able to provide the slightest proof, I had the pretension of being a writer. And I really believed I had genius. I was itching to write. Megalomania and impotence, hope and despair, exaltation and distress. How could I get out of that intolerable, ridiculous situation? My friends were calling me a failure. And I couldn't find anyone who had faith in me as a writer.

BRASSAÏ But June . . .

MILLER Yes, June. But we were so close that she was almost another self.

BRASSAÏ And your old friend Schnellock!

MILLER He stimulated me, of course! But he was also a friend, my best friend even. What I needed was the encouragement of a stranger who would have said: "Go on, you're a writer!" But I never encountered that person in America. And since I had left my job, I found myself in an awkward position. I was a failure in the eyes of society and had not earned the slightest place in the world of the arts. An uncomfortable situation, especially in the United States. Woe to you if you deviate from the crowd. You become an exile, an outlaw, in your own country! Seeing no way out of my situation, my mother was always lamenting: "In your old age you'll be begging in the street." She didn't know it had happened much sooner than she thought. I could even write the beggar's manual: (1) Always borrow from inferiors, never from superiors. (2) Learn to debase yourself, since anyone who borrows is always guilty, a potential thief. (3) Accept without flinching the moralizing sermons that usually accompany the charity given you. Etc., etc.

MME P.B. So then you really became a beggar.

MILLER Yes. Fortunately, that's in the past. But since then I've always had a certain fondness for anyone who asks for handouts.

BRASSAÏ Two years ago, in the Bowery, I saw New York bums. What a depressing sight! Already drunk in the morning, staggering, idle, covered with wounds and bumps, they are truly human refuse. Did you know that, like sheriffs, they wear official badges that authorize them to beg? And take advantage of them to extort contributions. The Paris bums have a more human face.

MILLER You're right. One night, when Fred and I were coming home from Montparnasse to the Villa Seurat, an old man accosted us. To get a better look at his face, I grabbed him and dragged him under a streetlight. And I was reassured. It was not the mug of an inveterate drunk but the open and honest face of an old man who was hungry. Without hesitating, I rifled through my pockets—that day, a rarity, I had a fair amount of money—and I stuffed my entire fortune into the bum's hands. We were already a long way off when the beggar started to run after us: "Messieurs! Messieurs! You've made a mistake! You've given me *too much* money!" The poor man couldn't accept the idea that a man would offer him bills and not just small change. "Take them back, I beg of you," he pleaded with me, "You don't look like you're rolling in money." I had to insist that he accept half. And he asked me for my address so he could reimburse me "in kind," by washing the windows, the floor, or by cleaning the toilet.

Henry, having emptied a fair number of glasses, was spirited in his conversation. Nothing could stop him now. But it was one o'clock in the morning, and early the next day the television ordeal would begin!

BRASSAÏ It's a shame the taping didn't take place this evening. You're in top form.

MILLER That's exactly what I find wrong with television. Instead of capturing the voice when it's warmed up, they record you cold. For me to be able to say something interesting, I need a friendly atmosphere, a certain warmth. You can't order inspiration at a set time! This evening, I ate well, drank well, I was off and running. But tomorrow morning? I'll be only half awake, I may say nothing but nonsense.

Miller and Brassaï in Pacific Palisades (Los Angeles), June 28, 1973

Hans Reichel at L'hôtel des Terrasses, circa 1933

Miller atop the Eiffel Tower, 1959

Lawrence Durrell at the Mazet Michel (Nîmes), 1964

Miller and Brassaï in Cannes during the film festival, 1960. © Yoshi Takata

Miller and Brassaï playing with Tony Miller in Paris

Miller in front of his swimming pool in Pacific Palisades, 1973

Miller at the door of his home in Pacific Palisades, 1973

CHAPTER 9

Tuesday, May 10, 1960

Yesterday at the Hôtel Montfleury, Henry, already up, complains he hasn't slept well. And he continues to grumble:

"I have no gift as a speaker. Talking doesn't come easy to me. So I'm always hesitant to express myself 'live,' especially in French. I mumble. I always feel inferior to that other self who expresses himself in my writings. And, on most questions, I've already replied better in my books. This will probably be my last broadcast on TV."

In the park, someone places the cameras, loads the film; the boom, or *giraffe*, straightens out its neck with the microphone at the end. The motors roar.

QUESTION Henry Miller, today you are a famous writer. For twenty years you have been considered an expert on eroticism more than anything. Does this verdict seem absurd to you?

MILLER Yes, absurd! I'm always asked about sex, as if I were an "expert" on eroticism. I'm taken for a pornography giant! But I'm the most normal of men. No vices or perversions. By stripping sex of all its hypocrisy, I simply wanted to liberate myself from the puritan mind, and also liberate others. Isn't sexual life part of human life? And isn't it absurd to treat is as if it did not exist because of some principle, some sense of shame, some taboo? If I've insisted on it in my books, it's precisely because it was a *forbidden* topic. Where some peevish or prudish people blame me for my obscenities, other criticize me for putting too much philosophy and spirituality into my books. So what?

The questions keep coming, the motors whir and, contrary to what he feared, Henry is full of ideas and expresses himself with ease.

Suddenly Georges Simenon appears in the park. Everyone admires his big, unusual pipe.

SIMENON Don't think it's the largest, the most valuable, the most expensive pipe I own! In Switzerland I have a very large collection. But in my luggage I usually carry only about eighteen or twenty. The jewel of my collection was carved out of a block of French briar by an English pipe maker and was covered with seven coats of gilded shellac from Japan.

But Simenon is in a rush. As chairman of the jury, he has a thousand obligations. Now he's in front of the cameras, extolling Henry's merits:

"I am happy and proud to have Henry Miller as a friend. An exceptional individual, he rebelled like no one else against conformism and established morality. Without men like him there would never have been any progress. His work is a sort of chanson de geste, the chanson de geste of our age. It undoubtedly plays a large role in the revolution against puritanism, hypocrisy, and lies. I will add—and this will probably shock some people—that I consider Henry Miller a lay saint. For a long time he lived on the fringe, only a few friends recognized his genius. Now his friends, or rather, his 'followers,' have multiplied in the world. Thousands of young people see him as their liberator."

As suddenly as he appeared, Simenon disappears and the taping ends.

Today we have lunch in the Cannes harbor.

MILLER When you see films from different countries, you travel around the world. It's crazy the extent to which each reflects its own temperament, its own atmosphere. Everything from the north is slow, heavy, sometimes childish. The Slavic films, though often bad, are always full of humanity. But I deplore the sadness, the excessive length of so many films—two or even three hours of viewing—for the most part slow, incoherent, weepy, morose.

BRASSAÏ What about *La Dolce Vita*?

MILLER Fellini's film also lasts three hours, but it doesn't seem long. It moves faster than the others, is teeming with characters and events. You hardly ever get bored with it.

GILBERTE It's very rich. But Fellini puts too much in. It would have been better if it'd been a good half hour shorter, or so it seems to me. It could have ended at the point where Marcello, after the bitter argument, after abandoning his wife at night on a road, comes back to get her in the early morning, overcome with remorse, and takes her with him.

MILLER You're judging that from a woman's point of view! That would have been a comforting, moral ending, a happy ending! Was that really the author's intention? On the contrary, didn't Fellini want to produce a great deal of discomfort at the end? Express the *loneliness* of the man of today?

BRASSAÏ That film is an indictment, to be sure. But do the idle people of the Roman haute bourgeoisie, who seek their salvation in alcohol, drugs, and orgies, really represent the man of today? The demonstration is not conclusive. Fellini, it seems to me, is showing not the "mal du siècle" but only the ills of a few Roman degenerates who no longer know how to kill the boredom in their idle lives.

MILLER What is marvelous in this film is the satirical depiction of the tabloid press. The obsessive presence of the pack of paparazzi in every circumstance.

BRASSAÏ Have you seen any stars?

MILLER Not one! I'm exhausted by the length of the films shown in poorly ventilated halls and I don't have any elbow room. Since I arrived in Cannes, I haven't been myself. As for distractions, I was promised the moon: Brigitte Bardot, Lollobrigida, Sophia Loren, and all the rest. I've been served up nothing but widows. And middle-aged ones. Beginning with Nadia Léger. She writes me, telephones me, bombards me with messages. I don't have the slightest desire to go to that famous opening in Biot. And the other widows! I've received four or five letters: one invites me to live in her country house, another offers me her deceased husband's studio. No thank you to the macabre atmosphere!

While we were talking, Henry kept staring at a young man eating at a nearby table.

MILLER (*addressing him*) You're undoubtedly American. Only an American can stare at people with such insolence. When I came in here, I immediately saw you had spotted me. I was expecting at any moment to see you pounce on me, ask me for an interview, an autograph, to sign a book, what do I know? [Turning toward us:] Such things have become an obsession with me. This morning it was an Italian journalist who assaulted me. I must have really baffled him with my responses. He left sheepishly. In Bremen, in an extraordinary rathskeller, I was shocked by the strange look given me by a waiter. A look so sharp that it literally went right through me. I was suffering so much because of it that, abruptly, I stood up, caught him, and said: "You're a professional boxer, aren't you?" "How did you know?" he exclaimed with surprise. "Good Lord, by your stare!" He couldn't get over it.

The young man is not American but French. But he had recognized the author of the *Tropics*. He lived in the United States for a long time and even knows Big Sur. He vaunts its wild coast, the beauty of the cliffs, and the reefs peopled with cormorants, pelicans, and otters.

MILLER You're forgetting the seals, the sea lions. I hear their cries, their raucous barking. The vast areas around Big Sur are devoid of human beings. Beyond the ridge, it's virgin forest, almost impenetrable. You can't clear a path through it unless you're equipped with an ax. The state of California has made it a national park.

BRASSAÏ Do you still have bears, as in the Pyrenees and the Carpathians?

MILLER The grizzly bear, which used to live in those mountains, has disappeared. On the other hand, in that dense jungle we have mountain lions, deer, coyotes that howl at night. Above all, that big forest is rich in birds, perhaps the richest in North America. Growing up in the city, the only birds I knew were pigeons and sparrows. There you find every species, even hummingbirds. Yes, yes, we also have hummingbirds. I especially like the birds of prey: falcons, eagles, buzzards. They soar silently above the desert canyons, circling above their prey. Sometimes you also see condors shooting past. And all the migrating birds from north and south meet there.

BRASSAÏ And you also have rattlesnakes.

MILLER Yes, a lot of them! We're infested with them! I myself have killed three in my garden. How do you kill them? With a pickax. Above all, you mustn't panic. You just have to be quick and aim accurately. Cut the snake in half with a single blow. But we also have black snakes and scorpions.

The young man with the "insolent" look asks Miller which writer, in his view, has best described the American continent.

MILLER Nobody! No American writer has yet succeeded in producing a work that embraces the *whole* continent, the *whole* of American life. It's always been treated partially, here and there, the South, the frozen North, the Rocky Mountains. The subject is too vast. So no one has yet been able to express the American man in a single novel or in a cycle of novels. And, as usually happens, it took a *foreigner*, fresh eyes, to give us the most accurate picture of our continent's soul. No author of American stock has aimed as accurately as Jakob Wassermann, a German. He was the only one, in *The Maurizius Case*, to pin down a few truly American types: solitary, strong, generous, of the stature of Walt Whitman, the author of *Leaves of Grass*. Those giants exist no doubt, but, as in all things, to find them, to describe them, it took an eye and a pen. A rich, fascinating book, I read and reread it I don't know how many times. And did you know that Wassermann greatly influenced Thomas Mann? I believe he's superior to him in terms of profundity, mystery, style, everything. *The Maurizius Case*! What intrigue, what skill, what a marvelous, torrential style. And so many dramatic episodes, so many extraordinary characters! For example, the young Etzel Andergast is almost the personification of Rimbaud. You absolutely must read that novel, I mean that trilogy. It begins with *The Maurizius Case*, with the main character Dr. Kerkhoven, a marvelous spiritual healer, a sort of genius psychoanalyst who also shares a few character traits with Professor Jung. Reading it took my breath away, especially since the character is very similar to me.

BRASSAÏ You yourself wrote a book on the Maurizius affair, didn't you?

MILLER During the war, in 1941–42, I spent horrible years in Hollywood. [*Miller's marginal note:* "That's right. H. M."] To escape my poverty at the time, I tried to write a few screenplays. A job to get by. Without the slightest positive result, in fact. Then, one day, I got a vague commission: write a synopsis based on *The Maurizius Case*. I bravely launched into it. Naturally, the film was never made. But that little job earned me a hundred dollars, and, one day, a publisher had the idea of publishing my version of Wassermann's trilogy.[1]

The young man remarks that another foreigner, Jean Cocteau, in his *Letter to the Americans*, had also captured the American soul with great accuracy.

BRASSAÏ In it, didn't he say, among other things, that the Americans have two tits, one for whiskey, the other for milk?

MILLER About thirty years ago, Georges Duhamel published a very violent book on the United States. Many French people were shocked by that diatribe against technology and the ills that afflict humanity. But I feel that Duhamel really put his finger on a few wounds of American civilization.

After a short tour of the harbor, we pass alongside La Croisette. Suddenly, Henry exclaims: "Good heavens! I have to return right away to the hotel. I left all my money with the concierge. I don't want to be robbed."

CHAPTER 10

Friday, May 13, 1960

On the sea sparkling with strass, four American cruisers and a submarine come to drop anchor nightly in the roadstead of Cannes. What a boon that shipload of sailors must be for the whores of Golfe-Juan!

As I am preparing to be announced at the Hôtel Montfleury, I hear the warm and sonorous voice of Henry, who is talking in the telephone booth.

"I learned from the newspapers that Michel Simon was to come to Cannes," he tells me, radiant with joy. "He's just arrived, it was him I was speaking to."

And here is Luis Buñuel. Last year, his film *Nazarin* won a prize in Cannes. This time he is presenting *The Young One*, also made in Mexico with American actors.

BRASSAÏ So you've returned to Spain.

BUÑUEL Yes, after twenty-five years of voluntary exile.

BRASSAÏ A great event in your life! Have you also reconciled with Salvador Dali?

BUÑUEL (*darkening*) No! It's all over between us forever.

BRASSAÏ And your latest film?

BUÑUEL I like it very much. But I wonder if others will like it. For once, I wanted to make a film in which all the characters are sympathetic, but not without flaws. I wanted to show that men are not fundamentally wicked.

We head for La Croisette. Gilberte remarks that Buñuel is always excellent when he can give free rein to his obsessions.

MILLER A marvelous creature, don't you think? The artist as well as the man. Simple, direct, warm. Like most men, sensitive and softhearted. Yes, a softhearted man, that's the right word.

BRASSAÏ Have you known him for a long time?

MILLER I met him in Paris. [*Miller's marginal note:* "I'm not altogether certain of this. I think I met him before our encounter in Paris on a steamship coming from New York. H. M."] One night, at Studio 28, I saw *The Golden Age,* by a certain Luis Buñuel and Salvador Dali. What a revelation! I felt a great affinity for him. A desperate man, a rebel who defied society. And that sensual, savage, almost mystical love! I wrote him a note at the time to express my enthusiasm and my admiration. He replied, and we met at the Café Sélect in Montparnasse. I immediately saw that I was dealing with an instinctive creature, an intuitive creature like myself, and not an intellectual. I liked that Spaniard from the start, a little crazy, passionate, violent, a dreamer, torn between his Catholic upbringing and his sexuality.

I find in my notes: "Miller told me, 'One day, I saw *Le chien andalou* at Studio des Ursulines. I immediately wrote Buñuel, who made an appointment to meet me at the Café de la Paix, at the Opéra.' But, on another occasion, Henry told me he had made his acquaintance during his crossing of the Atlantic, coming from New York." [*Miller's marginal note:* "Yes, I think I met him on the boat. H. M."]

BRASSAÏ Was it then you wrote an essay on him?

MILLER Yes, and it was my first article published in France: "Buñuel, or How the Golden Age Always Ends," which appeared in *The New Review* in May 1931. [*Miller's marginal note:* "No, I think my very first article was on the 'Cirque Médrano,' published in the *Herald Tribune* in Paris, thanks to Paul Eliot. H. M."][1] In that film, Buñuel had already developed his essential themes—his opposition to prejudice, taboos, superstitions—with great liberty, but also with lyricism and humor.

BRASSAÏ Have you seen him often since then?

MILLER Never again. So it was our great joy to run into each other in this hotel *thirty years* later! Buñuel told me: "No one has ever written so well about me as you in *The New Review.* I was really very happy and very flattered." And I saw *The Young One,* his latest film, with pleasure. But hush, hush [he puts two fingers to his lips], I can't say anything about it.

We leave Cannes. Today the festival is idle. All of La Croisette will be taken to the Léger Museum in Biot, which is being inaugurated with unprecedented solemnity. In charter planes, hundreds of guests will arrive from Paris, Oslo, Stockholm, New York, even Moscow. There will be a banquet and an evening of ballet. Henry prefers to spend the day with us, away from Cannes and the hubbub of the crowd.

MILLER Nadia Léger badgered me again, I don't know how many times. I

wonder whether that down-to-earth Norman would have even liked these official, high society displays. Picasso and Braque, I've been told, also declined.
I knew Léger well, but we didn't really get along.

Glorious weather. The first day of the Mediterranean spring, hot and
sunny. We drive along the seashore. Henry is terrified of drafts. In this heat
he wears an undershirt, a thick wool shirt, a sweater, and a corduroy jacket on
top. He's too hot, he's too cold.

MILLER Five hours spent in the heat of that airless auditorium has exhausted me. I felt a draft on my left shoulder and that entire part of my body
is sore now.

BRASSAÏ Did you meet Michel Simon?

MILLER Yesterday, at the Carlton, in Simenon's suite. A marvelous man, full
of warmth, humanity. He's just been through a terrible ordeal: three years of
illness, of inactivity.

BRASSAÏ Poisoned by a hair dye, wasn't that it, and he couldn't remember
his lines. In the middle of the scene, he'd draw a blank.

MILLER What worse can happen to an actor? No one offered him roles anymore. They thought he was done for. It's only now he's getting a little life
back, and a little hope. So, to demonstrate my friendship and my admiration,
I decided to go spend a few days on his property at La Ciotat.

BRASSAÏ You stayed there last year as well. [*Miller's marginal note:* "I think
my first visit to his home was in 1953. H. M."]

MILLER His "Eagle's Beak," perched on a rock that juts out as a promontory
into the pine forest overlooking La Ciotat, is a little earthy paradise. Thanks
to the cachet of his films and his roles in the theater, he managed to buy the
land surrounding the house parcel by parcel, along the coast, between the sig-
nal station and Cap d'Aigle. His property now extends over three kilometers.[2]

BRASSAÏ And have you met Rossellini?

MILLER Yes, at the Carlton, at Simenon's. He was with his pretty Hindu girlfriend. I especially admired her shimmering sari. Rossellini made a confession to me. He would like to rest, he told me, but he can't. Women torment
him too much. He's exhausted but he hasn't managed to have a single day of
rest in years: a day *without a woman*, to himself.

Henry speaks of his new love: *Margery*. She arrives in Paris on Sunday
and will join him in Cannes. It's her first trip to Europe.

MILLER I wouldn't want to have her live at the Hôtel Montfleury. Photographers and journalists could be counted on to make a fuss about Henry Miller's
new "favorite." Could she stay at your hotel in Juan-les-Pins?

BRASSAÏ Yes, probably. Where did you meet her?

MILLER   At Big Sur Inn. She's the daughter of the innkeeper in the area. [*Miller's marginal note:* "No! Not true! She worked at the hotel. That's all. H. M."] The innkeeper is a little crazy and his wife, an enormous woman, can no longer move. She sits at the window and spends the day counting the cars go by, her only distraction. Margery is thirty years old. She's divorced. But it's the father who has custody of her two children, a rare thing in the United States.

And like a schoolboy in love, Henry takes a little color photo of Margery from his wallet.

"I adore that creature. Isn't she beautiful? I love her lips, made for kissing. Yes, I'm in love. I'm impatient to see her. This may be my last love."

BRASSAÏ   How can you say that? You're way off!

MILLER (*with a big, resounding laugh*)   After all, it's possible. Yes, I've had a lot of lovers in my life. Many women and four wives. And I know I'll die alone and abandoned.

BRASSAÏ   You're still probably under the influence of *La Dolce Vita*! In a big scene in that film—do you remember?—the abandoned mistress screams in her lover's face: "You'll be alone and abandoned, you'll croak and no one will love you." You're thinking of the fate of that old skirt-chaser destined for loneliness and abandonment.

MILLER   It's one of the best moments in the film! It particularly struck me. But I especially remember what the man replied to the abandoned, weeping woman: "All you want to do is eat and sleep, make love, and hang on my neck. All you want is for me to stay with you night and day. But I am a man and my life is elsewhere." Now those are male words I like to hear.

For Henry, that matrimonial quarrel in *La Dolce Vita* evoked his own marital disputes. "You never had any human respect for me," "You insult me in front of your friends," "You chase after other women," "You aren't even interested in your children," "You leave me loaded down with all the chores," "You deceived me from day one," "You're an egoist, as harsh as you are cruel, an inhuman being."

MILLER   It's odd how much wives seem to delight in those furious altercations, those chaotic arguments. At least, that's my bitter experience. Maybe the stormy relations with my wives are written in my astrological constellation. The conjunction of a bellicose Mars and a stubborn Uranus. Several astrologers have told me so. And it's a fact: in the long run, every one of my marriages turns sour. Every one fails miserably. With Lepska in Big Sur, it was hell from the beginning. A damnation! Never a truce! Not a day of peace! As soon as she opened her mouth, it was war. A fight to the death. Until the day she dumped me, leaving me alone with Tony and Val.

Henry would no doubt have approved of Restif de la Bretonne, to whom he is sometimes compared. At the time of the French Revolution, making fun of the equality between the sexes, he denied wives "any imperiousness at home," "any authority they claimed in order to place themselves above the head of the family," and professed: "The weaker sex is made to be submissive" (*Le paysan pervers*). To arm himself for the war between the sexes, Henry adopts as his own D. H. Lawrence's male words, advice to a young man who was about to get married: "Be gentle with her when she is gentle, but if she tries to impose her will on you, beat her." An astonishingly good, almost magnificent piece of advice, observes Miller. "You don't know how swell that sounds to me. . . . Essence of wisdom in man-to-woman matters. I feel if I had known that before, I might have averted so much trouble, useless trouble" (letter to Anaïs Nin, April 1932).[3] But that cruelty will always remain indecisive in him. When he did sometimes beat Lepska, because she had slapped him, he always felt ashamed about it: "You cannot imagine," he wrote me, "how diminished I feel after that."

GILBERTE   You are incapable of loving. Eve is so nice, so beautiful. And devoted—she mothered your children as if they were her own. Don't you think so?

MILLER   Hmm, hmm. Yes, very nice. I still love her. Believe me. She's the one who wants to get a divorce. We're going to send her a postcard, that will make her happy. Obviously, when you love a woman, you always run a risk, the risk of losing a different one. But that's also the worst thing that can happen to you. There are plenty of fish in the sea.

Miller also repeats: "Another one will come along in a moment," "Lose one woman, gain ten." Curiously, Proust had the same feeling. What prevents him from attaching himself exclusively to Albertine is the idea that he is depriving himself of the enjoyment of other women, still anonymous and off in the shadows, but who, once Albertine is out of the way, might very well fill him with pleasure: "Life, in gradually revealing to me the constancy of our needs, had taught me that, lacking one person, we must be content with another, and I felt that what I had asked of Albertine, another, Mlle de Stermaria, might have given to me. But it had been Albertine" (p. 233).[4] He also writes: "It is more reasonable to sacrifice one's life for women than for postage stamps. . . . It is simply that the example of other collections ought to warn us to change, to have not one woman, but many."[5] And he says hypocritically: "To the person we have loved most we are less faithful than to ourselves, and sooner or later we forget her in order . . . to begin to love again, and thus, to be faithful to her even in infidelity."[6] Is that cynicism, apathy, hard-heartedness? I see it rather as the desire for a *total detachment,* to which Miller always aspired.

In *Hamlet* he wrote that sometimes it is friends one leaves, or a woman, people who are already dead for you. And, he added, in the end, one can manage to see the world as a whole in that manner, but without sadness, without regret. Detachment already opens another world to you. He says, of the man with the "sublime indifference" he is dreaming of, that every step he takes, every word he speaks is a definitive break with his past. He has no memories, no hopes, no regrets. No women or friends. No loyalties either. He proceeds full of cold compassion, the supreme master of irony. He also wrote: "If your best friend dies, you don't even bother to go to the funeral; if a man is run down by a streetcar right before your eyes you keep on walking just as if nothing had happened. . . . Sympathy alone flourishes, but it is not a human sympathy, a limited sympathy—it is something monstrous and evil" (*Tropic of Capricorn,* p. 64). And that is why Miller would like to identify with the "happy rock."

GILBERTE You're only looking for adventures and not love. You're a knee-jerk. I wouldn't trust a writer's feelings. I wouldn't want a novelist for a husband for anything in the world. Wouldn't his intentions, his acts, and even his passion be warped by his literary preoccupations? How would you know? Would he know it himself? Can any woman love a man she suspects of writing a short story or a novel based on their love? Of seeing the woman he is supposed to love only as the guinea pig for his experiments? Who could tell me whether his joy or sorrow is real or feigned? Literature corrupts true feelings. Perhaps only women are capable of selfless love.

MILLER Dear Gilberte, you judge me unfairly and too harshly. I have never loved in order to make a book out of it. The need to write has always come *afterward,* to relive my joys, and usually to reopen my wounds. Believe me, despite appearances, I too am a sentimental man capable of true love. Often I play the blasé cynic so as not to cry. With the exception of my passion for June, none of my great loves appears in my books. Affairs, passing fancies, purely sexual relationships, I speak of them at length, but I keep silent about my true loves, especially since most of them were, in fact, frustrated loves.

CHAPTER 11

Friday, May 13, 1960 (continued)

Golfe-Juan, Juan-les-Pins, Antibes, Gros-de-Cagnes, Cagnes-sur-Mer. We are still driving along the seashore.

MILLER In 1928, during our first stay with June in Europe—a tourist trip if ever there was one—we did a grand tour across France on bicycle. And do you know who made up the itinerary for us? The sculpture Zadkine! He strongly advised us to stop in Vézelay. Then we descended the length of the Rhône Valley toward Avignon. We visited the château of Beaucaire. But it was Tarascon that especially interested me, because of *Tartarin* and Alphonse Daudet. I read that book late, I was already thirty-five, and after that I dreamed of that city. We arrived there in a tropical heat. June couldn't go on. So I visited Tarascon alone and it did not disappoint me.

BRASSAÏ You were a cycling enthusiast.

MILLER Yes, when I was young, I belonged to an athletic club, the Xerxes Society, and for five years I trained like a madman. I dreamed of becoming world champion, Olympic champion even. Still on bicycles, we arrived at the Côte d'Azur. I have only some vague memories of it. But I remember my delight at the marvelous gardens of Monte Carlo.

BRASSAÏ And you never came back to the Riviera?

MILLER Oh yes, in 1939, before I left for Greece. And around the same time of year as it is now. No, a little later, in June. It was only then I discovered the Mediterranean, its pale blue horizon the color of lavender, its green and opal reflections, its light air, and also the mistral, which washes clean the sky and makes the sea foam. And I understood why Renoir, Matisse, Bonnard, Picasso, and Chagall came to live here. I liked its medieval cities. I explored the old Nice, climbed the Haut-de-Cagnes. My great discovery was Grasse, its old streets on the side of the hill, its cypresses, its fields of olive trees and roses. Maybe I would have spent a winter there if I'd known about it earlier. War was coming, I was leaving soon for Greece with no hope of return. That last stay on the Côte d'Azur felt like my farewell to France.

We leave behind us Saint-Laurent-du-Var, drive through Nice, the Baie des Anges, the old harbor with its pink, mauve, yellow, and orange houses with green shutters already evoking Italy. Then it's the Moyenne Corniche. A glimpse of the roadstead of Villefranche. In 1928, Miller and June spent one night there, at the Hotel Welcome, a favorite of Cocteau's. And here is Beaulieu-sur-Mer and Saint-Jean-Cap-Ferrat. The road rises alongside the wooded ravines, and suddenly, crowned by its demolished feudal château, the rock of Eze stands out against the sky.

MILLER I remember now: we also visited Eze-Village. Where did you get the idea to buy a house there?

BRASSAÏ Just after the Liberation, we took a trip to Monte Carlo. I was not acquainted with Eze, but that odd place intrigued me. One morning, I proposed to Gilberte that we visit it. We left from the seashore, walked for two hours in the Midi sun, and reached the charred village perched on its peak. And we were captivated. Those steep little streets covered with arches, broken up by staircases, that maze of houses, ruins, rocks leaning on one another. And not a living soul! The eagle's nest was deserted. "This is where I'd like to have a house!" Gilberte exclaimed. Finally, in a little courtyard, we discovered an old woman dressed in black, knitting—Mme Rosalie. "A house for sale? I have one on the ramparts." We bought it. It was a beautiful ruin with a superb view. Now that it's fixed up, with a room dug into the rock, and with its semicircular fifteen-century vault and slate staircase, it has a great deal of charm. Our windows look out partly on the sea, partly on that hill across the way.

MILLER I prefer the view of the hill. The reflection of the sea tires the eyes. I could not work facing the Pacific. I have nearly the same view in Big Sur, and at about the same height. In fact, this rocky part of the Mediterranean resembles the coast of California. But nature is wilder there and almost devoid of human presence. Even on the ocean we never see a white sail. Here, you have an ancient land, old houses, bistros. Oh, yes, from time to time, I could sit on a terrace with nice people and have a drink! I miss that terribly there! And I sometimes tell myself: "If only Big Sur were on the Mediterranean."

BRASSAÏ We're really suffering from the influx of tourists. The village was a desert in 1945, now it's invaded. Dozens of buses unload their cargo every day here. And we're infested with postcard salesmen, souvenir salesmen, bric-a-brac salesmen. It's like Mont-Saint-Michel. So now we only stay here during the off season.

MILLER And what is that château you can see on the hill across the way?

BRASSAÏ The "château Balsan." The wife of Colonel Balsan was the super-rich Consuelo Vanderbilt. To build their château, they looked all over the coast for the "ideal spot," "the most beautiful view." They chose this hill. And so that no one could build around it, they purchased all the property from the sea to the Grande Corniche. More than two dozen owners, brought in to the notary in a bus, signed the bill of sale. The château is immense and almost gloomy. Since Colonel Balsan is now dead, his widow has put it up for sale.

We go through the village on carpets of pink bricks set into the pavement, which run through the middle of the streets and up the stairwells. And we arrive at the summit, at the ruins of the old château, destroyed, like so many others, under Richelieu. From that platform, the view is very vast. It extends from the Esterel to Italy.

BRASSAÏ Do you see the path that runs along the coast from Villefranche to the rock of Eze? Well, that's the path Nietzsche took when he discovered that old aerie overlooking the coast.

MILLER Nietzsche in Eze? I knew nothing at all about that.

Henry is surprised. The author of *Zarathustra* has always figured among the "four horsemen" of his "personal apocalypse."

BRASSAÏ Now do you understand why I so wanted to know this village? Nietzsche's presence attracted me. It was when he climbed the harsh mule trail during that "most painful" ascent that he had a fit of vertigo and composed the "decisive" part of book 3 of *Zarathustra*. He himself recounts his "ecstasy" in Eze in several of his letters and also in *Ecce Homo*: "The following winter, under the halcyon sky of Nice, which shone for the first time in my life, I found the third *Zarathustra*—and that is how I ended it. Many hidden corners and silent peaks in the landscape of Nice were sanctified for me by unforgettable moments. That decisive part of the third book bearing the title *Of Old and New Tablets* was composed during one of the most painful ascents from the train station to the marvelous Moorish village, Eze, built among the rocks" (*Ecce Homo*).

MILLER That's exciting. But did Nietzsche live in Eze-Village?

BRASSAÏ No. But he came back when he felt the need for a solitary haven.

The Zarathustra of the Great South and Eternity was Nietzsche seated exactly where we are, contemplating the Mediterranean from this height.

MILLER It's impressive! I've always wanted to see Sils Maria and the upper Engadine Valley, that spiritual high point!

BRASSAÏ In the north, Nietzsche had suffered so much from the cold that he decided to spend his winters in the south. He tried Genoa, then Portofino, then Venice. He was then advised to go to the French Riviera. In 1883 he established his winter quarters there and his "experience of Nice" began on the Côte d'Azur. His first stop was Villefranche-sur-Mer. He arrived in late November and spent a week there. It was while passing along the seashore on the way to Monaco that he suddenly perceived the aerie of Eze, more isolated and less accessible than it is today, since the Moyenne Corniche and its viaduct did not yet exist. Nietzsche would no doubt have felt the same thunderbolt upon discovering Peille, Gourdon, Tourette, or Levens, any of those strange towns perched on peaks. But those towns are inland, whereas Eze overlooks the sea.

MILLER And how long did he stay on the coast?

BRASSAÏ Six consecutive winters, from 1883 to 1888. He stayed in modest boarding houses. He was only thirty-nine, but, with his prematurely gray temples, his thick glasses, his enormous mustache, he was taken for a retired old German professor. He was so self-effacing, so modest, so likable, so polite, kissing the hands of women and fussing over the children, that no one guessed this was the giant who practiced philosophy with a hammer.

MILLER So he liked the Côte d'Azur.

BRASSAÏ No doubt. But there was one odd thing: when he discovered Nice, he was so enthusiastic about its pure sky "of a blinding whiteness," its "cloudless rays of sun," and its sea "of tropical blue," that he was overcome with rage at the idea of "*having discovered it so late.*" But, six years later, when he abandoned it for Turin, his new love, he was so disgusted with Nice and "its contemptible and venal race," that he begrudged it for the six winters spent on that "stupid charred Riviera," because he "*had escaped it so late*"! "Nice was pure folly." He complained that cities such as Nice, "given over to the pace of modern life," at length made him irritable, indecisive, discouraged, sterile, ill. But that irritation may have been only the first sign of the madness that was lying in wait for him that same year, 1888, in Turin, "an enchanting place, however," which he loved for its "aristocratic calm."

MILLER My very first essay was on *The Antichrist*. I wrote it at the age of twenty-three, in my father's tailor shop. Oddly, at every crucial moment in my life, I came across the author that suited me. It was the example and the philosophy of Nietzsche that sustained me for many long years, in my physical and moral distress. That man was a hero! He valiantly struggled to have his brainchild recognized. That's what made him so admirable in my eyes. Call everything into question, become an iconoclast, that's what I instinctively got from him. It's only now I realize it. Some of his sentences went so deep inside me that they transformed me. Once we understand the truth of an idea, it changes us profoundly. And did you know I was once fired because of Nietzsche? I'd been hired to compose a mail order sales catalog. Well, I was caught reading *The Birth of Tragedy* and I was sacked. Nietzsche captivated me. What a magical use of language! Even now, after I've read him ten, twenty times, the fascination remains. An indisputable sign of genius. It's strange, in fact, ever since you told me the role this village played in his life and work, I see Eze with completely different eyes. I'm always astonished how much a writer's or artist's birth, sojourn, or even brief visit to a place can affect our impressions. For example, Uzès. I don't know Racine very well at all. He's intrigued me, by the way, ever since I read a brilliant essay on *Phaedra*. Now that I know he lived in Uzès, I can't go through that city without thinking with emotion of Racine.

BRASSAÏ Proust was very sensitive to the relations between geniuses and the flavor of a city or region, and was astonished that people usually visit the place where a genius was born and where he died but not where he loved, where he really lived.

MILLER That's quite right. Can you think of Amboise without bringing Leonardo to mind? He lived there, painted there, died there in the arms of Francis I. Aix-en-Provence still radiates the prestige of Cézanne, and Arles, of Van Gogh. And what about Toledo? I went there to visit El Greco's studio. All the places where great minds have lived irresistibly attract me.

BRASSAÏ Have you been to Chinon?

MILLER Yes. That city is as inseparable from Rabelais as Uzès is from Racine. I visited his estate there, the "Devinière." In Avignon itself, it was not the popes I thought of, but again Rabelais. It was in that city—one of the most licentious of the time—that he had a brief affair with a woman. And in Paris, so many streets have suddenly acquired prestige in my eyes when I learned that one of my venerated authors once lived there, like rue Saint-André-des-Arts, the street of secondhand clothes shops! When I arrived in Paris, I still owned two suits, marvelously tailored by my father—one of the major tailors on Fifth Avenue. One day, desperately poor, I sold them for a ridiculous amount of money. And even that street, which I ought to have hated, was suddenly lit up when I read that Rabelais had lived there.

BRASSAÏ And you made a pilgrimage to Stratford-on-Avon, even though you don't like Shakespeare very much. And you told me about your trip through a forest to the abbey of Groenendaal, near Waterloo, where Ruysbroeck the Admirable had lived.

MILLER I'll never forget the wood of beech trees we went through to get to the convent of that great mystic. I felt like I was dreaming, like I was hearing the music of *Pelleas and Melisandre.* It didn't look like any forest I'd gone into before. The meditation and philosophy of Ruysbroeck had transformed it into a magical forest.

BRASSAÏ In Paris itself, I remember, you were eager to visit the Orfila boarding house, to see the room where Strindberg lived and, on rue des Beaux-Arts, the hotel where Oscar Wilde and Maupassant stayed.

MILLER In the Saint-Séverin district, is there any trace left of Abelard, Dante, Saint Thomas Aquinas, or François Villon?

BRASSAÏ I don't think so. On the other hand, did you know that Boccaccio, the author of the *Decameron,* was born on rue des Lombards in the early fourteenth century? That street of brothels that intersects rue Quincampoix and is teeming with prostitutes? Curious, isn't it?

MILLER I was impressed by the countryside of Saint-Rémy-de-Provence, where Nostradamus was born. I even felt its strangeness. What philosophy adds to the walls, the stones, even the landscapes, is imponderable but ineffaceable.

BRASSAÏ Proust, who was very primitive in certain ways, assumed that places conserve something of the eyes that have looked at them.

MILLER No doubt. So many regions have been enriched by the gaze of the great painters! I'm thinking of Île-de-France in Paris itself. Think how much the eyes of Daumier, Lautrec, Manet, Seurat, Pissarro, Monet, Renoir, Utrillo, have fertilized them. That's the richness of France. And that's what's missing in the United States. There, no one has looked intensely enough or lovingly enough at things. Here and there, a few oases exist, however. For example, the home of Jack London in Glen Elle, California, or Mark Twain's old house in Hannibal, Missouri, a miniature house to fit the man, which reminds me of Mozart's house in Salzburg. I almost cried with emotion when I visited them. But here's the difference: in Europe, wherever a poet, a great painter, a sculptor, or a musician is born, there are also streets and monuments named after him. But just look for them in the United States! You'll have trouble finding a Walt Whitman Street, a Thoreau Street, a Melville or Jack London Avenue.

BRASSAÏ The fountain of Vaucluse has also conserved something of Petrarch's poetry.

MILLER The same way that Les Baux-de-Provence makes you think of Dante, who was inspired by it, I think, for the description of hell.

BRASSAÏ That's only a legend! I verified the facts and the dates. The Val d'Enfer could not have inspired *The Inferno*. On his way to London, Dante probably stopped in Arles—it's not certain—but he was already the author of *The Divine Comedy*! Obviously, it's in the interest of southerners to make you believe that Les Baux inspired Dante. I can mention another legend to you. Do you know the Grove of Apollo on the grounds of Versailles? It's closed to the public and is not very well known. A marvelous place! Apart from the Parc de Trianon, the only "romantic" spot at Versailles. Under Louis XVI, all the splendid geometry of Lenôtre was almost plowed under. At the impetus of romanticism! Fortunately, only the "Labyrinth" was destroyed, to be replaced by the Grove of Apollo. Hubert Robert, a specialist in ruins, had enormous rocks carried there from Fontainebleau, had caves and splendid groups of horses built. In the center, you see Apollo nude after his bath, surrounded by goddesses wiping him dry. It's the *Bath of Apollo*. In a peremptory voice, the guard explains to you that it's Louis XIV surrounded by his mistresses, and he points out Marie Mancini, Mme Montespan, Mme de Maintenon, and so on. If you check the dates, you find that it's pure legend: the Sun King was only eighteen when the *Bath of Apollo* was created. Therefore, he didn't know his future favorites and mistresses. Legends can withstand anything.

The mistral is blowing violently. Nietzsche liked that icy wind from the Alps, which sweeps through the Rhône Valley, surges in gusts over Provence and the Côte d'Azur. He even composed a hymn in its honor. Descending from the village, I show the trail by which, after two hours of "the most painful" ascent, completely out of breath, Nietzsche reached the village gate. Henry is astonished that no marker recalls his passing.[1]

At the foot of Eze-Village, on the esplanade called the "Colette," Henry and I have a glass of wine. The terraces, swarming with people in summer, are deserted. Only an old man, seated at a nearby table, writes on sheets with a fierce energy. Henry nudges me with his elbow.

"My word, if it isn't Nietzsche! Look at his eyes, his glasses, his mustache."

I glance at the stranger. On the table in front of him, an English newspaper, a briefcase stuffed with papers, and a book: *Thus Spake Zarathustra!* Stupefied, intrigued, Henry can no longer hold still in his impatience to speak to him. The man stands up. On his feet, he looks even more like Nietzsche. He has the same stiffness of the Prussian officer.

THE STRANGER Henry Miller? I know your name well. Brassaï? You have a house in Eze-Village. As a matter of fact, I wanted to write to you.

And he brandishes the *Herald Tribune*. On the front page, displayed in bold type, is the event of the day: an air incident and the photograph of the American spy plane downed by the Russians.

"It's a sign! A bad omen! It is an announcement of historical inevitability."

MILLER Are you involved in politics, sir?

THE STRANGER I am a thinker and a philosopher. And I am involved in *political meteorology*, a science invented by Friedrich Nietzsche. A hundred years in advance, he predicted our chaos, our upheaval, our nihilist world. What were taken for the ramblings of a madman were the *scientific* predictions of a scientist. It was from him that I learned to sound out the political climate.

MILLER And what is the forecast by that political barometer?

THE STRANGER Nothing good: a heavy sky loaded with electricity, growing tensions. A hurricane is approaching. But no one wants to look the truth in the face! Do you really believe that the delicious "balance of terror" will incite the superpowers to give up the use of force forever? Only *political meteorology* tells us the truth: it records the *facts* and not verbiage.

MILLER And what can be read on the recording strip?

THE STRANGER 1815: Waterloo; 1870: Sedan; 1916: Verdun; 1943: Stalingrad. Do you think the needle *will stop there?*

Was he a madman, a fanatic? He spoke like an oracle. And he began again worse than ever:

THE STRANGER Is there still a chance to avoid the catastrophe? Yes, if people listen to me! What we need is a "Supreme Tribunal of Humanity." And only an "International Philosophical Center" can create it. I tried to found it in Lausanne. Without success! I was counting on Baron Coubertin. I bombarded him with letters. No answer! I wanted to convince Colonel Balsan. The billionaire did not offer me a cent! Now I'm pestering all the major groups, foundations, bankers in the world. I almost made contact with "Moral Rearmament" in Montreux. I can still save humanity, but, for the love of God, give me the means to do it! Money is the sinews of war, they say. It is also the sinews of peace! House me, feed me. And time is fleeting. I'm seventy-seven years old.

BRASSAÏ But why are you in Eze?

THE STRANGER I have my plan! It's here I want to set up the "International Philosophical Center"—at the Balsan château, to be precise. It's for sale, in fact. What a boon! They're only asking a million dollars. A trifle to definitively assure peace. I would live there, I would make it my center, and humanity would finally be able to breathe.

These words fall on us like a shower running hot and cold. So the prophet is only the first atom bomb blackmailer. We run away from him! He chases after us, handing us brochures, asks Henry to find an American publisher for his *Political Meteorology,* "a new scientific discipline," asks me to lend him my house, a temporary headquarters for the "philosophical center."

We tell Gilberte about our strange encounter.

GILBERTE That doesn't surprise me much. Eze attracts eccentric types and nutcases.

BRASSAÏ Yes, nothing but madmen and fanatics on the coast! Wealth combined with idleness produces strange and laughable aberrations of taste. Almost everywhere you see "Scottish châteaux" with machicolation. Even here in Eze. Do you know who had the "Scotsman's château" built? The son of Alfred, Lord Tennyson, poet of the Victorian age. One night, at the casino in Monte Carlo, after he'd lost his entire fortune, he had to hand over his château to the Sunbathers' Society.

CHAPTER 12   *Friday, May 13, 1960 (continued)*

We leave Eze-Village for La Turbie. That's where the Via Aurelia crossed the border between Italy and alpine Gaul. Still standing there is a piece of the "Trophy of the Alps," a gigantic monument. Henry has too often repeated that he would not take one step for a ruin, a historical curiosity, for me to show it to him. I am certain, however, that I have only to point out to him that Gaius Petronius, the author of his cherished Satyricon and a Gaul, probably passed this way to awaken his interest in the site. Very close by, in a verdant valley shaded by the austere Nice hinterland, is Laghet, the pilgrimage site in the Alpes-Maritines, an antiquated little Lourdes. An Italian fragrance still floats in the air; you'd think you were in Umbria. But Laghet is also one of the centers of folk art. The walls of the four galleries in the church vanish under hundreds of ex-votos. Among them are true masterpieces, the "fixed ones" from the early nineteenth century, executed no doubt by families of artists: their style and technique sometimes achieve the beauty of the pre-Renaissance Italian masters.

But the surprise I had for Henry on this site of pilgrimage and devotion is the strange presence of the author of *Alcools*. An alerted ecclesiastic discovered and enlarged a text on Laghet written by Guillaume Apollinaire. And we read: "The wonder-filled and meticulous awkwardness of primitive art that reigns here has what it takes to touch even those who do not have faith. . . . All the possible accidents, the fatal illnesses, the profound suffering, all the human miseries are depicted here naively, devoutly, ingenuously. . . . The raging sea tosses a poor dismasted hull, on which a man, larger than the vessel, is kneeling. All is lost, it seems, but the *Virgin of Laghet* is watching over him in a shining nimbus in the corner of the canvas. The devout man was saved. . . . That was in 1811. . . . And even now, every year, every month, almost every day, blind people see, mute people speak, consumptive patients survive, thanks to the *Lady of Laghet,* who smiles sweetly, haloed in yellow, in the corner of the canvases." Signed: Guillaume Apollinaire.

MILLER It's surprising to run into the author of *One Hundred Thousand Rods* in this holy place.

BRASSAÏ Even more strange, I discovered that Marcel Proust also speaks of it in *Remembrance of Things Past.*

MILLER Proust? Really?

BRASSAÏ Odette Swann, the former demimondaine, who led a loose life in Nice, Paris, and Baden-Baden, felt profound devotion for the virgin of Laghet. Proust says she had once been healed there and, after that, she always wore the gold medallion of Laghet on her chest, to which she attributed unlimited power. And we learn from Françoise, who heard it from the Swanns' governess, that Odette never went on a trip without her medallion. Swann is well aware how much his wife venerates it. Therefore, when he questions her in a fit of jealousy about whether she has slept with women, which she ferociously denies, her husband orders her: "Can you swear to me on your medallion of Our Lady of Laghet?" You see, he knows she would not perjure herself on that medal for anything in the world. And since she still tries to avoid the issue, the furious Swann screams at her: "Tell me on your medallion if, yes or no, you ever did those things."

MILLER And she confesses?

BRASSAÏ Yes, she confesses. She confesses to him that "without realizing it she did those things two or three times."[1]

This evening, dinner at the home of Mme P. B. in Juan-les-Pins.

MILLER Tony was barely eight years old when a girl of eleven, who had fallen in love with him, wanted to initiate him into the ways of love. She had already had a few experiences. She had even dragged him to the bed. I had to grab him from the arms of that budding vamp. "Sexual awakening" is a big, confusing time for children. One day, we were having dinner with a few friends, and Tony asked me point-blank: "Papa, will you show me how to make love?" A strange question, don't you think? And yet what is more legitimate? A child ought to be able to ask his parents *anything.* But it was so unexpected and so embarrassing in front of strangers. Naturally, they must have thought: "Like father, like son."

BRASSAÏ Didn't you reply that it cannot be shown *at the dinner table?*
MILLER I did what parents usually do out of cowardice and hypocrisy in such cases: I put off the response.

The lesson in love that little Tony had vainly asked of his father at age eight, he received at twenty through his father's books, as he recounted in an afterword to the French edition of *Quiet Days in Clichy.*

"Last summer, when I was in Sweden," Tony writes, "I happened to get my hands on a book by my father: *Quiet Days in Clichy,* which I immediately began to read. I had no sooner read the first page than I was off on a lively gambol of love, passion, beauty, and wisdom—things so rarely found in these sad and dreary times.

"It seems that, lately, people are very prompt to condemn a piece of literature the moment they perceive a word that baffles or embarrasses them—too bad! For myself, I have drawn so much life and compassion, so much humor and wisdom from that book, that I find it incredible that anyone could have the nerve to say: 'My God, what a pornographer!' as I have often heard.

"It would take a twisted and very malevolent mind to find obscenity or unfairness in that description of Miller's life in Clichy. Not only was I captivated by its liberal analyses of people strewn throughout the book, but I was never so aware of that man's sense of humor, a humor both satirical and sarcastic and very down-to-earth, a humor to make us die laughing as tears stream down our cheeks.

"*Clichy* was a second birth for me. . . . A reflective and soulful spirit emanates from the printed word, passes through the reader's eyes and, in the end, saturates the entire body like the euphoria that takes hold of us after a good bottle of red wine" (Tony Miller, Santa Monica, California, April 1967).

I ask Henry if he had seen his interview broadcast on television the night before.
MILLER I left the palace too late. But even if I'd been free, I wonder if I would have had the heart to watch it.

He says this without regret. If he had really wanted to see it, he could have. But he doesn't like to see himself and even less to hear himself.

"I don't have a very pleasant voice," he says. "It's monotonous and guttural. It's like a big bear singing softly to himself. It quickly becomes irritating. When I was young, I loved to read out loud, but I had to acknowledge with sorrow that my voice had a soporific effect."
BRASSAÏ The program was good. As always, you spoke with a great deal of naturalness. But Simenon seemed to be reciting a lesson. Not the slightest hesitation.

MILLER   What do you expect, the man is diabolically clever! He has an extraordinary vivacity, an ease of elocution. His intelligence is so quick, so sharp, that he can say anything without even thinking. Obviously, that gives you the feeling he is not "natural," that he's reciting a lesson. But he can assimilate anything, get inside any character. I even wonder how he manages to find his own voice again.

Mme P. B. shares her memories of the Occupation, which she spent in Die, in the Drôme.

MILLER   Die? A city I love! A marvelous town with the Vercors in the background. The Drôme is not well known, an admirable region! Last year, I spent a few weeks there with Eve and the children.

MME P.B.   How did you get the idea to go to Die?

MILLER   One day, in Big Sur—it was 1950, I think—I was visited by a young French writer, Albert Maillet. To make my acquaintance, he had crossed the Atlantic, then all of America to California, hitchhiking all the way.

BRASSAÏ   He had a "dramatic" incident during that trip, or so you told me.

MILLER   More than a dramatic incident, a terrible adventure! In the Rocky Mountains, he stopped a truck driver, who picked him up. But he was a gangster determined to rob him and even kill him. To perpetrate his crime, he suddenly drove his car out into a wild, desert region. Albert Maillet saw that his life was in danger. He knew it. The other man had already grabbed the heavy jack to knock him out. Fortunately for my future friend, he was an English teacher. Without losing his presence of mind, he began to tell him about his wife and children, to express his yearning to see them again soon. His words were so moving that, finally, as boorish as he was, the gangster dropped the weapon, dissolved into tears, and asked him for forgiveness. In 1953, during our first trip with Eve to Europe, I saw my friend Maillet again. We even lived with him for a time in Vienne, in the Isère, where he was teaching. He's now at a different high school and lives in Die. That's where I saw him last year.

BRASSAÏ   And you, Henry, have you done much hitchhiking?

MILLER   At age twenty-one or twenty-two, when I first ran off to the West as a farm worker, I stopped all sorts of cars on the road and sometimes they picked me up. But I was first frisked to see that I wasn't hiding any weapons. And I always had to sit *next to* the driver so that he could watch my every move. What trust! It was really humiliating! But I had no choice! Sometimes I ran across jovial men who treated me like a friend, invited me to eat and drink, even gave me money. Later, when we were with June in North Carolina without a red cent in our pockets, we again hitchhiked. With June, it was child's play. She was so pretty, so attractive. She had only to raise her little finger and the most beautiful, the fastest cars stopped to pick us up. But the heyday of my hitchhiking was the beginning of my stay in Big Sur. I was so broke that I could not even consider having a car. But if there is one place in the world where a car is indispensable, it's truly on that high cliff, seventy kilometers from the nearest city. Lepska and I were really forced to hitchhike then.

Since it is very hot, Henry opens his shirt collar. I see a chain around his neck with a gold talisman, engraved with Arabic or Hebrew characters.

MME P.B.   What, you wear a talisman?

MILLER   Yes, I've worn it for a very long time. It's four hundred years old. It's a Hebrew medallion, and so worn down by contact with the skin of everyone who's worn it or touched it that the characters are almost effaced. Rightly or wrongly, I think it will bring me luck.

MME P.B.   Do you really believe so? Then let me touch it.

CHAPTER 13

Tuesday, May 17, 1960

This morning, Henry telephones me: "I have only one film to see today. I'd like us to have dinner together. And here's some good news! Margery arrived in Paris this morning. I hope you'll be in Cannes to make her acquaintance."

I call Picasso.

PICASSO What a surprise! Come to see me whenever you like. Are you free tomorrow at two thirty? We can spend the whole afternoon together. We'll be alone. Then I'll expect you tomorrow at the Californie. The door will be open for you.

In the evening we meet Miller.

I had learned that, during the Occupation, the Hôtel Montfleury was the domain of the Gestapo. But I am careful not to breathe a word of it to Henry. It might spoil his tranquility in that place.

MILLER Today, I feel relaxed. But tomorrow will be terrible. Then Thursday's the big day! Screenings from ten o'clock in the morning till midnight, maybe till dawn. We have to award the prizes. Just between us, no actor or actress seems to deserve the prize. Oh well, yes, perhaps Melina Mercouri.

GILBERTE But you haven't seen everything yet. Wait till *Moderato cantabile.* You'll see Jeanne Moreau, the heroine of *The Lovers.* A great actress.

Juan-Luis Buñuel, who helped his father during the shooting of *The Young One,* is having dinner with us, along with an American actor and his wife.

I ask Buñuel's son, who is sitting next to me, how he became a filmmaker.

J.-L. BUÑUEL I was not at all attracted to film. As I child, my parents often dragged me to the sets where my father was shooting. That left a rather bad memory. I wanted to devote myself to literature, especially English literature. But at the age of twenty, I spent my vacation in Mexico. Orson Welles was looking for an assistant who spoke English as well as Spanish. In order to earn a little pocket money, I accepted the job. That's how I became a filmmaker. Usually, I shoot with my father, sometimes with other producers. And I hope, naturally, to be a director myself one day.

BRASSAÏ   I talked to Picasso on the phone yesterday. His voice was astonishingly young. I arranged to see him tomorrow afternoon.

MILLER   So you'll see him.

BRASSAÏ   I'll see him and you can come with me.

MILLER   But it's a bad time. I won't be able to. I'll have too busy a day.

BRASSAÏ   Ten times, twenty times, you've asked me to introduce you to him in Cannes. You even wrote me that you agreed to be a member of the jury at the Cannes Film Festival only in the hope of making his acquaintance.

MILLER   That's true. Cannes is forever associated in my mind with Picasso's name. But it's a bad time. The festival is coming to an end and we're in a terrible rush. Tomorrow, I have three showings instead of two, and the third begins at three o'clock. To know Picasso! Of course, that's one of my greatest desires. But I don't like to rush things. I could probably go to his place with you, but the very idea of leaving him at a set time would poison every minute of our conversation. What would be the point of such a hurried meeting? You need more time and more serenity to make friends.

BRASSAÏ   You can go back to his place another day. You're in Cannes, just a short walk from him. Soon you'll be in Big Sur, Greece, Tibet, Japan, God knows where. And Picasso may be in Vauvenargues. It will be a missed opportunity.

MILLER   You're probably right. Hmm, hmm, ha-ha-ha. Don't tempt me! You have to let chance do its work. The opportunity may present itself one day. I'm a fatalist. It's possible Larry will take me to Vauvenargues from Nîmes someday.

BRASSAÏ   You'll never get him on the phone. The door will be closed. You won't even get a response from him. To be able to work, he must create a void around him.

MILLER   If I can't meet him in this world—I'm sixty-nine years old and he's eighty—I'm sure to meet him later, in ten million years, I don't know where, since such forces, such energies always remain active.

GILBERTE   Do you really think so? Do you believe in immortality?

MILLER   Immortality? Hmm, hmm, ha, ha, ha. Yes, I believe in it in a sense. I think that no one dies, that death does not exist. One simply achieves a different vision, a different consciousness, one reaches a new, unknown world. Just as you don't know *where* you come from, you don't know *where* you're going. Or, as Nietzsche said: eternal return. Why not? I firmly believe that there is a *before* and an *after*. I too am a philosopher when I like. In any case, tell Picasso how much I like and admire him, how much I would have liked to know him.

And we speak of the Ingmar Bergman film presented at the festival.

MILLER *The Virgin Spring* is very spare, very strong, based on an old ballad. It's the story of a young girl who is carrying candles to the Virgin Mary. On the way to the church, she is raped and murdered by three shepherds. The rape scene in the forest is of an almost unbearable brutality. I've never seen anything like it. But the film is more poetic than realistic and very pure, almost chaste, in spite of the rape.

GILBERTE Is Bergman the Scandinavian Buñuel?

J.-L. BUÑUEL I don't think so. Bergman is much more philosophical than my father. Buñuel's films are free of philosophy or spiritual messages. He often uses childhood memories. And his humor is typically Spanish: cruelty and permanent defiance of death. By the way, I saw Jacques Becker's *The Hole*. An innovation even more interesting than *Breathless*. That so-called bold and revolutionary film doesn't appeal to me.

I ask Henry about his "schedule" after the festival.

MILLER Sunday we leave with Michel Simon for La Ciotat. Then I'll go see Larry in Nîmes for a week. Then I'll go to Italy to see my publisher, who is brave enough to publish *Tropic of Cancer*. He doesn't even want to make any cuts! It'll be a power struggle with the pope! Nevertheless, I told Feltrinelli that the stakes were high, that he could lose his money and even go to prison. But he's not afraid. I would also have liked to see Greece again. But if I go to Athens, I would be immediately cornered. I made a great number of friends there. But I prefer to have elbow room. Nevertheless, I'm burning with the desire to see Crete again. The museum attendant is the poorest man in the world. Many Cretans still walk around in the clothes I sent them, hundreds of garments, in I don't know how many packages.

BRASSAÏ Did Michel Simon tell you his tragic adventure?

MILLER You mean his agony. Yes. He was not in love with the prostitute of Porte Saint-Martin, just great friends with her. What a story! A real detective story! That whore killed someone only a few minutes after he'd left her! There he was is in his bath. He's grilled, interrogated. And, like me, he's afraid of the police, of judges, of all the judicial machinery that's set in motion and grinds you down.

BRASSAÏ Two years ago, someone rang my doorbell. I open up. The visitor flips open his jacket: police inspector. He puts a little photo before my eyes: "Do you know this boy?" I look at him. He is blond, fairly good-looking, thirteen or fourteen years old. "No, I've never seen him." "Look closely. You ought to know him." "No, you're mistaken! I've never seen that boy, I repeat, I'm sure of it! But can I know why you're asking me that question?" "Because he disappeared. Three weeks ago." "So what? Are you assuming, then, that I played some part in that disappearance? It's beyond me!" "You see, among the few names written in the diary of his that was found, yours also appears, with your address and telephone number. So he knew you. What do you have to say? Can you provide an explanation?" Imagine! I was suspected of nothing less than murder! My name scrawled in that diary made me one of the suspects. I found myself in a Kafkaesque maze.

MILLER But how did you get out of it?

BRASSAÏ I told the inspector that my name is fairly well known and that it was natural for a boy, if he was interested in photography, to write my name and address in his notebook. Maybe he wanted to see me, like many other young people. In fact, in my view, that's the only plausible explanation. But the inspector was a tough nut: for an hour and a half he grilled me. He also made inquiries about my morals with the concierge. He asked her if I entertained a large number of young men. Two weeks went by. I thought the matter was closed. And then I receive a summons from the "investigative services" at the police prefecture. I was so apprehensive that I asked Gilberte to go with me. "If you don't come with me, I'm afraid I'll confess that I'm that boy's murderer."

GILBERTE (*laughing*): He only wanted me to come to prove that, flanked by a deserving spouse, he was normal as far as morality was concerned.

MILLER I understand you. Going through the doors of the police prefecture has always been a nightmare for me. In my role as an "alien" I also had a feeling of guilt. What a horrifying maze that building is! Fortunately, I had an admirer among the high officials, François Raoul. In his office, I forgot we were at the prefecture. With great serenity, we spoke of writers and literature. He was the one who made it easy for me to obtain my visas.

BRASSAÏ And what about your imbroglio with the judge in the Seine—in 1953, I think. Your summons regarding *Sexus*.

MILLER I was very frightened. Fortunately, my lawyer was up to the task. Seeing me come forward, livid as a condemned man, in the "pacing" hallway near the judge's chamber, he did everything to raise my morale. "Mr. Miller," he said to me, "don't be discouraged, be *proud!* You are walking in the footsteps of François Villon, the marquis de Sade, Zola, Balzac, Flaubert, Baude-laire." And, in fact, at that moment, the "Miller case" all the newspapers were talking about was beginning to resemble the "Zola case," the "Dreyfus affair." I say that as a joke. All the same, I was in excellent company. And the words of my lawyer restored my peace of mind a little.

BRASSAÏ What about the judge?

MILLER A total surprise! What an open mind! What humanity! "Mr. Miller," he told me, "I would like to know what your intentions were in writing this book. What did you want to express in it?" I was very distracted by an urgent need to piss, due no doubt to the emotion. In spite of that, I somehow or other explained myself. The clerk was eating up my words. Deep down, even the judge agreed with them. Yes, that was my impression. He repeated several times: "Mr. Miller, don't worry." Then he asked me this question: "Do you claim total freedom of expression for your thoughts?" I reflected for a full minute. "Yes, total freedom of expression!" "So you maintain that a writer has the right to *say everything, everything, absolutely everything*?" "Yes," I replied with conviction, "he has the right to *say everything, absolutely everything*!" At each of my affirmative responses, he made a gesture as if he agreed with me and the clerk's hands also applauded me silently under the table. I spent an hour with the judge. When I left his chamber, I had already forgotten all my mortification, I was reassured, contented. His loyal, almost friendly attitude showed me the true face of France. I took myself for the author of *Justine, Madame Bovary,* or *The Flowers of Evil*! And I observed with pleasure that, in this country, it's sort of an honor and a privilege for a writer to be dragged into court.

BRASSAÏ But I remember that the trial made you profoundly bitter.

MILLER Yes, because France passed for the most liberal country in the world, where art and literature had the greatest freedom, and where the public was the least easily shocked.

BRASSAÏ It's for that reason, I think, that Joyce, when he left Trieste, chose to live in France. Proceedings against obscene books were rare there. He also thought it was the only country where even the little-known writer was respected. Stuart Gilbert reports that, while traveling with Joyce, the writer gave him this advice when he had to fill out a hotel card: "Don't put *pensioner,* put *man of letters*. You'll see, they'll take better care of us knowing we're writers."

MILLER I thought that myself. I had assumed that French censorship was less harsh than that of the English-speaking world. But when *Tropic of Capricorn* was published, my publisher, Maurice Girodias, had to cut five pages at the very last minute, so as not to have the police on his back. And, in spite of that, as with *Tropic of Cancer,* the publishers were prosecuted for "public indecency." Fortunately, they were granted amnesty the next year.

BRASSAÏ That was the first "Miller affair." The second was triggered by *Sexus,* wasn't it?

MILLER That book was seized as soon as it was published. The "expurgated" edition, with many blots and blank pages—all the somewhat scabrous passages were suppressed—was banned as well.

BRASSAÏ The trial lasted a long time.

MILLER A very long time, more than four years, and ended with a—how do you say that?—with a *non-lieu,* a dismissal. Nevertheless, *Sexus* was banned by a special decree, not only in the French language, but also in English and in every other language. By the way, that judgment did not prevent *Sexus* from selling under the table. It was also banned in Norway and even in Japan. And not only in Japanese, but also in English. *Sexus* is truly my most forbidden book, the one most often taken to court, even more often than *Tropic of Cancer.*

BRASSAÏ Have you seen many people today?

MILLER When I got back to the hotel, I had a very agreeable surprise. A man was waiting for me in the lobby. It was Jean Renaud, my old friend from Dijon, the prefect of Carnot high school! He found out in Toulon that I was a member of the jury in Cannes and came to see me.

BRASSAÏ Wasn't he the one who brought you a bottle of burgundy wine one day at the high school?

MILLER A *latricière-chambertin* from the wine cellars of the dukes of Burgundy. Unforgettable! Beaune was his native city and it was the first time I was able to drink a vintage burgundy. We enjoyed ourselves. To make our pleasure last, Renaud served it in driblets. Since then, I've gotten my education in good wine. France is so rich in it, so very rich. But I can no longer drink a *chambertin,* a *clos-vougeot,* or a *hospices-de-beaune* without thinking of my friend from Burgundy.

BRASSAÏ And it was Renaud who came to see you in Clichy, and for whom you served as guide in Paris.

MILLER Yes, at the time of *Quiet Days in Clichy.* It was then that Fred's young girlfriend, a girl of fifteen, who lived hidden in our house, was struck with very violent pains due to her period. She was a minor. If we called a doctor we risked going to prison. I was the one who applied my two hands to her belly, as healers do. And miraculously, I made her pains go away.

GILBERTE Perhaps you have the gift of a healer. Mme P. B. told me that she was relieved of her symptoms after touching your talisman. It's curious, she's both frightened of you and attracted to you, as if you were the angel and the devil at the same time. "When I read Miller," she told me the other day, "I find him dreadful, weak, egotistical, cynical, without the slightest moral sense, smugly displaying all his vices, all his defects. But when I see him, he's a man radiating kindness, generosity, humanity, intelligence. And whatever my aversion in reading his books, in his presence I once more fall under his charm. There's something about it that escapes me. Because of all the horrors he recounts about himself, I ought to hate him, but when he speaks to me, I forget everything, as if I had a different man in front of me."

Oddly—and before Marcel Proust—that gap between the author and his work preoccupied the young Balzac. In a "psychological essay" that precedes *The Wild Ass's Skin*, he examines the phenomenon of those "ill-matched peculiarities that exist between a writer's *talent* and his *physiognomy*"! It is a mystery, according to him, from which no law can be deduced: there is as much resemblance as difference. Whereas Petrarch, Lord Byron, Hoffmann, and Voltaire were "men of their genius," Rabelais was not at all "Rabelaisian": a temperate man, he drank nothing but water. Similarly, Brillat-Savarin was frugal and not at all a gourmet, and thus did not resemble the writer who celebrated good food. According to Balzac, it would be easy to multiply these examples of "cohesiveness" and "disunity" between the man and his thought. But what interests him even more is the attitude of readers: "They never remain impartial regarding a book and its author. Involuntarily, they sketch out a figure in their minds, build a man, supposing him young or old, tall or short, likable or mean." In short, as we would now say, they draw up a "profile" of the unknown author. But the uncertainty of the laws governing literary physiognomy is such, says Balzac, that most often, suddenly finding himself in the presence of the author, the reader exclaims: "I didn't imagine him like that!" Proust expresses the same surprise: "We are stupefied, when we encounter in the world a great man whom we knew only through his works, to have to superimpose, to make one thing coincide with the other, to introduce the enormous body of work . . . into the unyielding nature of a completely different living body" (preface for Jacques-Emile Blanche). In fact, that was the case for Proust himself. The "profound disunity" between his work and his person even fooled André Gide, who saw his novel as only the amusement of a dilettante who spent all his time in salons. For Balzac, as for Miller, it is instead the author who suffers from the "bad reputation" of his work. Balzac complains bitterly that his readers take him for an old roué and cynic, a sensualist, a pleasure seeker. And yet, he says, he can show his birth certificate saying he is *thirty years old.* And he lives a solitary and sober life, he asserts, "without which fertility of the mind does not exist."

In Miller's case, the distance between the real man and the character his readers imagine is enormous. Early on, Anaïs Nin was completely astonished by it: "He was so different from his brutal, violent, vital writing, his carica-tures, his Rabelaisian farces, his exaggerations" (*Diary,* winter 1931–32).[1] And there have been so many other, similar reactions! "What surprises me," a Hindu writer remarks, "is the contrast in Miller between the writer's style and the man's personality. As frank and audacious as his literary work is, his nature seems equally calm, meditative to me. . . . The man surprised me with his almost Oriental sense of contemplation" ("Budhadeva Bose," *Synthèse,* February–March 1967). Miller, aware of that contrast, laughs about it: "No matter how violently disagreeable a reader's reaction may be to the writer's work, when we meet face to face he usually ends by accepting me whole-heartedly. From the many encounters I have had with my readers it would seem that antipathies are quickly dispelled in the living presence of an au-thor" (*The World of Sex*).[2] He has had the experience a thousand times. In 1934, after the publication of *Tropic of Cancer,* he sometimes distributed his book himself. I remember that once when he identified himself to a Parisian bookseller, she exclaimed: "But you don't look so obscene at all!" No one, looking at that fine, delicate, meditative, even discreet man, wants to believe one is dealing with the horrible pornographer. His distinction makes you think rather of a spiritual preacher, an ascetic, a saint. Perhaps he followed Céline's advice: "One must be the *opposite* of what one writes."

MILLER You were speaking, Gilberte, of my gift as a healer. I don't know anything about that. In any case, I believe in psychic forces. The other day, I had a rather extraordinary visit from a Swiss jeweler. He wanted to do my portrait, since he is also a painter. But he only executes *abstract* portraits. He did one of Eisenhower, of Khrushchev, and even of Picasso. I was very in-trigued. He explained to me that every person elicits certain signs in him, cer-tain symbols, whose meaning he himself does not understand very clearly: the "abstract portrait" is formed altogether intuitively in his head.

BRASSAÏ And did you see those abstract portraits?

MILLER He showed them to me. And I found them to be very good like-nesses. Mine as well. In fact, I was flabbergasted. In it I discovered my char-acteristic sign: the image of "protection" that the astrologists—and even the graphologists—have always detected in my "psychic" chart; a column rising from a vase and supported by three leaning pillars. Official science neglects the powers that dwell within us, that may even determine us.

GILBERTE Brassaï doesn't want to hear about such occult things. For him, the visible world contains everything, explains everything. He thinks that "elsewhere" doesn't exist. But I am persuaded of the existence of the psychic forces you're talking about. Sympathies, antipathies, attractions, repulsions, loves, hates, are often inexplicable, and undoubtedly depend on those powers, I'm convinced of it. And I feel such things very keenly. It's rare that my feelings or presentiments steer me wrong.

MILLER I'm like you. All my life, I've been attracted to everything that so-called exact science doesn't take seriously. And increasingly, I'm turning to the Orient, where these psychic, occult forces are not only recognized and respected but studied, cultivated, even taught, like yoga.

BRASSAÏ Have you heard of a graphologist named Schermann? He had his hour of glory in Vienna, then in Paris. He left for the United States. He was the most extraordinary graphologist. He undoubtedly had the gift of clairvoyance. For him, handwriting was only a medium. Looking at a person's face, he could reproduce his handwriting. Looking at a canvas, he gave you the painter's signature. Reading a few pages of the poet Lise Deharme, he discerned that that eccentric woman wanted to have a streetlamp in her apartment! He went from the physical person to the psychic person or vice versa with stupefying ease.

We are at a café and Henry orders a Chartreuse. It's now his favorite liqueur. He used to end his meals with a Benedictine or a kümmel.

CHAPTER 14

October 1960

In a hotel in the Montparnasse district, where the poet René Char and other writers and artists stay, I find Henry in top form.

MILLER I'm doing marvelously! Better than in Cannes, even better than in Big Sur! I thrive remarkably well in the Paris air. In Los Angeles—and this is something very rare for this time of year—it was dreadfully hot: 100 degrees Fahrenheit. In New York it was not quite so hot, but the air was more humid, which is worse.

We order our lunch at La Coupole. The hardest thing is choosing the wine. As he goes over the list of vintage wines, Henry's nostrils dilate, as if their names alone were already giving off their bouquet.

MILLER How far away the festival and Juan-les-Pins seem! I feel like it all happened six years ago, not six months.

BRASSAÏ I can now reveal a secret: the Hôtel Montfleury, I learned, was the headquarters of the Gestapo in Cannes. I didn't want to tell you in Cannes, to spare you nightmares. The other thing that reminds me of Cannes is the Paris opening of the films shown during the festival: *La Dolce Vita*, *L'Avventura*, the Japanese film *Kagi* or *Odd Obsession*. You remember the big scandal it caused when the prize went to that film? The public was unhappy to see it honored, they booed the jury, accused it of awarding the prize only to "failures" and of brushing aside the good films. Six months after the decision, people are still arguing. Last night, while I was reading a critic's review, I thought of you. Out of "charity," he said, he doesn't want to name the members of the jury who preferred the Japanese film to what he considered a masterpiece, Antonioni's *L'Avventura*. It was you especially he was targeting.

MILLER No doubt! I'm in great part responsible. I'm willing to recognize it.

I fiercely defended the Japanese film *Kagi*. What do you want? I liked it and I didn't understand a thing in *L'Avventura*, which was incoherent, interminable, absurd, and basically boring. I may have committed an injustice.

BRASSAÏ You're not the only one to have that opinion! Many critics, irritated by the "gratuitousness of the sex scenes" and the "incredibly morose" story, wrote that "it was impossible to be so damned annoying with so much talent," and that Antonioni is sending "soporific and indecipherable messages."

MILLER I'm reassured by that. It appears, however, that *L'Avventura* has been successful in Paris.

BRASSAÏ True. Especially among the younger critics. They speak of a "new language" of film, of "open film," where the characters don't have a determined character, where the actions remain unmotivated. In short, one leaves to the viewer's imagination what ought to have been the work of the screenwriter and producer.[1]

MILLER I'm rarely wrong, I rarely change my mind. But it happens sometimes. I had to revise my admiration for Thomas Mann, whom I had taken for a genius when I was young. In my eyes, he fell from that pedestal to the rank of a skillful literary writer. I ought to see *L'Avventura* again, and also *Odd Obsession—Kagi*—with new eyes.

BRASSAÏ It's my feeling that no form of expression elicits so many *contradictory* judgments as film, as if, in that medium, you could only love something or hate it.

MILLER That's because films are addressed more to our guts than to our brains, more to our emotions than to our reason. And when a film touches us, it's very difficult to establish whether it touches us subjectively or objectively.

BRASSAÏ It's true. The faces, landscapes, and situations of a film can bring up personal memories that have nothing to do with the screenplay. Because of that, even a bad film can move us if it projects itself against the background of our memories.

MILLER And what about the circumstances under which you saw a film! As a result of watching a string of them one after another every day in Cannes, my sense of judgment began to get clouded.

BRASSAÏ It often happens that critics modify their judgment—for better or worse—when they see a film presented at the Cannes festival a second time, in a Paris theater.

I ask about Eve.

MILLER Hmm, hmm. We live apart now. I live in Los Angeles, she in Big Sur.

BRASSAÏ Yet it was Eve who absolutely wanted to leave Big Sur, and you were the one who wanted to stay. What happened?

MILLER Set your mind at ease. She's not unhappy. She's living at present with a sculptor and is devoting herself to painting. They get along very well. Everything is happening for the best. As for me, I've changed. I've even changed sexes. I'm now traveling with a man. His name is Vincent, Vincent Birke. He's charming, without ambition, without pretensions, and so courageous! You'll see. He's delighted to accompany me, a dedicated secretary. At this moment, while we're having lunch, he's typing my letters at the hotel. What devotion! Vincent has knocked around a great deal. He was in the navy and the air force. He knows a bunch of languages. He speaks French, English, Italian, Portuguese, Spanish.

BRASSAÏ Did you stop in New York?

MILLER Only for two days. And it was right during Fidel Castro's visit! All the Americans hate him, even the taxi drivers, even the Jews, even the blacks. A surprising unanimity! What a comedy! That bearded man arguing with the manager of a hotel, one of the rare ones that agreed to take him in. When he learned the price of the room, Castro replied: "This is surely a misunderstanding! I don't want to *buy* your hotel, only to *rent* it! Your price is no doubt the sales price!" When the hotel manager refused to accept payment with Cuban bills instead of dollars, Castro moved to Harlem and a hotel run by a black man. There, it was a real circus! P. T. Barnum, what have you! Daily scandals. The Cuban leader was seen surrounded by live chickens, which he killed and plucked with his own hands for roasting. He went to bed with all his clothes on, with all his weapons, he was afraid of being poisoned or murdered. And what a spectacle to see Khrushchev, Fidel Castro, and all the rest come to New York to insult the Americans *at home* under the aegis of the UN, with the Soviet premier taking off his shoe in the middle of the session and rapping it on his desk! The way they told us off!

End of the meal. After a few hesitations, Henry orders a green Chartreuse.

CHAPTER 15

Friday, April 20, 1962

Henry has just arrived in Paris and we will have dinner with him this evening at the Rattners'.

But what's going on? Gendarmes, state police, police vans in the street. All the streets bordering La Santé prison are blocked off. General Salan, head of the supporters of French Algeria, has just been arrested. From the crowd, thronging everywhere, rise shouts of "Death to Salan!" "The firing squad for Salan!" while, in the prison, activist convicts are shouting: "French Algeria!" "Long live Salan!" Having finally crossed the police cordon, we arrive at our hosts' home.

Abraham Rattner, Henry's old friend, had participated in the second battle of the Marne and had been wounded in Château-Thierry. A painter, he led the camouflage operations for the 75-millimeter guns. After World War I, he lived in France for about twenty years and was part of the École de Paris. He has recently produced very beautiful stained-glass windows for the Chicago synagogue. In 1940, he accompanied Henry on his tour of the United States, which resulted in *The Air-conditioned Nightmare*.

RATTNER When Henry returned to New York from Greece, he told me of his plan for a trip and suggested I go with him. He was thinking of a deluxe edition illustrated with my gouaches. On principle, Doubleday and Company was willing to publish it. But, instead of the five thousand dollars promised, Henry received only seven hundred and fifty.

Regarding that modest "advance" from the publisher, Henry later wrote me: "After the manuscript was rejected, over the next two or three years, I gradually reimbursed the money that had been advanced to me. It was hard, since I was penniless at the time. But it was a question of pride! One day, I received a letter from Doubleday telling me I was the *only author* who ever returned an advance for a book rejected by them!" (letter to Brassaï, July 31, 1965).

BRASSAÏ And you accompanied him.

RATTNER I liked the idea. There was a sizable pitfall, however: neither of us knew how to drive. After a dozen lessons on an old Ford we had bought—we barely knew how to hold the steering wheel, brake, and change gears—we were off!

BRASSAÏ But Henry didn't like to travel very much.

RATTNER After ten years of absence, he felt the need to come to terms with America and to take an objective look at his country. He hoped to be able to revise his judgment and to find the cities beautiful, his compatriots kind, cheerful, happy. What a disappointment! Almost everywhere, we ran into nothing but ugliness, bitterness, skepticism, cynicism, despair.

BRASSAÏ But what about the landscape?

RATTNER Magnificent, naturally. But you very quickly grow tired of the monotony of the cities, the roads, the highways. We suffered a great deal because of them.

BRASSAÏ You produced your washes of landscapes at sixty miles an hour, Henry told me. What about him? Did he take notes?

RATTNER Rarely. But he reconstituted everything we saw and heard with extraordinary fidelity. He was very sensitive to what things suggested to him. Merely the name of a city or town could make him take a detour, could sear into his brain. Mobile, Natchez, Savannah, Baton Rouge, Tallahassee—what curious, mysterious, alluring names. They awakened glorious memories of the past in him, visions of the great poets he'd been weaned on. His disappointment was that much more cruel! The name "Mobile," for example, in the state of Alabama, evoked water, music, light to him. He thought he'd find a unique, extraordinary city. But Mobile is just one city among others, no more beautiful or interesting or fantastic.

I thought of Proust, who felt the same disenchantment with names. "Names," he said, "are fanciful artists, giving us sketches of people and countries that are such poor likenesses that we often feel a kind of stupor when we have in front of us, rather than the *imagined* world, the *visible* world. We leave to seek in a city a soul it cannot contain . . . but that we no longer have the power to expel from its name" (*A la recherche du temps perdu*, vol. 2).

BRASSAÏ How long did the trip last?

RATTNER We traveled more than fifteen thousand kilometers! Alas, in most of the cities and towns—hundreds!—there was almost nothing to see: the main street, a group of houses, the church, the town hall, the bank, the school.

The monotony and ugliness of the cities suffocated us. There were certainly a few oases: New Orleans, Charleston, Biloxi, Mississippi, where we felt we were again becoming "civilized beings." Rare places where people still grant the pleasures of the senses the importance they deserve, where you can take a stroll, savor a good meal accompanied by good wine. And those magnificent eighteenth-century plantation houses, surrounded by imposing rows of giant oaks covered with Spanish moss hanging from the branches.

BRASSAÏ You also went to New Iberia, didn't you?

RATTNER Yes, it was the last place we saw together. Ten days of rest on the magnificent property of my friend Weeks Hall, near Avery Island. Then we went our separate ways.

BRASSAÏ Five years ago, I too visited that region with Gilberte, in the heart of Cajun country. Magnificent! I admired the bayous, their variety, their shimmering colors, the forests loaded down with Spanish moss, which rise up from the arms of the Mississippi and are reflected in the water along with the sky.

RATTNER Well, you may have seen the colonial house of my friend Weeks Hall: "The Shadows," surrounded by a thick hedge of bamboo. It dates from the eighteenth century. And do you know what name we found in its visitors' book? Paul Claudel! Astonishing, don't you think? The ends of the earth. And right next to it is the Bayou Teche, a Japanese print.

In fact, amazed by the Bayou Teche, Henry wrote: "Sky and water had become one: the whole world was floating in a nebular mist. It was indescribably beautiful and bewitching" (*The Air-conditioned Nightmare*, p. 105).

Henry arrives. I say to him: "So you're again a member of a jury. But this time, it's the Formentera Prize in Spain."

MILLER I was weak enough to accept. Happy all the same to get to know the Balearic Islands. Formentera is an agreeable and restful site, I've been told. Are you familiar with it?

BRASSAÏ The hotel is luxurious. But a little too isolated. Cut off from all life around it. No village nearby. A few villas is all. So you must have read a lot of novels?

MILLER No, but what does it matter? Literary prizes are politics, diplomacy.

And we speak of Dali.

MILLER I had a funny adventure with Dali and Gala. Do you know Caresse Crosby?

BRASSAÏ No, but I just learned that, at one of my graffiti exhibitions in Rome, at the del Corso "Obelisco," she bought two of my panels for the property she's just acquired in Italy.

MILLER A generous woman. A patron of the arts. And also a poet. Ten years ago she published her memoirs: *The Passionate Years.* When did you make Dali's acquaintance?

BRASSAÏ In about 1932, in Picasso's studio on rue La Boétie. He was working at the Villa Seurat. It was there, I think, that I photographed him with Gala for the first time.

MILLER In summer 1940, when I came back to the United States from Greece, very broke and very depressed, even poorer and more unknown than I'd been when I left, Caresse wanted to help me. In 1944, she even held an exhibition of my gouaches in Washington. She'd invited me to spend some time on her magnificent property: "Bowling Green" in Virginia, in the heart of the South. A very large, very beautiful colonial house. And do you know who built it? A famous architect, you probably know him: Thomas Jefferson, the third president of the United States! That's where I wrote *The Colossus of Maroussi* and also *The World of Sex*. Caresse did a great deal for Dali in America. At the beginning, she was the one in charge of his public relations. Dali and Gala were enjoying her hospitality at the same time I was. He painted for many long months in "Bowling Green," and that's also where he wrote *The Secret Life of Salvador Dali*. He worked all day. We saw him only at mealtime. Over dinner, he was intent on distracting us with his clowning. Sometimes—rarely—he made us laugh, since he's teeming with comical ideas. But, at length, his exhibitionism got on my nerves! In that large house, we guests were on our own. Caresse had left for a long trip. One night, at about three in the morning, strange noises woke us up: the noise of an engine, the slamming of car doors, shouting, an argument. I get up. Through the window, what do I see? In the middle of the yard a taxi from Washington! The "fare" was shouting, waving his revolver at the driver: "I won't pay you! Not a penny! Get lost! Otherwise I'll kill you." Frightened, the driver took off in a cloud of smoke. And then we heard the heavy feet of the ranter climbing the stairs. He entered the Dalis' room and pointed his revolver at them, shouting: "Get the hell out of here! You bunch of lazybones! You bunch of bastards! What the hell are you doing in my house? Clear out! This is my room! I don't want anything to do with the good-for-nothings my wife is putting up and feeding here!" And he began to pull Dali and Gala from their bed. Then it was my turn. Threatening me with his revolver, he chased me from my room: "Put all your money on that table and get the hell out of here! I want it!" A dramatic situation, really. Dali was scared, he feared for his life, and for his canvases. Nevertheless, he didn't lose his sense of humor: "I know all about surrealism," he whispered to me, "but the surrealism of a drunk leaves me defenseless, makes me impotent." After the death of Harry Grew Crosby in 1929, Caresse had remarried several times. The man who threatened us was her fourth husband, I think. After getting good and drunk in Washington, he'd returned to Virginia in a taxi. What were we to do? "What if we called the sheriff?" Gala suggested. "The sheriff?" I exclaimed. "You're one of the aliens here, and I'm a Yankee, which is worse than a foreigner, worse than even a black in the South. We're certainly not the ones the sheriff would find in the right! He's at *home*, it's *his* house! The law is on his side! He can chase us off, kill us even! That's his right! We're intruders."

BRASSAÏ What a story! And what happened?

MILLER I took it upon myself to soften him up. I'm a chicken. I fear for my life. But I'm used to drunks. I got a bottle of whiskey and filled two glasses with it. We emptied I don't know how many together. The struggle lasted three hours. I was drunk myself. But finally, I managed to vanquish the giant. We became almost friends. He fell asleep peacefully. And the Dalis breathed easy. But what is he up to? Have you seen him recently?

BRASSAÏ With Gilberte, we spent a few days in Port Lligatt, near Cadaquès. Not *at their house* but *with them*. You see, even though their house is very large now—a row of several fisherman's cottages put together—Salvador and Gala never put anyone up at their place: "Even if we had ten times the room," Gala explained to me, "we would never have a guest room." So all Dali's visitors go to the only hotel in Port Lligatt, which overlooks their house. In the hope of seeing the "master," many curiosity seekers come to that place. Then, so as not to disappoint them, Dali makes furtive appearances, taking care to change his costume—and what costumes!—at every moment. "I always dress like Salvador Dali!" he told me. For him, to go out is to make a stage entrance.

The next morning, I learned that the previous night's demonstration regarding the arrest of General Salan had degenerated into a true riot. Political prisoners had succeeded in leaving their cells and setting the straw mattresses on fire. Late that night, with the help of tear bombs, the state police managed to control the riot and the firemen put out the blaze. In the street itself, violent fights broke out between sympathizers and opponents of "French Algeria." The Denfert-Rochereau pharmacy tended to the casualties all night long.

CHAPTER 16

Summer 1962

The breakup with Eve, another failed marriage for which he believed he bore the responsibility, profoundly depressed and unhinged Henry. Remaining alone, rooted to one spot, to work on *Nexus II* no longer appealed to him at all. "I'll be in Tokyo or Paris in a month or in September," he writes me. "If it's Paris, it will be to look for a place where I can spend the winter in comfort. People have mentioned Saint-Jean-de-Luz and the surrounding area as having the best climate in France. Is that true? They've also spoken of Cadiz (Cadix) in Spain. I wrote an amusing letter to Paul Morand (the globe-trotter) to ask him for information about the 'Winter Quarters.' According to him, such a place does not exist. But I know that in Siam, Burma, and Cambodia, the climate is mild in winter" (letter to Brassaï, from Big Sur, July 7, 1960).

And that was the beginning of a mad ride through Europe that would last two years, Miller flanked by his factotum, Vincent Birke, like Don Quixote and his Sancho Panza. But Henry's "Rocinante" would be the old 1953 Fiat that had been rusting away for a year in Die, Drôme. Having retrieved the jalopy, Henry heads for "Epalinges," Georges Simenon's luxurious property in Switzerland. "I met Charlie Chaplin at Simenon's, where I spent a few enchanted days," he wrote me. "It was quite an event!" Then it's Vienna. He visits Austria in the company of his old friend from Big Sur, Emil White, an Austrian who has not seen his country in forty years. "I really like the atmosphere here, turn-of-the-century Vienna," he writes me. "The people are so likable, so civilized. No neurotics, but very contented peacocks or cows. I went to the restaurants and cafés (old-fashioned) to listen to gypsy music and also to the zither players. It's enough to make you weep! Especially for an old whimperer like me!" And he adds: "At this point, I don't yet know where I'll go this winter. From here, I'll go home to Hamburg in three days—for sentimental reasons" (letter to Brassaï, from Vienna, November 20, 1960). Notice he does not say, "I'll go to Hamburg," but rather "I'll go *home* to Hamburg."

His first visit to that city, just before the Cannes festival, had enchanted him. Not Hamburg itself, which he feels has done only a poor job of rising up from its ruins, or the *Bierstuben,* which are too sad, but the warm welcome he received there. At the hospital in Hamburg, he greeted the old publisher Rowohlt, who, with his jovial beard, resembled "a monarch who has abdicated." He also wanted to meet Hitler's famous astrologer. But the "sentimental reason" was naturally a woman. "I had the good luck," he wrote me, "to have as my guide Frau Renata Gerhardt, who heads the Rowholt publishing house." After seeing her again in Reinbeck, near Hamburg, he informed me: "I'm in love with a charming German woman (who, fortunately, speaks English and French). We'll go to Berlin together for a week after Christmas. And there I'm going to see the actress Hildegard Knef. I have everything I could wish for in the way of work, visits, and—love!" (letter to Brassaï, from Reinbeck, December 19, 1960).

Now Henry is plunged back into his origins. Before going to school, he spoke only German and grew up in the atmosphere of a Germanic colony. His yearning for the forgotten language sometimes came out in his letters. One day, I quoted the saying of Goethe's inscribed on my oriflamme: "Objects have gradually lifted me to their height," and he replied: "What you quote from Goethe is *wunderbar.* I would like to have it in German. When I want to, I can understand that damn language! Just finished reading Herman Hesse's *Siddhartha in German,* a language I have not read for thirty years or more. I recommend this book to you, a masterpiece!" (letter to Brassaï, April 4, 1948). In Reinbeck, he is even trying to write a text in German: "Ungebummelte Fuchselbiss," for the review *Rhinozeros.* "I wrote it in a German no one can understand," he writes me.

The doors of the house where Renata lives in Reinbeck open directly onto the beautiful countryside of Schleswig-Holstein. Miller has the impression he is "contemplating the *Vaterland.*" "I never get tired of looking at the landscape, which is truly beautiful," he writes, "a region rich in farms and dense forests. It's a different sort of beauty from the French landscape. It looks more like the beauty of parks with rich soil and a verdant lawn, a little like England." And he exclaims: "I don't understand how my ancestors could have abandoned that landscape for horrible New York City and Brooklyn!"

He also visits Dortmund, the native city of his maternal grandfather,

Valentin Nieting, born around 1850, whose name Henry has sometimes borrowed, and other cities where a great artist or loved one was born, lived, or died: Heidelberg; Lüneburg; Tübingen, where Hölderlin died; Maulbron in Baden, where Herman Hesse studied; Ulm, the native city of Hildegard Knef.

After spending the whole month of December with Renata in Reinbeck and Berlin, Henry sent his chauffeur Birke back to Paris. He wanted to join him on January 15. On February 3, he was still in Reinbeck and wrote me: "I will be in Paris in three weeks, I believe." But he stayed with Renata for three months, until March 5. Still in the old Fiat, eight years old and constantly breaking down, he headed for Italy. After passing through Switzerland, which he does not like very much, Ticino, and the St. Gotthard tunnel, they arrive in Milan, where Marino Marini is making a bust of him. Feltrinelli invites him to his property. In Verona, the Italian city he prefers above all others, he visits Juliet's tomb; in Ravenna, Dante's tomb; in Forte dei Marmi, the sophisticated house of d'Annunzio and, near Milan, the native city of Eleonora Duse. After a short stay in Venice, he returns to France. A stop in Nice to consult the rich collection of Rimbeau manuscripts belonging to the autograph dealer Henri Matarasso.

"Since March 5, when I left Reinbeck," he writes me, "I've had the feeling I've been halfway across the world. But I'm a long way from finding the ideal place. Perhaps in China, in Persia, or in India. But surely not in East Germany!" (letter to Brassaï, April 2, 1961). In late April, he writes me from Montpellier, in Languedoc: "A little depressed or discouraged at present. It seems to me I haven't managed to find the place that can make me happy. I'm beginning to think about Switzerland again (Lake Geneva or thereabouts), or of Austria, a charming little village on the *Donau* (Danube). Are there any left? Next week we're going to see Roussillon—the last prospect around here. I gave up on the Côte d'Azur and even on the region beyond the coast. I'm left with only Gascony now, someplace like Pau. Are you familiar with it? If you have suggestions to make, write me immediately!—because my children are flying to Paris from Los Angeles (polar route) on June 10. I really must hurry. I need a (furnished) house with five rooms and two baths, with toilets if possible. Near a river or the sea—and healthy!—no mosquitoes! But if I find a place for the summer only, I can look for a permanent one with all the comforts later on" (letter to Brassaï, from Montpellier, April 22, 1961). Since, in the meantime, he has gotten a fifty-thousand-dollar advance from Grove Press for *Tropic of Cancer*, which will finally be published in the United States in June—a significant event—Miller can allow himself a few comforts, if not luxury. But he is more indecisive than ever. Should he settle definitively in

Montpellier near the Delteils and the Durrells or continue his infernal rounds searching for an impossible-to-find place? How men and situations change! Is this the same Miller who wrote in 1937, and with considerable irony: "I see my friend Fraenkel trotting his legs off searching for the right place and never finding it. Loewensfels too, always seeking, seeking. They make me laugh. I feel sorry for them. I went through all that years ago. I went through everything—that's how I feel" (letter to Durrell, April 5, 1937).[1] It was also a long time ago that Henry approvingly quoted Emerson, who said: "Travel is a fool's paradise. Stay put and watch the world go round."

It was no doubt the breakup with Eve, then the passion for Renata, that had thrust him back into that state of depression, discouragement, and incessant flight. Then there was the obsession with his age: that year he was to celebrate his seventieth birthday! Was he thinking of marrying Frau Gerhardt? The idea probably preoccupied him. It was an unrealizable plan, however. His own life was now centered in California and Renata's was in Berlin, where she was launching her own publishing house. And she too had children. Henry, flanked by his factotum, heads toward the Basque region. "I don't like the Basque region, not Ainhoa and especially not Biarritz, Hendaye, etc.," he writes me from Banyuls in Roussillon. "I dislike the entire Basque region. And the Basques don't interest me at all! They're just like the Swiss, even in architecture. I'm staying here for two or three days. Afterward, I don't know. The children won't be coming. I canceled their visit. I am in a very poor state (morally)" (letter to Brassaï, from Banyuls, June 9, 1961). Henry, indecisive, returns to Montpellier and leaves immediately for Portugal, because, according to F.-J. Temple, "his German fortune teller had given him notice to go to that country."

In early July, he is again with Renata: "My dear Brassaï," he writes me, "do you have the address of that Japanese woman who returned to her home in Japan? If you do, give it to me. It's possible I'll go to Japan—not yet certain. But I found nothing in Europe that pleases me and can't stay here any longer—it's too sad! I'm always ill at ease—out of sorts. Nothing pleases me. The success I have at home—in America—leaves me cold. Even money doesn't interest me. I could do anything I please now, but I have no desire. *I'm fed up!* I even believe I'm a failure. A good-for-nothing. A zero ('for conduct')" (letter to Brassaï, from Reinbeck, July 9, 1961).[2]

In late July, Henry again leaves Renata to go to his publisher's in Copenhagen. He also goes to Amager Island to meet Antonio Bibalo, the composer of his opera, which is going to be performed at the Hamburg Opera. In London, he looks up Fred Perlès and they go to Ireland together. In Dublin he visits the house Oscar Wilde lived in and is sorry to miss George Bernard Shaw's. He returns home to Big Sur, then leaves it definitively in September for Los Angeles, where he writes me: "I'm still in love with that woman in Germany. Hence *capable of anything!* In two months I'll be in Paris—en route to Berlin. Have you seen Renata in Paris recently?" (letters to Brassaï, November 23 and December 11, 1961). Depressed, Henry falls sick and stays in bed for a few weeks. He is asked to be a member of the jury for the Formentera Prize. He agrees and asks Frau Gerhardt to accompany him to Majorca in April. And the idyll continues. After Formentera, where Henry is again ill—he "goes home" with Renata to Berlin. "The 'Beauty of Hamburg,' as you have nicknamed her, is doing well here, now on her way as a *Verlagerin.*" And Miller asks me to send manuscripts to the young "Gerhardt Publishing House." Nevertheless, the idea of traveling still obsesses him. "Japan! Do you really intend to go there? It's very possible I'll join you. Everything depends now on the advice of my doctor. . . . To see Japan through your eyes—What a treat that would be!" (letter to Brassaï, from Berlin, May 27, 1962).

On May 31, he returns to the United States and learns that the Kings County Court of Brooklyn has convicted him for publishing *Tropic* and that he can be arrested and thrown in prison. In Los Angeles, he again returns to the trip to Japan: "Are you thinking of going to Tokyo? If everything goes well, it's very possible I'll go with you. I am beginning my medical visits" (letter to Brassaï, June 17, 1962.). But all his letters are still full of Renata: "She's going to publish books on the 'fringe,' first a Max Ernst, then a Jarry, an Artaud, etc. She could also publish something of yours. She knows your photographic work, but not your writings. Think about it!" (letter to Brassaï, July 5, 1962). In August, Henry is with Lawrence Durrell at the Edinburgh festival. Then, via Copenhagen and Berlin, he goes to visit Hildegard Knef, near Mühlberg, in Perscha on Lake of Starnberg in Bavaria. He spends the whole month of September there. And while the actress is making *The Great Catherine* in Yugoslavia, he visits the country, especially all the baroque castles, gaining new strength from his Germanic atavism. "I find myself in my grandmother's country," he writes me. "I went to the 'Schloss Nymphenburg,' where a few scenes of *Last Year in Marienbad* were filmed—in the park. *Es war wunderbar!* And especially the 'Amalienburg' pavilion in white lead and lemon yellow. *Wie ein Traum . . . Nicht war?* Or like 'a mild winter,' I think" (letter to Brassaï, September 2, 1962). Four weeks later, he writes me: "I took a little trip to Austria in the Salzkammergut. More lakes and castles. Unforgettable! With the three *Schloss* I saw, I better understand the film *Marienbad*, which I am crazy about. But that madman Ludwig II is way out!!! With his ideas of grandeur and madness, he's a little like Gilles de Rais (except he had only Wagner in his life—and not a Joan of Arc!)" (letter to Brassaï, September 28, 1962.) He also visits Salzburg and, naturally, Mozart's house: "An enchanted, verdant, cheery country, clean as a whistle." And, a few days later: "Yes, I'm enjoying myself here in Bavaria, and especially in Salzkammergut. *It's my country!* . . . I like the book on Ludwig II and am going to devour it. Tomorrow another *Schloss*. Yesterday I visited Schleissheim. *Scheisslich!* (Shitty!)." But Bavaria does not make him forget Renata: "After Perscha," he writes me on September 8, "I will go to Berlin to see my Renata. She is in Frankfurt *jetzt beim Book Fair. Verstehen Sie?*" To his great joy, Frau Gerhardt joins him in Bavaria. "I'm here with Renata and Sunday we go to Berlin, I think." And since I mentioned the two years I had spent in Berlin, between December 1920 and April 1922, he replies: "I too saw Wegener, the plays of Reinhardt, Georg Kaiser, Ernst Toller, and others of the same period—but in New York!" And he adds: "Ever since I saw the big Georg Gross exhibition at the Academy of Arts, I see nothing but 'Gross' types in the street here" (letter to Brassaï, October 14, 1962). These are also the last days Miller spends with Renata.

When he has returned to California, in November 1962, Henry writes me: "No news from the 'German Joan of Arc.' Very moved by the fact that you and Gilberte found her so beautiful, so charming."[3] In the same letter, he writes that he is buying a house in Pacific Palisades "to live there with the children, as a family. Oof!" (letter to Brassaï, January 1, 1963). And by March, his letter is coming from 444 Ocampo Drive. It is the end of his great love affair and also of probably the most agitated time in his life.

CHAPTER 17   *Wednesday, August 15, 1962*

"We're in Paris! And guess who we ran into on boulevard Raspail! Larry! Yes, Larry! Before he leaves for Edinburgh, he's spending two days in Paris. I'm looking forward to spending the evening with two old friends. Come to the Hôtel Royal. We're going to have dinner with Durrell."

I was expecting this telephone call from Alfred Perlès, who was coming from London. Six months ago, we agreed to have dinner together on August 15. Age has embalmed rather than wrinkled Fred's face, mockingly adding a touch of purple rouge to his nose, his cheeks. But the "angel of the comical," as Henry nicknamed him according to Cocteau, is not by himself. He is with his new wife, a Scotswoman dressed in black with a rather martial appearance. She teaches in an English high school.

Lawrence Durrell arrives with Pebita, his girlfriend from Argentina. What a curious face: long, calm, sculpted, yet not at all hard.

DURRELL   The only country where I was truly unhappy in my life—so unhappy I wanted to die—was Argentina. And it had nothing to do with the climate—which isn't bad in Buenos Aires—but with the ambience of the country. Fortunately, I met Pebita there. Without her I might have wasted away.

Pebita, as Larry told me, belongs to a rich Argentine family, but rather than choosing a life of idleness, she preferred to make herself useful, joining Dr. Schweitzer in Africa or taking care of patients in a leper hospital.

I ask Durrell why, again this year, he will go to the Edinburgh festival.

DURRELL   To make it more interesting, its organizers had the idea of inviting about forty writers every year from now on. Not to give lectures, but so the public can meet them, ask them questions about their lives and their work.

BRASSAÏ   And which French writers are invited?

DURRELL   Jean-Paul Sartre and Nathalie Sarraute, I think. It's a shame Fred and you aren't free, we would have had a good time together.

BRASSAÏ   I was at the Edinburgh festival twice, and I always had the impression I was being followed, watched. One evening, I attended the lord mayor's reception at city hall, in honor of the big orchestra conductors, Bruno Walter, Sir Beecham, etc. After I took a few photos, I went to find Gilberte, who had remained back in a room at the end of the other wing of the building. I went from room to room. A man accosted me: "Are you looking for your wife? She's sitting in the reading room, reading a newspaper." I was disconcerted, and asked him: "How do you know?" There were more than a thousand people at city hall. "Are you Sherlock Holmes?"

"A little bit, a little bit," he answered in French, with an enigmatic smile that made me shiver. "Last year, they presented your *Sappho* in Edinburgh."

DURRELL   In an official performance. But those matter less than what goes on on the side, at the "Fringe Festival." About forty troupes of amateur actors and students, from Cambridge, Oxford, and London, making do with what they have in improvised places: churches, courtyards, caves, or ruins, converted into theaters. It's all often chaotic, confused, but full of life and originality: poetry is mixed with jazz, the stage invades the room. A unique and very agreeable phenomenon.

Fred has decided to leave England and settle in Greece. He questions Larry on life in that country.

DURRELL   For fifteen years, alas! I haven't seen Greece. But nothing has changed there, I suppose. In any case, I advise against going to live in a little village. There you'll be dependent on four or five people: the mayor, the grocer, the baker, the butcher. If you don't know how to manage, your life becomes hell. It takes a great deal of tact and diplomacy to remain on good terms with them, and I'm afraid your wife is not so flexible. Otherwise, in three days, you'll have everyone against you.

I am astonished at Durrell's progress in French, which he now speaks without searching too much for words. And I remark: "Soon you'll be able to speak French with the accent of the Midi."

DURRELL   And what about you! You also manage in English! Do you know, Fred, that Brassaï signed a book *in English* for an American reporter who was at my place in Nîmes? I still laugh when I think about it: "I love you because you love me."

BRASSAÏ   I even earned a hundred guineas with my English at the BBC. I went back and forth between Hildegard Knef and the king of Nigeria. And I must have made English ears suffer enormously.

Dinner at an inn. We are on our third bottle of Sancerre. I ask Larry if he enjoyed collaborating on the film *Cleopatra*, for which he wrote the screenplay.

DURRELL It meant earning a fair amount of money. But, as I learned, I wasn't the first to be involved with that film, or the last. Do you want to know the number of writers on that film? *Seventeen!* With none of them knowing any of the others. After me, there was surely an eighteenth and many others, to further turn what we had done upside down. Did I write dialogue? Oh yes! I'm visually oriented. That wasn't a major problem for me. As for my novels, I got many offers. But almost all asked me to collapse *Justine, Balthazar, Mountolive,* and *Clea* into a single screenplay. An impossible task, just nonsense! If it had been rewritten that way, not much would have been left of my *Quartet.*

On our way to Montparnasse, we pass the Odeon Theater, one of the darkest buildings in Paris, which is immaculately white since its repointing. It's a beautiful night. We walk alongside the Luxembourg Gardens and find ourselves on the terrace of the Dôme café, as in the old days. We speak of Henry, of his new German girlfriend, his astounding and quixotic ride through Europe, flanked by Vincent, his Sancho Panza. Ten thousand kilometers on the road, from the North Sea to the Atlantic, from Hamburg to Saint-Jean-de-Luz, through Switzerland, Austria, Germany, Italy, France, Portugal. And always in quest of the "dream" spot, filled with all the beauties of nature and all the virtues of comfort and hygiene, neither too hot nor too cold, on the water, but without mosquitoes, civilized, but without noise, wild, but with two toilets and two bathrooms. All his letters revealed his distress.

Fred says he often writes Henry solely to lift his spirits. "They're not letters, they're shots of tranquilizer." But Larry wonders: "Can his 'distress' always be taken seriously? In the space of a second, it can turn into *euphoria*, can't it? I got two of his letters dated *the same day,* one announcing his imminent suicide, the other overflowing with energy, joie de vivre, with a thousand plans for the future." In fact, total frankness reigned among the three musketeers. Everyone had his home truths to express to the others. Fred criticized Durrell's *Quartet* for lacking warmth, the human touch. Larry criticized Perlès's sentimental outbursts. And the admiration these two friends had for Henry did not diminish their critical faculties.

DURRELL *Journey Paris–New York* is not his most felicitous text. He must have written it in a single night and published it without rereading it. That happens to him sometimes. In fact, Henry has changed his style in the United States. He's gained in power, but he's a little lacking in self-discipline. For example: the portrait of Reichel, written in Europe, is compact and dense. The one of Rattner, done in America, is much looser.

Fred maintains that Henry is becoming too personal and mentions his book on Rimbaud. Isn't it unwarranted, he says, for him to compare himself to that dazzling star, that nova, who shone with all his brilliance at seventeen, when it wasn't until Miller was forty that he found his voice?

Durrell is a little jealous of our "prehistory," the six-year period we spent with Henry before he came to France. He would like to know more and mentions with deep yearning the six months spent at the Villa Seurat. Eight years later, he wrote from Rhodes: "Oh, the heat and fury of the days at the Villa Seurat! The good glasses of wine and the pleasant muffled madness of the typewriters!" And even ten years later: "I must walk along the Seine in Paris, on rue Saint-Jacques, I must see the Villa Seurat again."

DURRELL It was a time of camaraderie, solid friendship, a rich, perfect, un-forgettable era. Every moment of my stay in Paris is still engraved in my memory. I can recall each one as if it were today. I've traveled a great deal, lived a great deal since, but nothing could take the place of those memories, much less erase them.

And Larry mentions the airy figure of Betty Ryan cooking, Hans Reichel's big drinking bouts, Conrad Moricand's prophecies, the good bottles of *volney* and *chateauneuf-du-pape,* the gatherings at the Brasserie Zeyer, the Closerie des Lilas, the long walks in the fog and cold among the ghostly scaffolding of the 1937 Exposition, and naturally, Miller the "giant" in the middle of his studio, a cigarette butt between his lips, furiously typing on his typewriter. Larry finds even the trash cans of the Villa Seurat touching. He remembers them with tears in his eyes. But, curiously, at the time, after the first en-chantment with Paris, Durrell felt rather ill at ease living that "dissolute and putrid" bohemian life. He even thought of running away and returning to the bewitching atmosphere of Greece. I have rarely felt so strongly the embel-lishing power of my memory.

With the help of the little glasses of white wine, and with the saucers be-ginning to pile up on the marble table, we plunge, drunk, back twenty-five years. At two o'clock in the morning, we are kicked out of the Dôme. We drink more glasses at other counters. Our wives are away: Claude in Nîmes, Gilberte on Lake Leman, Anne, tired, already in bed. We have become three bachelors, suddenly mixing with the human dregs the late hour was catching in its net, at the counter of the last open bistro in Montparnasse. Oddly, this world that once excited me hardly moves me anymore. And I have long since lost the habit of sleepless nights. Nevertheless, one has only to open one's eyes and ears to see and hear strange things. We were almost the victims of a settling of accounts. After a bitter discussion with the owner, I saw Colts gleaming in the hands of two "customers." A racket? A pimp in a cap and two whores, their elbows on the counter, are chatting. "One of these nights," exclaims the blonde, "I'm going to turn on the gas." I prick up my ears. Marilyn Monroe's recent suicide had left an impression on the minds of thousands of prostitutes. She was their idol. Her universal appeal and fame fascinated them. And many were tempted to follow her in death. "What's the point of living?" continued the same raucous voice. "I'm not joking. One of these nights I'll turn on the gas." Her friends admonish her. She replies, imperturbable. "I know what I'm saying. I know what I'll do. It's my life. Can you imagine me old, disgusting, dragging myself to the cafés or through the streets? You can't, can you? That's not the stuff I'm made of. So? I know what I'm saying. I know what I'll do."

Dawn is already breaking when we part ways, after drinking a cup of coffee with warm croissants in a bistro that has just opened near the Gare Montparnasse. And, as in the old days, when I went to sleep at sunrise, fleeing this Paris that is waking up only to rush down into the hole of the metro, I am going to put myself to bed with the fresh morning paper and the good smell of its printer's ink.

CHAPTER 18

Tuesday, April 6, 1965

Left Paris yesterday afternoon. Descending into the Rhone Valley, we came up with the idea of taking a detour to the Durrells in Nîmes, via Pont-Saint-Esprit. Beginning in Uzès, the road follows a deep riverbed and wends through the garrigue as far as you can see. In Engance, on the outskirts of Nîmes, a stony road forks to the right and leads to the "house of the Angliche,'" the Mazet Michel. The garage is empty and no one answers our calls. The large sign to scare people off, leaning against the house with white lettering on a black ground, is still there: "If UNINVITED and UNEXPECTED: UNWELCOME—This is a WORKSHOP—Please write." The only sign of life: a shirt of Larry's, still wet, swaying on a line. Suddenly, the noise of an engine on the bumpy road. There they are! Claude, thin, blonde, with delicate features; Larry, stocky, sturdy in his lumber jacket. His blue eyes sparkle on his tanned face. A sign of prosperity: the old jalopy—a gray Simca purchased from the baker—has been replaced by a comfortable Opel.

GILBERTE Last summer when we came by, you were at Saintes-Maries-de-la-Mer.

DURRELL When the kids arrive from London, we go all over. We swim in Camargue, camp two or three days on the beach, or we go to Avignon to the Pont du Gard. There are plenty of pretty spots in Languedoc. We have forests, lakes, mountains. The Mediterranean is my kingdom! I've always dreamed of living in France. In the end, it's the Midi that's the most propitious place for work. Without France, I'd never have been able to write my *Quartet.* This ambience is found in no other country. A few English and American writers owe more than they can repay to France, especially Joyce, D. H. Lawrence, Katherine Mansfield, Samuel Beckett. They could work and get themselves published here. Miller, Faulkner, and myself were discovered and respected in France well before we were in the English-speaking countries.

GILBERTE How long have you lived here?

DURRELL Seven or eight years. If it hadn't been for the riots on Cyprus, I might still be in Greece. Misfortune is good for something! In my little house on the side of the hill in Bellapaix, I had just finished *Justine* when the revolution chased us out. Claude and I decided to settle in France at that time. It was Homeric! Loaded down with bundles, luggage, packages tied with string, and our typewriters, since Claude also writes, we arrived one night in Nîmes, then, on the bus, in Sommières. I'll never forget the first night spent in the cottage we rented. A terrible night! The first visit of the mistral. The icy February mistral, gusting through doors and windows! Fortunately, a short time later, we were able to move into the Villa Louis, which was more livable.

GILBERTE Your property is very "Irish." It's only on the Aran Islands that you see so many stones.

DURRELL I'm not acquainted with Ireland. This wild garrigue and this soil burned by the sun remind me instead of Greece, Attica. In fact, the people of the Midi came partly from the ancient Greek colonies. I like them! They're cheerful, they like laughter, good food, good talk. They're all straight out of Rabelais.

GILBERTE Your walls are similar to the stone walls we saw in Inishmore on the Aran Islands.

CLAUDE Larry's the one who put up all these walls. Also built these rooms for the children, whitewashed the bedrooms, built new cisterns. Since water is rare and precious here, he's very stingy with it: he watches every drop. We need it for our vegetable garden.

GILBERTE Are you of Irish origin?

DURRELL Yes, ninety percent! I have only ten percent English blood. I probably inherited Irish laziness and also an overdeveloped sense of humor. But I don't know Ireland very well. It's Greece that counted the most in my life as a writer. I was twenty-three, I didn't know anyone on my island. I was on the brink of despair. It was then that, by chance, in Corfu, I bought *Tropic of Cancer*. I was bowled over by it. I immediately wrote to Miller and our correspondence was under way.

GILBERTE Miller was also stimulated by your letters.

DURRELL Stimulated, yes, I think so. But as far as I'm concerned, he *saved* me. His letters were so warm, so encouraging. Of course, I was already writing poems, but as a "man of letters" I was stammering. It was owing to Henry that I wrote *The Black Book*, under the influence of *Tropic of Cancer*, naturally. It was my "season in hell." I sent him the only copy of my manuscript, and can you imagine, that man, at the expense of his own work, retyped three copies of it himself, and offered it to his own publisher, Obelisk Press, which in fact published it, sending one copy to T. S. Eliot, another to Cyrille Connoly. A magnificent, generous gesture, don't you think?

GILBERTE Brassaï said so as well. Henry always encouraged him too, in his photography and in his writings. But explain this to me—you were comfortable in Sommières: why did you move here? All the military firing ranges must bother you.

CLAUDE It wasn't by choice. We loved that delicious little medieval city, its Roman walls, its cobblestone streets, its beautiful freestone houses, its calm river, its vineyards. We also liked the Villa Louis, up on a peak. But then all of a sudden the owner wanted his house back. Where to go? What to do? We explained our situation to a real estate agent in Arles. And especially, the state of our finances! When he learned that Claude's father had lost his fortune in the Suez affair and had been expelled from Egypt, he immediately sympathized and took our fate to heart. He was a Frenchman born in Algeria, and had himself lost all his worldly goods over there. "I have something that might suit you. Get in my car, I'll take you there." The owner of the Mazet Michel had just died. His family didn't want to leave his wife alone in that wild garrigue. And luckily—for us!—during the extraordinarily cold winter of 1956, all the olive trees—eleven thousand!—had frozen, the only thing of value in this sterile region. But there was yet another reason we were offered this little country place for a song: next to us there's a shooting range for infantrymen with automatic rifles. Every Tuesday, to the delight of our children, there's a big show: shooting exercises on ground targets, firing of antiaircraft guns, assaults by tanks, airborne infantry, supersonic booms, the whole kit and caboodle.

BRASSAÏ But your olive trees have grown back!

DURRELL Those trees can't be stopped, their root stock is tough. So I bought a power saw and cut all the dead trunks to the ground. And these bushes, now nine years old, already produce as many olives as the trees used to do. We cook in our own oil. Oh, you're looking at my telephone line. It's one-way. We can call anybody, but no one can call us, no one knows our number. An arrangement with the phone company. Otherwise the Mazet Michel would be hell.

CLAUDE In the beginning, it was very, very hard. Now we love this spot. And especially before the hot season. Spring is delicious here. If only the mistral didn't exist! In autumn, and especially in winter, it's dreadful! Sometimes, even in January, you have beautiful, very hot, sunny days. You can have lunch outdoors. Then, abruptly, the temperature falls thirty degrees and you're withered, frozen. The cold of the mistral chills you to your soul.

Although we are "neither invited nor expected," the Durrells have us stay for dinner. And while Claude grills the lamb chops, Larry tells us: "It's odd, isn't it? I lived in Alexandria at the same time as my wife, Claude Ford. We frequented the same circles. But we never met! It was only later, on Cyprus, that we made each other's acquaintance. I don't know how I could have managed without her. Claude's the one who gave me courage. A marvelous, inventive, cheerful, and extremely gifted woman. She writes novels."

We sit down to eat.

BRASSAÏ Do you know Henry was supposed to have surgery on his femur? It hurts when he walks. But his heart condition didn't allow it. The operation had to be postponed twice.

DURRELL That concerns me a little. After all, he's seventy-four years old. But he's built like an athlete, very tough.

BRASSAÏ And he's been forbidden to smoke. Five cigarettes a day. He complains about it, because he coughs as much as before. But I don't think he was ever a big smoker.

CLAUDE Oh, yes he was! When he was irritated, he could smoke two packs a day! We liked Eve a great deal.

DURRELL She came into his life at the most critical time.

CLAUDE And he was so happy to introduce his young wife to his friends and acquaintances! The vanity of showing off a beautiful girl is a big part of his love affairs. Now he's taken the same tour with Margery, but the beautiful doll didn't elicit as much sympathy as Eve. She couldn't stand up to the comparison.

DURRELL She's not one of those wives who takes care of her husband, relieves him of cares, of life's chores, the way Eve did. She's careless, she doesn't give a damn. That's who she is. Henry understood that all of a sudden in a taxi in Paris, when she lost not only their airline tickets but also their passports, their money, and all their papers. A disaster! Miraculously, the papers were returned. But Henry sent Margery back to her native California on the next plane.

CLAUDE Once, he brought his conquest here in the company of a young poet, who had an extraordinary beauty. I've rarely seen eyes so marvelous. And Henry, though usually so jealous, was very prepossessing toward him. The young poet undoubtedly belonged to the other camp and Henry had no fear of danger from that side. I have a nose for such things.

DURRELL Do you have any news about the film that's supposed to be made from *Tropic of Cancer?*

BRASSAÏ The filming is supposed to begin in Paris this June. Henry will be part of it. It'll bring him a fair amount of money. He asked for my collaboration as a "specialist on the brothels of Paris." I was familiar with them thirty years ago, but since then they've changed a great deal. Henry will be the "adviser" for the film; they probably won't listen to his advice. He's very skeptical, in fact.

DURRELL What will they be able to draw from that great book, which I admired and still admire? A few characters? A few episodic stories? There's really no action or plot. All the novel's interest lies elsewhere. Above all, they wanted the name "Henry Miller" and the tantalizing title of the "great scandalous novel."

BRASSAÏ Nevertheless, Henry hopes that the director, J. Strick, the one who wrote the screenplay for Joyce's *Ulysses,* will remain faithful to the spirit of the book. According to the producer, Joseph Levine, Henry was too realistic and too violent for the censor. So they sent him to a few experienced Hollywood screenwriters. [*Miller's marginal note:* "No! I never wrote that screenplay. It was done by one of my friends. H. M."]

DURRELL What do you expect, the author is always at the mercy of businessmen.

BRASSAÏ What about you, are you still working for the film industry? How's it going with *Cleopatra,* which Liz Taylor is supposed to star in? Three years ago, you were talking about the seventeenth screenwriter.

DURRELL The number has undoubtedly grown since then! I did my job as conscientiously as possible. I wrote scenes and dialogue, about sixty pages. Nothing at all was respected, or maybe even used. When I protested to the producer, since on principle I'm the *author* of the film, do you know what he replied with a cynical laugh? "Mr. Durrell, you probably don't know that, for *Spartacus,* we had sixty screenwriters working on it!" And each one thought he was unique, the only one! That's their method! They swipe an idea here, a scene there, take dialogue or a character from one person or another.

BRASSAÏ But will your name appear in the credits?

DURRELL I didn't allow them to use it. Now I understand. What do those producers want? To buy your name. You can allow yourself to be tempted by film, but you mustn't have any illusions! It'll bring in a little money, that's all.

BRASSAÏ What about the film with Sophia Loren?

DURRELL I wrote a short story for her. The story of a young German Jewish woman expelled from her country who emigrates to Palestine and joins a kibbutz. I wanted to show the transformation of that middle-class girl within a community where she'll achieve great serenity and find happiness.

BRASSAÏ Did you participate in the filming?

DURRELL Yes, and that brought in some cash, enough to pay for my children's schools. We have four, two of mine, two of Claude's. Sophia Loren is a very agreeable person, simple, intelligent. I was happy to work with her. Do you want to see our photos? But since even in that film, conceived entirely by me, there were also other screenwriters, I required them to put on the credits: "Film *based on* a short story by Durrell."

The interior of the Mazet Michel is as modest as before. Claude, who is writing her second novel, complains she doesn't have a room of her own. As for the walls of the library, they are now entirely lined with Durrell's books, published in countless languages.

Larry shows me his work table turned toward the wall, with no view, no window.

DURRELL When I'm writing, I dread the light of day. Artificial light is more favorable for creating. Henry was astounded when he saw that: "How can you work in such a dark corner?" he asked me. "Me, I need a vast landscape before my eyes, and especially light."

BRASSAÏ What's your brother Gerald up to? He was eleven when you published his article in *The Booster*.

DURRELL He became one of the best animal writers. At this moment he's in Africa to bring back new animals for his zoo. If you ever get a chance to go to Jersey Island, I strongly urge you to go see him. For six or seven years, he's been set up there with his entire menagerie. There are probably richer and vaster zoos in the world, but none where the animals are so well off. It's enchanting! They "dwell" in the stables of an old manor house. I say "dwell" because they possess real animal "apartments." We were there a few years ago. It was winter, and snowing. Sometimes, you know, we're awakened at dawn by the chirping of birds. But there, at dawn after our first night, it was a regular symphony of cries, bellows, screams, whinnies, bleats. Then the racket stopped all of a sudden. It was as if all the animals were greeting the sunrise. A sort of prayer. One morning, my brother called us: "Come quick if you want to see the most beautiful sight in the world!" We followed him and what did we see? Two young lions beside themselves with joy were playing with snowballs! We also saw two escaped chimpanzees go into the kitchen and hang onto my mother's shoulder. Here are the photos. It was priceless.

BRASSAÏ Is your mother living in England or in India?

DURRELL She died recently. She fell asleep peacefully at my brother's house on Jersey. What a beautiful death! In her sleep, without suffering. And, in fact, she wanted to go to India to see the places where we'd lived one more time.

BRASSAÏ How's Fred doing?

DURRELL Still in Greece and still writing. But his style has changed. It had a Viennese charm, a lightness, a grace all its own. And a Schnitzler-style humor. But since he's become an English citizen, he's turned terribly serious, even moralizing. I'll see him soon, since we're about to leave for Greece. In Corfu I found a little house next to the water. And we'll also have an inflatable boat, but with a motor that transforms it into a "motor boat." It doesn't reach very great speeds, but no matter!

GILBERTE Can you tell me what sign Alfred Perlès was born under?

DURRELL Cancer or Capricorn. Are you interested in astrology? [*Miller's marginal note:* "Wrong. He's a Virgo. H. M."]

GILBERTE I was once keenly interested in it. Not anymore. What the stars say often seems compelling to me as far as character is concerned. As for events, destiny, that's something else again.

DURRELL When I was in Paris, at the Villa Seurat, Henry was infatuated with occultism, excited by astrology, and he converted me. Each of us had to pay ten shillings for his horoscope, made up by Moricand. I remember the day at the Villa Seurat when we received a voluminous package: it was our horoscopes. Then Henry had an idea. Instead of giving each person his own, he proposed to read them aloud one by one so we could guess which of us it applied to. It was extraordinary! As soon as someone had read out a few lines, we could make out if it was about Fred, Henry, Fraenkel, Reichel, or myself. Moricand's portraits had a striking likeness. [*Miller's marginal note:* "Correct, yes! H. M."]

GILBERTE Do you see a few people in Languedoc? Douglas Cooper, the English critic, a great collector of Picassos, lives at the Castille château on the road to Uzès, near the Pont du Gard.

DURRELL I know him. But we don't see him regularly. Claude and I each work in our own little corner. We get up at about five thirty and go to bed very early. Going out at night and frequenting "society" would disturb the rhythm of our life. But I don't work all day long anymore. I stop at noon. In the afternoon I take walks, deal with my mail. And in the evening we listen to music.

BRASSAÏ There's also Jean Hugo at the "Fourque," near Lunel, the Godebskis in Saint-Gilles, the Colomb de Daunants in Nîmes and Cacharel, right in Camargue.

DURRELL Do you know Denys Colomb?

BRASSAÏ Yes, very well. Because he loved horses and bulls, he moved to Camargue. His greatest ambition was to fill the void left by the marquis of Baroncelli, who introduced the manners and customs of the cowboys into this country. In fact, Denys married the marquis's granddaughter.

DURRELL I'm familiar with the house belonging to the Colomb de Daunants in Nîmes. Extraordinary! An enormous greenhouse where palm trees and hundred-year-old philodendrons grow.

BRASSAÏ When you have lunch at their place, you'd think you were under the luxuriant, subtropical vegetation of a jungle. I nicknamed the four Colomb de Daunant brothers—Edmond, Denys, Gilbert, and Alain—the "brothers Kamargazov." But only Denys was really crazy about bulls and horses. I made several visits to his farmhouse, "Cacharel," and in particular, when the lovely *rejoneador* Conchita Cintrón was staying there. One winter, Denys dragged me on a horse ride through the frozen ponds, the tamarisks, the reeds loaded down with hoar frost, to the herds of bulls at the mouth of the Petit Rhône. It was magical and exhausting. Thirteen hours in the saddle! We returned in the dark, late at night, in a blizzard. It was like the retreat from Russia.

DURRELL I don't know Denys. But one day, on our way through Camargue with Henry Miller, we stopped at Cacharel. The master of the house was absent. In the oppressive afternoon heat, even the servants were dozing. They were awakened by our visit, and those somewhat worldly young women received us very kindly and offered us tea.

BRASSAÏ You wrote *Bitter Lemons* on Cyprus. Aren't you thinking about writing a book on Provence or Languedoc?

DURRELL God forbid! Several publishers have already proposed I do it. I refused. I have no desire to attract more tourists to our region. Happily for us, the mistral and the mosquitoes still protect us a little from the "invaders." I hope Henry won't write a book on Languedoc either, the way he did on Big Sur.

The next day, a radiantly sunny Sunday, we had our breakfast with the Durrells on the terrace of a café facing the Maison Carrée. I can still see Claude full of smiles, bidding us farewell as we drive off. It's the last time. Shortly thereafter, a cruel illness took away that creature full of life, that dispenser of joy, in just a few days.

CHAPTER 19

Tuesday, September 19, 1967

Returned to Paris to meet Henry. At the Gervis gallery on rue du Bac, where he will exhibit his works, the young director explains to me:

"Miller donated a great number of his gouaches to the Westwood Association, a cooperative of artists in Los Angeles that wants to build an art center. He'll arrive tomorrow with his Japanese wife and will stay across the way, at the Hôtel Montalembert. A swarm of supporters are accompanying him in a special airplane."

"Will they go to Marseilles after that for the premiere of Miller's opera, *The Smile at the Foot of the Ladder*?"

"No," replies Gervis, "it's been postponed."

"What an odd character, don't you think, that Antonio Bibalo, who wrote the music?"

"When someone told Miller about that Italian composer, who lives in the northern fjords, and mentioned his destitution, his poor health, he rallied the troops around him, even had him come to Big Sur. [*Miller's marginal note:* "I don't believe he came to Big Sur. But I may be wrong. H. M."][1] He discussed his opera with Bibalo. And Miller even paid him a monthly stipend, I think, so he could devote himself entirely to that work. When *The Smile at the Foot of the Ladder* was performed at the Hamburg Opera, he sent me the press clippings so I could translate them for him. "I thought I had forgotten the German language," he wrote me. "But no. I have not altogether forgotten it, but in these reviews many words are beyond me." It was a delicate task. Henry was expecting a triumph. He wrote me: "It would hurt me if the critics found his work without value. It's impossible!" But they were rather reserved. They criticized Bibalo for producing a hybrid work, part opera, part pantomime, part ballet. "Miller believes in the genius of his protégé," Gervis told me, "and pokes fun at the critics' judgment." In fact, after reading the translation of the clippings, he wrote me: "I believe the German critics, like the others, are assholes! I believe in Bibalo, despite his youth, despite his faults" (letter to Brassaï, May 28, 1965).

Bareheaded, with blond locks sweeping across his blue eyes, his shirt collar open, the lanky-looking "white smock" arrives at the gallery. Another of Miller's fans, he tried for a long time to get his address. In vain. Then, one day, hearing about the "Society of Friends of Henry Miller" in Minneapolis, he wrote to them. To his great surprise and even greater joy, it was the writer himself who replied. And, since then, Miller has continually showered him with advice, telling him to be fiercely intransigent: "You are not writing for the pygmies of our age, but for the giants to come," or, "Never do what the publishers ask you. Set aside the rejected manuscripts. Write another and then another. Throw them in their face when they've finally accepted you, when they say to you: 'So why didn't you show us these manuscripts?'" That had sometimes been the case for Henry. But not every young author is Henry Miller! At the idea of being able to make his acquaintance, the "white smock" couldn't stand staying in the Midi and went to Paris.

Faithful to his tradition of introducing a new wife on each of his returns to Europe, Henry, on the eve of his trip to Paris, remarried. The announcement of his "engagement" was revealed only two days before the wedding. It exploded like a firecracker in the world press: "At age seventy-eight, Henry Miller is marrying again." Hoki Tokuda, a young blues singer, actress, and pianist, was showing herself off in the nightclubs of Los Angeles. Her age varied—depending on the newspaper—between twenty-six and thirty-three years old. It was reported that Henry had met her at a party or during a Ping-Pong game. [*Miller's marginal note:* "At the home of Dr. Siegel, a physician in Beverly Hills. H. M."] The wedding took place just ten days ago, on September 10, in Beverly Hills, and at the courthouse in Santa Monica near Los Angeles, in front of Judge Elwin Brandt. [*Miller's marginal note:* "The wedding took place in Beverly Hills, at the home of Dr. Siegel and his wife. But it was registered [for the license] in Los Angeles. H. M."] One of Henry's witnesses was Jean Renoir. The author of the *Tropics* was very moved and declared, as he was getting married for the fifth time: "Marriage is a great adventure!" As for Hoki, who was wearing the emerald ring offered by her husband, when asked whether the half-century age difference didn't bother her, she replied: "Not at all! Henry is very young at heart, I see his youth in his mind and in his soul."

I was not surprised by the news of that event. For a year, Henry's letters, having become rather laconic, mentioned his love, but also his scruples, his torments, his hesitations. "I'm in love with three women, all three of them Scorpios," he wrote me a year before the wedding, "all different, but seductive. The principal one, the *Innamorata,* is a young Japanese woman from Tokyo—nicknamed the 'Shirley MacLaine of Japan'—the second, a Chinese woman, the third, a Polish woman." And he added in a postscript: "In any case, I'm in good shape, full of vitality, voracious, curious and, as Rimbaud said—'intact.'" And, in another letter: "I'm leaving now for a Japanese restaurant with a beautiful Chinese actress who wants to meet my beloved there, the Japanese woman. Soon, I hope, I'll be able to send you the clippings of a revue, where you'll be able to see us side by side. All of Japan is now advised of our love" (letter to Brassaï, November 18, 1966). And, one week later: "Don't send off a salute just yet! The story of our 'romance' is beginning to circulate throughout the country. It would be great if Henry Miller could add his name to those of Chaplin, Picasso, Pablo Casals, yes! The great love affairs of old men, right? But everything is a little premature" (letter to Brassaï, November 27, 1966). Two months later: "Still that romance, that devil-dance with the lovely Japanese woman. I have not slept well in six months. *Insomnia!* It's awful! In spite of that, I still look good, *rosy* face. I to be in love at 75, heart and soul, as they say, is no joke. But it is apparently doing us good" (letter to Brassaï, January 21, 1967).

At Orly airport, I learn that, propelled by favorable winds, Henry and his wife's airplane had landed an hour early. A dense crowd of photographers, journalists, and admirers surround gate 44. An intense discussion: "Is the little Japanese his fourth or fifth wife?" "Is Miller seventy-five or seventy-seven?"

Gradually I realize the crowd is split. Most of the people are waiting for a "showbiz" star on the same plane from California: "Mr. Dynamite," the American jazz singer James Brown. Others are there to welcome Ingrid Bergman and Lars Schmidt.

But here comes our Asian couple: the little Japanese woman, charming in a canary yellow suit, he, wearing his eternal beige houndstooth cap, tanned by the California sun. With the Chinese slit of his eyelids, his broad Oriental nostrils, his thick lower lip, he is more Tibetan, more Dalai Lama, than ever. He goes through customs leaning on a cane. In his recent letters he has complained of pain in his legs.

MILLER Oh, Brassaï! I'm still stunned. Where am I? Sixteen hours on the plane without a stop! I can't grasp it very well. Could I still be in the air? Could I really be in Paris? I can't believe it.

But already the pack of reporters closes in. Movie cameras, microphones appear from every side. Questions fly. Worried about his luggage, Miller constantly verifies it's following close behind him. Swept along by the officials of Air France, pushed by the crowd, we slip onto the escalators and go up to the large room where the popping of champagne corks and flashbulbs greet the guest who, twenty-five years earlier, had landed in Paris with ten dollars in his pocket—the poor devil in *The Gold Rush* who has become a billionaire and who, after so many tribulations, will be triumphantly received with a Havana cigar between his lips at the end of the film.

Collapsed on the sofa next to me, Henry empties a flute of champagne. Hoki, like a good American, asks for a Coca-Cola. "We'll get you to acquire a taste for French champagne," the Orly sommelier tells her, a bit offended. And the ring of microphones and movie cameras again tightens around us.

QUESTION Are you happy to be spending a few days in Paris?

MILLER I'm an old Parisian. But I haven't seen this city in five years. Yes, it gives me pleasure to see the places I knew and my old friends once more, and to show Paris to my wife.

QUESTION What is the purpose of your stay?

MILLER I'm on my honeymoon. And I'm doing an exhibition in Paris. I'm afraid. The art critics will be tempted to compare me to real painters. I hope they'll be indulgent. If they like the writer, I hope they'll forgive the painter! I am not Picasso! Maybe not even really a painter. I hope they'll find my gouaches amusing. I like to work with the colors, painting distracts me, it relaxes me. I look at the world with a child's eyes, I'm an amateur.

QUESTION The word "amateur" comes from the word "to love." Are painting and loving the same thing for you?

MILLER Perfectly so. That's the reason I called my book on painting: *To Paint Is to Love Again.* Love is more important than anything else! And not only for an artist. Without love, really, life is not worth living.

QUESTION Should we hail the painter or the writer in you? Has literature lost a writer?

MILLER I don't know about that. In any case, I'm done with literature. I've said everything in my books. Everything I had to say. So hail the painter in me now. In fact, I'm not an exception. Many other writers and poets drew and painted: William Blake, Victor Hugo, Baudelaire, Rimbaud, and closer to us, Max Jacob, Antonin Artaud, Henri Michaux. I could mention many others.

QUESTION What is the relationship between your painting and your writing?

MILLER No relationship! I do painting as a game, to sink back into my childhood. I like to wander aimlessly with a paintbrush in my hand, to imagine without preconceived ideas. For me, "painting" is a diversion, a recreation, a relaxation and nothing more. But "writing," what a responsibility! When I write, I tremble at every word. I'm divided: half of my being is the *angel*, the other half, the *devil*. It's really the devil who produces literature and the angel who paints. When I paint, I'm pacified, calmed, I become almost a saint. But in spite of my age and all my efforts at sainthood, I have not yet arrived, alas, at the state of a true saint.

QUESTION So you haven't yet closed the book on sexuality.

MILLER (*looking fondly at his young wife's face*) No, I haven't yet closed that book. Sexuality remains.

QUESTION You didn't like the United States very much, so why are you living in Los Angeles? Why haven't you come back to Europe?

MILLER Once I settled in Big Sur, I got married, I had two children and no money. I liked that wild country, but now, with age, I too have grown soft from the comfort and ease American life offers me. The dry climate of California suits me well, in fact.

QUESTION What has kept you so young?

MILLER The purity of my soul, playing Ping-Pong, and, above all, love!

QUESTION What advice would you give a young artist? And a young writer?

MILLER Not to do anything else. In a world like this one, it's difficult to devote oneself to art body and soul. To get published, to get exhibited, to get produced often requires ten or twenty years of patient, intense labor. I spent half my life at it! And how do you survive during all that time? Beg? Live off other people until you're successful? What a dog's life! I know something about that! You're always recognized too late. And today, it's no longer enough to have talent, originality, to write a good or beautiful book. One must be inspired! Not only *touch* the public but *create one's own public.* Otherwise, you're headed straight for suicide. To have passionate readers who follow you, encourage you, buy your books, is a long-term project, the work of a whole life. And so few are chosen! How many young people of promise fall by the wayside! How few break through! And what strength, what armor you need to take all the blows and scrapes you'll receive.

QUESTION You are considered the leader of the beatniks. Do you have something to say on that subject?

MILLER In this fucked-up world, everything is going by too quickly, and you're behind the times. There are no more beatniks. They're all dead. Now there are hippies. And just as there were true and false beatniks, we have true and false hippies. Those who smoke marijuana, who take LSD, and the other ones. I may have had a hand in triggering that movement, but really, I don't see them as my descendants. They haven't understood me very well.

QUESTION So you condemn the hippies?

MILLER I don't condemn them. I try to see the thing clearly. I'm sympathetic with many aspects of their movement. To violently reject this society, which thinks only of money, to reject a regular job, to prefer to beg, borrow, or steal, to look with contempt at their fathers and their "brilliant careers" in business. I have sympathy for all that! They also prove, through their way of life, that getting caught in the industrial machine is not an absolute inevitability, that one can move backward as well as forward. But I'm afraid that revolt is only a flash in the pan. It will never bring down the almighty dollar! For the moment, that movement is only a rejection, a protest. And I don't see at all what the hippies would like to put in place of the society they want to turn upside down. Yes, that's the important thing. It's easy to be a rebel at fifteen or twenty, to walk around naked, to wear flowers, to play the banjo. But when you have a family to feed, that's another matter! To be destitute with a wife and children on your back, that's the worst. We won't really be able to judge that movement until the hippies of today are themselves adults. I'm afraid they'll be reintegrated into the stupid social organization they execrate.

Miller is not entirely right to reject with contempt the idea that he is the father of the hippie movement. Of course, he never wore blue jeans or championed nudism or free love. He was eager to marry every woman he loved. He never got tattooed and never let his hair and beard grow long. And he never took drugs. Yet it was he who incited young people to "start out on a new foot," to undertake "anything at all," to "liberate themselves from any attachment." Whether he likes it or not, he was the spokesman for the *antiestablishment* at a time when neither the word nor the trend existed. For a long time before the 1968 revolts, he had predicted the "most horrifying prospect for adults: parents disconcerted by the anger and violence of protesters, governments losing face and composure."

His "antiestablishment" ideas are found in all his books. In *Hamlet* he wrote that at twenty-one he was closer to things than he had ever been since. He had chosen at the time to live "against the world," being incapable of bowing to its requirements or adhering to its norms. "Every genuine boy is a rebel and an anarch. If he were allowed to develop according to his own instincts, his own inclinations, society would undergo such a radical transformation as to make the adult revolutionary cower and cringe" (*The Books in*

My Life, p. 82). "Vengeance! Ravage, lay waste the land: make of Culture an open sewer, so that the stench of it would remain forever in the nostrils of memory" (*Nexus,* p. 248).[2] "I am not ready yet to throw my stick of dynamite. I nibble at it meditatively, ruminatively, cogently. Five more years, ten more years perhaps, and I will wipe these people out utterly" (*Tropic of Capricorn,* p. 222). "If I could throw a bomb, make the neighborhood go up in smoke, I would not hesitate. . . . I would like to annihilate the whole world. I want nothing to do with it" (*Tropic of Capricorn*).[3]

As he was being questioned, Miller twice knocked over a glass of champagne, and it spilled on his trousers and on his young wife's nylon stockings. An unexpected baptism upon their arrival in Paris!

The television cameras continue to whir, the photographers' flashes dazzle us. And it's a mess. The cart with Miller's luggage sets off again. In the airport terminal, the crowd escorting it runs into another, even larger one, from which barely emerges the big black bear cub head of James Brown, the singer inhabited by the demon of rhythm. Day after tomorrow, on the stage of the Olympia, he will enter into a trance like a disarticulated puppet, and, overcome by the shakes, will drag the entire room along with him in a collective fit of hysteria.

CHAPTER 20

Friday, September 22, 1967

Anticipating the zoo that was awaiting him in Paris, I have not tried to see Henry since his tumultuous reception at Orly. The next day, his "secretary" phoned me: "I am literally bombarded with phone calls. The Millers are still asleep. In spite of their fatigue, they did a tour of 'Paris by night.' And to complete the evening, they drank a glass of wine at the Brasserie Lipp in Saint-Germain-des-Prés. M. Pompidou, the premier, was having supper at the next table."

When, at about five o'clock in the evening, I arrive at rue du Bac for the opening, the gallery is already crowded, inaccessible. A dense crowd overflows onto the street, even blocks traffic. And what a crowd! Ecstatic hippies, bohemians and intellectuals from the Left Bank, Right Bank snobs, Parisians, Americans, Miller's friends, those who love him, those who hate him, those attracted by his bad reputation. A huge buffet has done the rest: three hundred bottles of champagne, two hundred of whiskey, a freightload of sandwiches and petits fours.

The gallery is completely blocked off: No one can get in or out. From that tumultuous mob, surrounded by a police cordon, in fact, a few familiar faces emerge and wave at me from a distance, as if marooned. Suddenly, a woman takes me by the hand. It's José Belmont: "I made a heroic exit to round up Henry's friends," she tells me in her raucous voice. "Follow me if you can. I'm going to try to get you into the gallery by the other door." And she adds: "If we get separated, come to the private dinner at the Reine Christine. Be there around ten. But don't tell anybody." And she sweeps me along, forcing her way through the crowd, jostling the police officers. Now we're in the gallery.

The little office where Henry and a few of his friends have taken refuge is now an overheated sauna. An untenable heat, unbreathable air. Perched on the wood boards around the edges of the room, about a dozen reporters point their lenses at Miller, collapsed on a chair, half asphyxiated, livid. A stocky man, with a fine beard in the style Gambetta wore while escaping the besieged Paris in a balloon, shakes my hand: "I am Temple, from Montpellier. I've been very much hoping to make your acquaintance." I hear other voices: "We have to do something, get Henry out before he faints. What if we asked for police reinforcements?" One brave soul goes out but does not come back. Two more volunteer messengers meet the same fate. But the police sergeant has been alerted, police reinforcements have arrived, the "exit" will take place in a few minutes. An epic exit. After the police have parted the crowd, like Moses the waters of the Red Sea, we reach the Hôtel Montalembert, whose door will immediately be barred. Finally, we can breathe!

Seated at the bar in the company of Prince Gikha, who has arrived from Athens, and two pretty young women, Larry Durrell begs me to join them. I have not seen him since Claude's death.

BRASSAÏ I heard the sad news from Henry. We were shocked by it. I can still see Claude on that sunny morning we left Nîmes, on the terrace of the café, so cheerful, so friendly, bidding us farewell.

DURRELL It was awful! So sudden and unexpected! She was taken in eight days. She died in Geneva on January 1.

BRASSAÏ Where's the château you bought?

DURRELL Let's not exaggerate! It's a large mansion with a lot of land around it. It belonged to a notary in Sommières. I've returned to my first loves. Take down my secret telephone number and come with Gilberte to see me.

BRASSAÏ And the Mazet Michel?

DURRELL It became almost unlivable. The shooting range was further expanded for the airplanes. If it continues, the "Vampires" will soon be choosing our house as a target. We were also beginning to feel too cramped there. But I've kept it. I'm returning from Greece. For six months I slipped back into its magic atmosphere. Yes, magic, bewitching, really. I can find no other adjectives to express what I feel there. I still yearn for my little Turkish house on Cyprus with its vaulted Venetian doors, its banana trees in the yard, a profusion of roses and almond tree blossoms in the garden.

At a nearby table, a glass of whiskey has restored Henry after the emotional experience and the horrors of that "very Parisian" opening. He is delighted with it. What a frenetic welcome Paris held out for him!

BRASSAÏ Now you're a "sacred monster."

MILLER You mean a *sacré* monster, a damn monster! What a fuss! Me, so disdained, so little used to success. I wonder if it's really for me that so many journalists, so many admirers, took the trouble. Now I'm a star, like Brigitte Bardot! After that reception, or I should say riot, I can die in peace, don't you think?

He stands up to stretch his legs, walks without his cane, hardly limping at all.

MILLER I can walk very well without a cane, but it tires me. The great rambles across Paris are over now! On the other hand—and it's surprising, don't you think?—I can ride a bicycle very well without feeling any pain or getting tired. I can also swim and take advantage of my swimming pool. And even play Ping-Pong! Does that surprise you? I often play a game with Hoki. I settle comfortably on my two legs and move only my torso and arms.

A short man wearing a mustache and goatee à la Napoleon III, Miller's "secretary," appears. He introduces himself: "I am Robitaille, Gérald Robitaille. We met at Henry's in 1959, eight years ago. Do you remember me? I have just translated *Quiet Days in Clichy*. Henry asked me to serve as his secretary during his stay in Paris. May I present Diane, my wife, a Canadian." The dark complexion and burning black eyes of that young woman betray her Indian origin.

Robitaille informs Henry: "The vicomtesse of Noailles just phoned. She would like to invite you to lunch or dinner. Whatever day suits you."

MILLER (*surprised*) The vicomtesse of Noailles? That rings a bell. Is that the person who financed Buñuel's *Golden Age*?

I remark: "Yes, she's the one, Marie-Laure, the wife of Charles de Noailles. They also financed the film by Man Ray and Jean Cocteau."

I ask Robitaille how he first met Henry.

"Like many young writers," he tells me, "I too was jolted by the *Tropics*. And, in 1950, I began to send letters to him from Montreal. Sometimes he answered. Not often. I hoped to meet him in the United States, but I missed him. It was only three years later that I met him in Paris during his first stay in France after the war, in 1953."

For several months, he and his wife had been living in Paris, as he would later recount in his book *Papa Miller*, moving from furnished room to furnished room, living by their wits. They had known only the bleakest poverty and were awaiting Henry's arrival as if he were the Messiah; Miller, however, had never seen that Canadian and owed him nothing. When Miller arrived in Paris eight years ago with Eve, Robitaille was indignant that, instead of getting in touch with him, he preferred, after fourteen years of absence, to see his old friends again. "His Eminence is in Paris and imagine! He did not rush to ring my doorbell!" he bellowed. And here is the Machiavellian stratagem he thought up: "I will get into bed and send Diane to his place, but as if I didn't know what she was up to. With a great deal of delicacy, but crying all the while, she will tell him that his thoughtlessness toward me has made me very ill." Diane played the comedy to perfection and since she is also fairly attractive, Henry fell into the trap. Frantic, he wanted to rush to the "invalid's" bedside, but the Canadian woman, following her husband's instructions, led him to understand that an invitation via express letter was all that was needed for Robitaille to get up and go at once to his place. After receiving the letter, the "invalid" revives and rushes to the Hôtel de Lutèce an hour before the time stipulated. He bursts in on Eve as she is ironing. "When she saw me, she got frightened, she stammered, she trembled." Henry comes home and the man with the black goatee bursts into sobs and falls into his arms. "I cry in his arms," Robitaille confesses, "I explode, but in a beautiful, feminine manner, that is, without ever altogether losing control of the streaming tears." "But where is Diane?" Henry asks. "Go get her! I'll take you to lunch." The Canadian then admits he is stone broke, doesn't even have enough to buy a metro ticket. Henry is frantic again. He takes a bundle of bills from his wallet. At lunch, he questions him about his plans, his future. The Canadian confesses he has no hopes in sight. "But fortunately," he says off-handedly, "I have my bicycle. I'm going to sell it." "Certainly not": Miller is roused again. "You will certainly need it." And, taking a hundred-dollar bill from the inside pocket of his jacket, he slips it discreetly into his hand. "So I'll see you later! God bless you!" But now it's Diane who bursts out sobbing, with the same "control of tears," since, her husband asserts, she more than he possesses the "talent for farewells." "Why is she crying?" asks Henry, frantic for the umpteenth time. "Diane is such a sensitive creature! The idea that you are leaving us has completely overwhelmed her." Unable to bear the sobbing, Henry tries to calm her: "Don't cry. Don't cry. We'll stay together the whole day. This evening I'll take you to the Grand Guignol and we'll have supper together. Are you happy? Dry your tears. Smile." "I made a good guess," Robitaille said to himself, proud of his Iago-style psychology, "that Henry has a talent for letting himself be snared by those tender tears." And he adds: "That is how, on the first day we met, we parted ways at two o'clock in the morning."

BRASSAÏ Are you satisfied with your "boss"?

ROBITAILLE He's extremely kind, extremely affable with us. He's at my feet. He shows me respect as if he were my secretary. His trust is boundless, without restrictions. I am profoundly touched by it. So I don't very much like the title of "secretary" or "treasurer." Am I not rather "his spiritual son," "his most faithful disciple"? I pride myself on that. And he'll be happy with my services. He wants to take us on *for life,* Diane and me, take us with him to California. His proposal enchants us. We're nomads. Whether we live in Canada, Paris, or Los Angeles is a matter of complete indifference to us. From now on I'll watch out for him. I'll be his ruthless Cerberus, chasing away the hangers-on and kicking them in the ass.

Ten o'clock, at the Reine Christine restaurant across from Picasso's old place, 7, rue des Grands-Augustins.

BRASSAÏ Did you know that Gertrude Stein lived on this street, rue Christine, after rue de Fleurus? With Alice Toklas, who recently died. This is where she had her collection. Did you know her?

MILLER Not at all, I never met her. On the other hand, one day I made the acquaintance of Leo Stein, her brother, and I chatted with him for a whole afternoon. In fact, I didn't know any of Gertrude's close friends, not Hemingway or Fitzgerald.

In a little room on the ground floor, the tables had been arranged in a square, and on the red tablecloths there are settings for about twenty people. It is not altogether an "intimate gathering" among old friends. Certain members of the Westwood Association will partake of the meal. Durrell and Ghika had been too hungry to wait. They will join us later.

MILLER (*pointing to the square of tables*) It reminds me of Leonardo's *Last Supper.* I don't like that fresco very much.

BRASSAÏ It's very theatrical. In order for the twelve apostles to be facing the "camera," Leonardo placed them all on the same side of the table. They're so cramped, piled one on top of another, that you wonder how they can manage to eat and drink. It's very Italian as well! All the apostles are gesticulating, talking with their hands.

MILLER I don't like Leonardo very much. And I have no affinity for Michelangelo. *The Last Judgment* exasperates me, *Mona Lisa* as well. I prefer her with Dali's mustache.

The room is beginning to fill, and the director of the gallery also arrives.

MILLER You're so young, you're already in charge of a gallery? Are you Parisian?

D. GERVIS I spent my childhood in Le Vésinet. We lived in a villa close to the one belonging to Utrillo and his wife, Lucie Valore. I saw him often.

MILLER I envy you. I adore Utrillo, one of my favorite painters! The only one to have grasped the poetry of the streets of Paris. And I like the person as much as the painter. In 1935, when I spent a few days in Le Vésinet, I went almost every day to the painter's home in the hope of meeting or seeing him. Alas, I never had that chance.

GERVIS If you had looked up into his studio, you might have seen his silhouette. He could sometimes be seen painting through the window glass.

MILLER I've been told that Utrillo had a prie-dieu in his house and, before painting, he got on his knees and prayed. It was not the act of a madman. He was perfectly right! Before beginning to write or paint, every artist ought to get down on his knees and pray.

Henry speaks to the writer Dominique de Roux, and, following his habit, asks him a question: "What region are you from? From Dordogne? The real France! A province I particularly like. Just before the war, I spent a few unforgettable days there. What natural, historic, prehistoric marvels. It's God's country. I could have spent the rest of my life there. In Domme, overlooking the valley from the top of the cliff, you get such an admirable glimpse of Dordogne, a mysterious river. And Sarlat! No other city like it in France! That region has been teeming with humanity for thousands of years. You can feel it. And the Perigord cuisine! The foie gras, the truffles, the goose confit, what a treat!"

Seated between Henry and Hoki, I venture to converse with my beautiful Japanese neighbor, who speaks no French. The fashion show at Dior's, which she saw the night before, did not excite her. "The dresses would be difficult to wear, not comfortable enough!" And on her artistic career: "I performed in four movie musicals, one of which was the Japanese version of *Irma la douce.* I played the role of a prostitute." In California, she was a blues singer. She has not been back to Tokyo in three years. "What is Henry's house like in Pacific Palisades?" "A beautiful white villa with black windows. Bright and spacious: a large living room with the master's gouaches on the wall, a painting studio, several bedrooms, three bathrooms. And a swimming pool Henry takes a dip in almost every day. The water has to be very hot, at least ninety degrees Fahrenheit" [*Henry's marginal note:* "Not ninety degrees, but almost. H. M."]

MILLER My plans? They change from one hour to the next. Perhaps I'll abandon my trip to Sweden and go spend a few days with the Durrells in Sommières. My filmmaker would also like to do a sequence with Jean Giono in Manosque.

BRASSAÏ Giono would be delighted with your visit. He told me so.

MILLER So you met him? I didn't have the chance!

BRASSAÏ This summer, I had an exhibit in Lacoste in the Vaucluse, the land of the marquis de Sade. And we went through the Haute-Provence. On the way through Manosque, I called Giono to say hello. He invited us to come see him. And we climbed the "Hill of True Riches," as the municipality has baptized the avenue that leads to his house. But did you know that another street in Manosque now bears the name "Jean le Bleu"?

MILLER How did he seem to you?

BRASSAÏ Very well. He's made a very good recovery from his heart attack. But since he's afraid of the sun and the wind, he lives completely shut up in his library and no longer smokes.

MILLER I have a hard time imagining Giono without his pipe.

BRASSAÏ In fact, he told me, "I could not imagine my life without tobacco. Well, since I haven't been smoking, a new world has been revealed to me, the world of *smells*. My sense of smell has become sharper, finer. I can now smell the most subtle fragrances. Ditto for the *taste* of food. It's only since I've had to eat *without salt* that I taste and really savor the flavors." Naturally, we also spoke of Henry Miller. He adores you! He was profoundly touched by everything you did in the United States to make him well known, and is very sorry that you came twice to Manosque without seeing him.

MILLER When I left France for Greece, the last person I ran into in Paris was Blaise Cendrars. And the last Frenchman I tried to see before embarking in Marseilles, in July 1939, was Jean Giono. It was his childhood friend Henry Fluchère who took me to his home. He's also one of my translators. And he's the one who wrote the introduction to the French edition of *Tropic of Cancer*. But Giono was out. He'd gone to take one of his walks in the country that have so marvelously enriched his novels. I at least had the privilege of wandering through his house, of meeting his blind mother and his mother-in-law, who were living with him. Then we walked around Manosque. It was the worthy conclusion to my ten years spent in France.

BRASSAÏ Well, Giono asked me to tell you he is counting on your *third* visit, which will undoubtedly be the charm.

MILLER I like Giono, a kindred soul! And if D. H. Lawrence had known him, he would have liked him. He too had the religion of life. I admire his courageous book against the war, against the draft—*Refusal to Obey*—and in Greece I was stupefied to learn that the government had thrown that great Frenchman in prison. Fortunately, he didn't stay very long.

BRASSAÏ But what movie is your filmmaker working on?

MILLER He's been working on it in California for several months already. A film about my life, the places I've lived, the friends I've known. It will be called *Henry Miller and His Friends*. We'll complete it now with the scenes shot here, in France. Naturally, you'll appear in it. In Los Angeles, the filmmaker shot a magnificent scene with Jean Renoir. We had as much fun as a couple of clowns.

BRASSAÏ Renoir was one of the witnesses at your wedding. Do you see him often in Los Angeles?

MILLER Not very often, alas! An admirable man! Intelligent, warm, and so humane. So humane. You absolutely must read his novel: *The Notebooks of Captain Georges.*

BRASSAÏ When my book *Conversations with Picasso* was published in the United States, I was surprised to see that the very warm article discussing it, three pages in the *New York Times Book Review,* was signed by Jean Renoir. You had a hand in that, I believe.

MILLER I spoke to him a great deal about you and I also praised your book on Picasso. It's quite natural, I like it. I reread it several times and underlined many passages. Everything Picasso says about the necessity of success and the flip side of success touches me personally. Words of gold I can cite almost verbatim. Apropos Picasso, have you seen him recently? Is it true he's gone deaf?

BRASSAÏ I saw him two weeks ago. No, he's not deaf, just a little hard of hearing, like all of us when we age.

MILLER I'm getting that way a little myself. But is he painting right now?

BRASSAÏ He doesn't paint. Since his serious operation, he hasn't picked up his brush again. But he's working on a series of etchings. Guess for what book. Fernand Crommelynck's *Magnificent Cuckold.*

MILLER My favorite play!

BRASSAÏ An idea of Picasso's. But he's also doing it to please Crommelynck's two sons. They're set up in a bakery in Mougins and are printing his plates on their press.

MILLER Is Picasso stingy? That's what they say.

BRASSAÏ I could cite many of his acts of generosity. A whole population has sponged or is still sponging off him. But he prefers that people take him for an old miser rather than a "benefactor."

Someone asks Miller if he has met Picasso. I reply in his place: "Alas, no! I could have introduced him when he was a member of the jury at the Cannes Film Festival. It was a unique opportunity, I knew it. Chateaubriand was always sorry he missed Goethe twice: in 1872, near Koblenz, then in 1821 in Weimar. To make the acquaintance of such men is worth a trip to Tibet or even the moon."

MILLER I too regret it now. But it was, believe me, more a result of my own timidity. Deep down, I'm shy. At the last minute, I was apprehensive about facing Picasso.

BRASSAÏ I took the "white smock" with me. How did you imagine him, based on your correspondence?

MILLER As he is. Bareheaded, no tie, irresponsible, rebellious, a little mad. With all the virtues and errors of youth. [Turning to him:] Tell me, was your novel a success?

THE "WHITE SMOCK" I had a few good reviews and I also took a pounding sometimes.

JOSÉ BELMONT That novel would be good if one didn't sense the influence of Miller so much.

MILLER That's not a flaw! Originality doesn't manifest itself spontaneously. When one is young, one imitates, one *must* even imitate someone. To identify with me is entirely natural at his age. To deliver ourselves from the confusion in which we necessarily flounder, we all must choose idols. Even *Tropic of Cancer* was under the influence of Céline. It took me a week to read his *Journey to the End of the Night,* with the help of a dictionary. And do you know where? In a hotel, next to the Folies-Bergère, where a charitable friend put me up. [*Miller's marginal note:* "A hotel whose name I don't remember. H. M."] And sometimes as well in a bistro next to the "artists' entrance" of the music hall, Au Rendez-vous des Machinistes, I think it was. Obviously, *Journey* is not the source of *Tropic.* But for certain passages, Céline certainly influenced me. Above all, I was inspired by the use he made of spoken language.

A dish of ice cream completes the meal. It is respectable. But Henry, having become increasingly demanding in the matter of housing, hygiene, food, and wine, tells me: "This ice cream, it's not rich enough, not creamy enough. It's more like a sorbet." [*Miller's marginal note:* "I've always noticed that the French don't know how to make good ice cream because they don't use enough cream. H. M."]

CHAPTER 21

Tuesday, October 3, 1967

The other day at the gallery, I glanced at the newspaper clippings. What press! "Miller, one of the masters of our age!" "Miller, one of the greatest writers in the world!" And no one criticizes him anymore for being "the biggest pornographer of the century"! The critics are rather disappointed. To be sure, they praise these "dreamscapes, more than real landscapes," and their "charming poetry," but they are sorry not to find in his multicolored gouaches any trace of the erotic delirium that Miller championed. "Where's the scandal?" they wonder nostalgically. "Where are the *Tropics* of yester-year?" They were expecting Miller's pictorial talent to be an illustration of his sulfurous books. They were hoping to find their own eroticism in it. But, they observe, "there is nothing more 'naively romantic' in painting than these 'good-natured' watercolors. Lovers of Japanese prints will think again."

An American professor enters the gallery. He looks disapprovingly at "all that publicity around Miller's name" and is surprised that Paris is making such a fuss about a writer whose name rarely appears on the list of the twenty best contemporary American writers.

"It's true," I tell him. "Lawrence Durrell also noted that one can scan a five-thousand-word study of American literature without finding Miller's name. But the situation is already evolving. Nietzsche said: 'The true author is the one who is ashamed to be a man of letters.' That saying fully applies to Miller. For him, the man comes before 'eloquence.' It was under life's pressures that he was led to write. He cannot be judged solely from the perspective of literature. Young people's infatuation with him is not directed so much at the writer as at the man liberated from his shackles who teaches the sacred value, a passionate love for life. But his exclusion from American literature is also explained by his aggressiveness toward American life. It profoundly shocked and wounded his compatriots! Even if one doesn't share the opinion of Durrell, who sees him as 'the greatest American genius since Whitman,' it is indisputable that he is a force of nature, one of the representative figures of the age."

The "white smock" in the gallery comes to my rescue: "Yes, that's right. For many young people, propelled into the universe of adults, Miller is the one who put in concrete form everything we bear within us secretly, confusedly, a world of purity, spontaneity, in total contradiction with the one that surrounds us, and which makes us abnormal, pariahs from the start. In demonstrating to each of us that we were not alone in feeling and reacting that way, Miller drew us out of our isolation."

One must emphasize the salutary uneasiness, the liberating effect that *Tropic of Cancer* exerted on young people. "Reading it," confessed the young Durrell, aged twenty-three, "liberated me in a single blow. I had the magnificent feeling of absolution, of liberation from my guilt!" Another disciple of Henry's, the young Dutch writer Henk Van Gelre, confessed: "Miller, a warm, liberating, and wise human heart. His books had a fundamental effect of deliverance on me, not at all limited to the sphere of sex. My life became happier, more colorful, and in many respects more profound." For a legion of young people, oppressed especially by sexuality, prey to the feeling of sin, Miller stood as a redeemer and his book was like a catharsis. One could cite a thousand witnesses to "miracle cures" thanks to the liberating, therapeutic effect of his work, like the confession of a young "prisoner set free," Philippe Derieux: "If my religious formation gave me a feeling of guilt, Miller exonerated me. I will be a free man, as free as Miller, who represents the maximum freedom a man can achieve. Miller, your work and your life avenge me with the priests, belie their thunderbolts!" (*La Tour de Feu*, special issue devoted to Miller).

At noon, appointment with Durrell on the terrace of the Dôme in Montparnasse. Tomorrow he will return to Sommières and he suggests I have lunch with him.

DURRELL   Henry hasn't aged a day, don't you find? He has that same mischievous, irresistible humor. And that marriage. What a phenomenon! With age, he has just become a little more serene. He resembles a Japanese Zen master more every day. Don't you think?

BRASSAÏ   I had the same impression when I saw him at Orly. He's so happy to be in Paris. This city is his birthplace, after all. Miller the writer was born here, on this terrace.

DURRELL   He still loves Paris, that's certain. But that love is now more nuanced. The other day, he told me: "One doesn't feel the need to be in Paris *all the time*. But sometimes, all of a sudden, it becomes an imperious and urgent necessity. Then I feel the irrepressible desire to go there, to assure myself with my own eyes that Paris still *exists*, that this city is still *there, within reach*. What would the world look like without it?"

BRASSAÏ   Obviously, it might have no longer existed. All it would have taken is for the German army to execute Hitler's instructions. The prestige of Paris prevailed over blind discipline. Even when he was living in Paris, Henry felt the need from time to time to "discover" the city. And I remember well his very apt remark: "One is not always conscious of the look of a city one lives in." That's profoundly true! One is always occupied with other things there. That awareness awakens only at rare moments, through fleeting images when you cross the Seine, the Tuileries, the place de la Concorde in a taxi or bus, or when, in the last glow of dusk, you perceive Sacré-Coeur on the hill of Montmartre from rue Lafayette. At bottom, to really feel Paris, you would have to leave it one day, to be able to come back with fresh eyes. Henry likes to discover it from the outside, from its peripheral districts: seen from Belleville, from Ménilmontant, from the porte des Lilas. He's been a prisoner of his success since his tumultuous arrival, and he now complains he's been unable to get in touch with the Paris he loves.

DURRELL   Isn't he a little bit responsible for that? That publicity ballyhoo! I understand he appreciates success. He was deprived of it for too long. But does he have to accept the thousands of requests? I've been in Paris for a week, expressly to see him, and I still haven't been able to have lunch or dinner with him even once. We were able to spend just a few minutes together with Hoki and Ghika in the Luxembourg Gardens and at the Closerie des Lilas. As for the "intimate" dinner the evening of the opening at Reine Christine, no thank you! Not with all those "supporters." It was really lacking in ambience. If only we'd been by ourselves!

And Durrell is also wounded that he cannot get close to Henry anymore without the irritating presence of his "secretary." "One can no longer exchange a private word in front of such a witness, who wants to know everything, listen to everything."

"I'm sorry," I tell Durrell, "not to see any letters from Anaïs Nin reproduced in Miller's correspondence with her. The dialogue has become a monologue: only Henry talks."

DURRELL I understand Anaïs. To publish letters, sometimes very intimate ones, while you're still alive, letters you never dreamed of making public, is an extremely delicate matter. For a very long time I too bristled at the idea that my letters would be divulged in my correspondence with Henry. In the end, I had to give in, but only after amputating everything that bothered me. And I was very annoyed when Henry, unbeknownst to me, donated our correspondence to the University of California. All the letters I sent him were in that batch. Since I was not considering publishing them, I sometimes got carried away telling secrets. It's very delicate, especially because of the wives, the children.

BRASSAÏ But in any case, they cannot be divulged without your authorization.

DURRELL Divulged, probably not. But all the academics have free access to that correspondence, can read it, consult it. [*Miller's marginal note:* "That's not true! H. M."] It's very troublesome. It may even lead to tragedy.

And Larry tells me the case of a person who learned through the publication of D. H. Lawrence's correspondence that he was a child conceived in adultery.

Robitaille telephones me: "As agreed, we'll be filming at your place this afternoon."

The filmmakers unload the equipment, set up the lights, load the cameras. Henry arrives. He tries to orient himself in the apartment and, when he rushes into the next room, the memories come back:

"It's around this table that we had dinner together, isn't it? What year was that?

BRASSAÏ 1953. Fourteen years ago! Two chairs are empty now: Reichel is gone, Eve as well. How did she pass away so young?

MILLER She drank whiskey at night. [*Miller's marginal note:* "Not only at night, but all day long. H. M."] And then, she took barbiturates. You know that certain tranquilizers, taken with alcohol, turn into lethal drugs. One night Eve went peacefully to sleep and never woke up again.

In my apartment, books, photos, negatives, and manuscripts are piled on the shelves up to the ceiling. The objects I like the most I had to box up and store away in my studio. Only a few naive paintings on the walls are left, and a few rare objects, beautiful or odd.

MILLER You like to amass things: Picasso, André Breton, the surrealists, they knew how to create a rather magical ambience around them.

BRASSAÏ Picasso's collector side always intrigued you. You asked me to tell you his horoscope and his planets in Virgo. Since I myself was born under that sign, for you that may explain my penchant for collecting. In fact, what is a photographer like me if not a collector of images, images that surprised him, that he liked?

MILLER   Yes, the virgin lighthouse. The house Goethe was born in. It's odd, but I never knew how to surround myself with things. I don't see a single object in my house to which I feel attached. Nothing worth preserving. Strange, isn't it? All my life I've been *detached* from everything. Everything was always replaceable and without too much effort, sadness, or pain. Of course, I like my house, but I don't like to be encumbered with furniture, artworks, or objects. If you ever come to Pacific Palisades, you'll see. There are only gouaches on the walls and inscriptions. I adore inscriptions! But, like you, I like the naïfs and the paintings of madmen. The first canvas that struck me in my life was a naive fresco painted on a dividing wall in my grandfather's house: a fat woman in profile with a poodle on a leash. That primitive picture impressed me for life.

Near my French window, I am working at an adjustable drawing table. In the foreground I see gardens, the chestnut trees on boulevard Arago and, in the distance, beyond the Seine, the hills of Belleville and Ménilmontant. But that view, which I like, is in part already obstructed by the growth of hideous new construction.

MILLER   It must be marvelous to work here with that view in front of you. And that big building in the foreground? Is that a prison?

BRASSAÏ   Yes, La Santé prison. In the very middle of Paris! An anachronistic relic, don't you think? Nine hundred cells and almost three thousand inmates! For the thirty years I've lived in this house, I've almost been part of the life of the convicts.

MILLER   I have sympathy for inmates, especially the adolescents who went wrong. I've always had a great desire to speak to them, to listen to their stories. "Real guys." As a child of the street, I myself might have become an apprentice gangster. That's why I'm interested in the fate of juvenile delinquents.

BRASSAÏ   In Missouri, I think it was, you even visited a lawbreaker who had become a good writer.

MILLER   Yes, in the state penitentiary in Jefferson City. His name is Roger Bloom, a bank robber. I corresponded with him and I went to the prison to boost his morale. I also took steps to obtain his freedom.

BRASSAÏ   Ilmer Gertz, your lawyer, says you were also involved in the fate of another convict, who also became a writer.

MILLER   Yes, Bill Witherspoon, a death row inmate. I had books, engravings, and tapes sent to him so he wouldn't feel isolated. I wanted to convey my feeling of friendship to him. And I was part of the campaign to save his life. I also wrote a letter to the governor.

BRASSAÏ   In France, it was Jean Cocteau who dedicated himself to getting inmates out of prison when they showed some poetic talent. Jean Genet was imprisoned here, at La Santé prison. A short while after he was liberated, he came to see me so I could do his portrait. I did it. One day, he came back in the company of a young "thug." He led him first thing out onto this balcony and showed him the prison. "See it? What is it?" "I don't know. No, I don't know." "You don't know? Look closely!" "No, really, I don't see . . ." "Imbecile! That's La Santé prison, where you just got out of!" "Really," responded the budding burglar, astonished, "I know it well from the *inside* but I'm seeing it from the *outside* for the first time."

MILLER   And can you see the inmates from here?

BRASSAÏ   Yes, sometimes I see their heads through the bars. They attach messages to the ends of string and pass them by swinging them from the window of one cell into another. Sometimes at night, they even emit Morse code. How? Well, simply by covering and uncovering the naked bulb that lights the cell. An accomplice writes them down and deciphers them in an apartment. And how many times have I heard a chorus of cries: "Our-bread-ev-ery-day! Our-bread-ev-ery-day!" or "Food-we-are-hungry! Food-we-are-hungry!" a chorus punctuated by the noise of saucepans and scrap iron. For me, it was almost a revelation. I understood how, when a crowd wants to express a common feeling, the strident cries, the thundering vociferations manage gradually to become organized into a rhythmic chant with a fixed form, so that it can be shouted in unison: "Our-bread-ev-ery-day," or "Food-we-are-hungry!" In that prison, I've seen fires, rebellions, executions. The most dramatic: riots broke out in the midst of the Occupation, on the night of a blackout. A few prisoners managed to break the heavy locks with their iron beds. I heard shouting in the corridors: "This-way-boys! Break-down-the-doors! This-way-boys!" In certain cells the torn-open straw mattresses were burning. Then, by the glow of that sinister fire, there was a fight to the death in the corridors. Guerilla warfare. By dawn, all the slave drivers were chased from the prison, the whole building was in the hands of the insurgents. Victory! But the heavy iron door remained hermetically sealed. No inmate could go through it, not one of them could escape. Then there was the backlash, the repression. With the help of German soldiers called to the rescue, and by means of tear gas, one by one the corridors were retaken by force, all the prisoners pushed back into their cells, and at dawn an improvised court martial condemned twenty-one "ringleaders" to death. I will never forget that sinister dawn! On three occasions, one hour apart, I heard the discharge of the firing squads. Every time, seven corpses bit the dust in the prison courtyard. And Marie, the housekeeper whose story I wrote down, who arrived at my place just as the second discharge of the firing squad was going off, kept lamenting like a Greek chorus: "What a pity, all those people they're shooting!"

MILLER   This adjustable wooden table, I like it very much.

BRASSAÏ   Do you know who it belonged to? Hans Reichel! During his move to the impasse de Rouet, for some reason he wanted to get rid of it and he sold it to me.

Miller, his eyes getting bluer and more transparent, looks at my "boxes," each bearing an inscription.

MILLER   Was it in one of these boxes that you buried the notes after your visits with Picasso?

BRASSAÏ   Yes, I found them again ten years later.

MILLER   What about these five or six boxes bearing the inscription: *Letters from Henry Miller?* Have we exchanged that many letters?

BRASSAÏ   You wrote me about two hundred letters. I must have lost some. Especially some of your first letters before the war. At that time you never dated them and often I didn't keep the envelopes. You usually put only "Thursday" or "Tuesday," and later, "March 6" or "June 10," without any indication of the year. Sometimes I had trouble sorting them.

MILLER   Anaïs was annoyed at my carelessness in that regard. She had the same problem as you. She's the one who insisted that I *date* my letters. And, since 1933, I have.

While we chatted, the filmmakers were shooting. We leave for my studio. The car heads up rue de la Tombe-Issoire, Henry's former stomping ground, the street the Villa Seurat opens onto. Here as well, an entire row of houses has been razed and an ultramodern building now stands there. In it, close to the sky, Georges Brassens and Jacques Brel compose their songs.

MILLER   The other day with the filmmakers, we went to the Villa Seurat to get a few shots. The current owner of my place gave us a very kind welcome. My studio has changed very little. But what a moving experience it was to see that place again!

My studio is very close by, in an old house of artists' studios, which are increasingly rare in Paris. They are unprofitable and are being destroyed so that ten-story buildings can be erected in their place. The little garden in the middle of the studios is filled with flowers and shrubbery. There are even vines that bear a few meager clusters of grapes in autumn. But the fig tree in the middle of the lawn died last year.

MILLER What a surprise! You carved all that in the stone? And in such hard pebbles? And all these marble sculptures! For me, they bring to mind the sculptures of the Cyclades and also their sensuality. You want to touch them.

BRASSAÏ Touch them, then, that's what they're made for!

My sculptures, my drawings, and also the engravings collected in the album *Transmutations* are filmed.

MILLER One questions is burning on my lips. You who practice all the arts, do you also have some connection to music?

BRASSAÏ My mother was a very good pianist and she wanted to play sonatas with her sons. So I learned the violin, as did my brother. I played fairly well for four or five years, and even in a symphony orchestra, then I abandoned it. If I had learned the piano, I might still be playing today.

We go by boulevard Saint-Jacques. There have been so many changes in this neighborhood! Almost nothing survives from the era of *Tropic of Cancer*! But, curiously, surrounded by new buildings, the large garden is still there. At the end of it, in a country house across from La Santé prison, lived Blaise Cendrars, Miller's dear friend.

BRASSAÏ Do you remember Cendrars's place? And here is a new building where Samuel Beckett now lives. I also run into him fairly often. He's almost my neighbor.

MILLER Samuel Beckett? It seems to me I met him for the first time in the office of Jack Kahane, the publisher at Obelisk Press. Some question of publishing the marquis de Sade's *120 Days of Sodom* in English. And Beckett was supposed to translate it. I don't know if he did. I also remember a discussion with Beckett about Joyce. I maintained that he was too attached to his god. Then one day, I read his play, *Waiting for Godot,* and I was amazed by it! [*Miller's marginal note:* "No! I didn't read it. I saw it at a theater. I even attended the dress rehearsal of the play. H. M."] And I observed: A great dramatic author is born. Samuel Beckett has found his way. One day, I was resting in a friend's apartment when a visitor rang the bell. I opened the door. It was Beckett. I embraced him warmly. Beckett is a great writer. He has learned how to create a strange world. I have a great deal of respect for him.

I ask him about his immediate plans.

MILLER Tuesday the 10th, we're probably leaving for Sommières, for Durrell's place, to spend five or six days there. The filmmakers are accompanying us. We may also go to Manosque. It would be very tempting to finally make Jean Giono's acquaintance.[1] At the end of the month, I leave with Hoki for Scandinavia.

CHAPTER 22

Friday, October 6, 1967

I have dinner with Henry in a bistro, near parc Montsouris.

BRASSAÏ That year you and June spent in Paris as "tourists" in 1928 is a riddle for me. What did you live on? You went all over France, visited Austria, Hungary, Romania, Poland, Germany. You stayed in good hotels, you lived the "good life"! [*Miller's marginal note:* "A slight exaggeration! H. M."] How could June have provided you with such a visit? Fred told me you did that tour of Europe "with pockets bulging with dollars" and that June had earned them thanks to her "talents as a taxi dancer." [*Miller's marginal note:* "Not true at all! She had earned them in a completely different way! And it was not at all a fortune! H. M."]

MILLER Fred's wrong. After all, he hated June. A violent, irrepressible hatred. He constantly inveighed against my wife, telling me repeatedly she wanted to destroy me.

BRASSAÏ Jealousy no doubt. Was he afraid she'd keep you apart?

MILLER That's possible. In any case, he was wrong! Brassaï, do you want to know where the dollars came from? At the time, June, to have more prestige with her "protectors," claimed she was a writer, that she was working on a novel. And one of her "patrons" had promised to finance its publication. So, to get the money, she presented him with one of my first novels, as if she were its author. And miraculously, the deception worked! She got her check. That's what allowed us to live in Europe for a year in 1928.

BRASSAÏ What astonishes me as well is your total silence about that year: "I had money, I visited Europe, I had no impediments and I was free." That's just about all you say about that period. One has the impression you mention it grudgingly. Was it because you were too unhappy?

MILLER   You're touching on a painful point. That year in Paris, I was in fact more unhappy than at any other time in my life. My suffering reached its peak. Until now I haven't said anything about it. It was too painful for me! In fact, it's the subject of *Nexus II,* the final book of *The Rosy Crucifixion.*

BRASSAÏ   Everything you say about that year attests more to your *disgust* with Paris than to your love of it. "Nothing had great meaning for me in Paris," you wrote. "I had had it up to here with the palaver. I was sick of the faces. I was tired of the cathedrals, the squares, the menageries, and the whole damn lot" (*Tropic of Cancer*). [*Miller's marginal note:* A big question mark. "H. M."] (Nevertheless, the quotation is accurate.)[1] And what you remember is not the streets you would later love so much, but the red wallpaper in your room on rue Bonaparte, the rattan armchair, the courtyard of the hotel with your bicycles, June's trunk, always open, with dresses scattered haphazardly, as if you had been sentenced to solitary confinement.

MILLER   At the time I was only a *tourist* in Paris. My eyes were not yet opened. For me, that city was limited to the Café Sélect, the Dôme, the flea market, the American Express office.

BRASSAÏ   Oddly, in that Paris of 1928, a single night stands out in your memory: the night before you went back to America, as if leaving that city was a real relief for you. Strange, don't you think? [*Miller's marginal note:* A big question mark. "H. M."] (Nevertheless, this passage appears in *Tropic of Cancer,* pp. 17–18.) But if Paris left you with such bad memories, why, once you were back in the United States, did you have only one idea: to come back as soon as possible?

MILLER   I wanted to escape America. And I didn't want to land in Paris, but in Madrid. You know that very well. It was for lack of money that I ended up in Montparnasse. I'll tell all about that in *Nexus II.*

BRASSAÏ   So how's that book going?

MILLER   I started to write it in 1959. I worked on it three years ago. I wrote some hundred and fifty pages. Then I had to interrupt it, and, since then, I haven't had the heart to pick it up again. Of all my books, *Nexus II* is the hardest to write, it's giving me the most trouble.

BRASSAÏ   Yet your keenest desire was to complete the cycle of *The Rosy Crucifixion.* You've often told me: "Only its completion will be the justification for my life."

MILLER   You're right. *Nexus II* should have tied up the threads of my autobiography.

BRASSAÏ   Maybe it's the finality you dread. You find the whole idea of an "ending" intolerable. Is that the reason for your lack of eagerness to finish *Nexus II*?

MILLER That's very possible! Basically, I'm loath to end it. Usually, when a man's task is completed, he dies, like Goethe after the second *Faust*. But there's another reason: there comes a time when talking about oneself becomes nauseating. And I'm weary of writing always and again about Henry Miller. As time goes by, the sequel to the autobiography is getting to feel increasingly pointless. I've already said enough about myself. I'm afraid I'll never finish *Nexus II.*

BRASSAÏ The unfinished symphony?

MILLER Yes, something must be left secret, mysterious.

BRASSAÏ There was also another project: *Draco and the Ecliptic,* which you said was to have been "the final stone of your autobiographical novels." Are you still thinking about it? You spoke of a "condensed, transparent, alchemical work, thin as a wafer and absolutely air-tight" (*The Books in My Life,* p. 52).

MILLER I've often thought about that book. You're right. And I imagined it would be very thin. It would have been a rapid overview, an explanation of all my works *seen from my point of view.* It would have contained my essential ideas about "autobiography."

BRASSAÏ Authors often remain blind to their own creations. Stendhal thought he was a "faithful mirror along a road." But his work is romantic, full of invention, daydreams, passion. It's far from a "mirror"! And what about Zola! Was he a cold "scientific" observer of the laws governing society? I see him rather as a lyrical author. And then there's Balzac. He wanted to be the "entomologist of the social species." But he was an ingenious creator of *types,* of *Balzacian* types. Don't you think so? The author is never the best judge of his work. He doesn't know any more about it than anyone else. Usually less. He doesn't have enough distance.

MILLER You're right: the author's voice is usually nothing but one voice among others. But it has its importance all the same. In my case, *Draco* would have been the voice of the medium who, coming out of her trance, begins to reflect lucidly on what has just happened to her, almost unbeknownst to her.

BRASSAÏ Isn't this Draco the white-bearded musician holding a heavy bunch of keys in his hand who has often appeared in your dreams? He looked like Noah or Mathuselah. You believed he held the key to the riddle, that he was at the center of your entire edifice.

MILLER That mysterious character is undoubtedly still myself, but another self, the oldest, the most intimate one.

BRASSAÏ What Proust called the *profound self?*

MILLER No doubt. It holds a secret. The secret of that something which I aspired with all my might to know and express.

BRASSAÏ   Henry, in your life you wrote a huge mass of letters. You were perhaps the greatest letter writer of the century. When all your letters come out of their hiding places, that will be very clear. Even in 1939—thirty years ago—you estimated the number of your letters at *twenty-five thousand*. The principal addressees were probably Emile Schnellock, Anaïs Nin, Lawrence Durrell, Alfred Perlès, June, and perhaps myself.

MILLER   I also sent many letters to three of my less well-known friends: Joe O'Regan, Bill Dewar, and Harold Ross.

BRASSAÏ   But since you often didn't keep a copy of them, the loss is enormous. Perlès, for example, didn't he lose all your letters? Hundreds of letters?

MILLER   Destroyed in the bombing of London.

BRASSAÏ   As Larry says: "Bombing can withstand anything." Many others are lost.

MILLER   That's clear, because I sent most of my letters not to artists and writers, but to unknowns I happened to meet in life, and who sometimes became my friends. No doubt they didn't think to save them.

BRASSAÏ   You often wrote just as spontaneously to writers and artists you didn't know, like Céline, John Cowper Powys, Jean Giono, Francis Carco, Hermann Hesse. The list would be long.

MILLER   There are people with whom one would like to be in touch. I don't find it at all ridiculous if someone writes me after reading my books. Nothing is more legitimate than to declare one's admiration for an author. Reading a book or magazine, I've often gotten all excited and have acted on my impulse without even wondering whether I'd get a response or not. And when that response came and I saw the signature of the one who had excited me, I was filled with joy. It brightened my whole day.

BRASSAÏ   You also wrote to Knut Hamsun, didn't you?

MILLER   Yes, at the time, he was one of my idols. His response was rather disappointing. An odd letter! Written by his secretary in very bad English. In it Hamsun complained that his books were selling poorly in the United States, and he turned to me, a poor devil who couldn't publish anything, for advice and help in remedying that sad situation.

BRASSAÏ   What about Count Keyserling, what did you write him about?

MILLER   In April 1936, after a four-month stay in New York, when I returned to Paris on a German steamship—huh, I've forgotten its name—from the library on the ocean liner, I borrowed *The Travel Diary of a Philosopher*. I was especially struck by the pages on Japan. But I also read the ones on China voraciously. One thing shocked me—revolted me—however. That great sage, that great "philosopher," was utterly devoid of humor! In China, he witnessed a "shocking" scene: Chinese sages surrounded by children were playing nonchalantly with kites. "An unworthy, ridiculous, distressing spectacle," he wrote. I, on the other hand, found it marvelous! The sign of superior wisdom, in the spirit of Nietzsche's "gay science." True seriousness is accompanied by gaiety, almost nonchalance. I thought of one of those good Chinese fellows, like Lao-tzu, prancing about on a zebu, with a large open smile. Yes, most philosophers in China possessed not only wisdom but humor! For us in the West, it wasn't until Rabelais that we saw humor given its true face, I mean its witty, emancipatory, iconoclastic face! When I arrived in Paris, I took my most beautiful pen and wrote a furious epistle to the sage of Darmstadt. "He'll never answer," I thought. But a few days later I received a long letter from him, written any which way, sometimes in French, sometimes in German, sometimes in English. That sage, that great old guy, wrote me with modesty and humility, acknowledging I was right and apologizing for having condemned the Chinese sages playing with kites.

BRASSAÏ And you answered him?

MILLER Yes, our correspondence continued. In his beautiful handwriting [*Miller's marginal note:* "No! An illegible handwriting! H. M."], I received several more letters from him—a dozen—all just as vehement. I then had Moricand make up his horoscope and also that of his eighteen-year-old son Manfred—who came to see me in Paris, by the way. We had dinner together one evening at the Villa Seurat. Alas, I never met Keyserling.

BRASSAÏ I heard several of his lectures, first in Berlin, then in Paris, in French.

MILLER You were lucky! I would have so liked to know him, to converse with him. I never had the chance.

BRASSAÏ Keyserling was a real volcano. At the end of the lecture, sweat was streaming from his forehead and his white goatee. He never had enough handkerchiefs to wipe himself off. I read almost all his books at the time. The most exciting was undoubtedly the one on the theme of "the reptilian world" in South America. Its title escapes me. [*Miller's marginal note:* "Its title in English: *South American Meditations*. H. M."]

MILLER I too consider that book his masterpiece.

BRASSAÏ Did you keep his letters?

MILLER They were all lost or destroyed, I think.

In fact, Miller did not keep any of the philosopher's letters. That is regrettable. And it was believed that those sent by him to Count Keyserling had been destroyed during the war, during the bombing of Darmstadt. But Henk Van Gelre, director of *The International Henry Miller Letter*, managed to recover four of them in the Keyserling Archives in Innsbruck. One of them is dated February 17, 1936, from New York, the other three from the Villa Seurat in 1938. Miller was thus mistaken in saying that his first letter to Count Keyserling dated from April 1936.

BRASSAÏ   And you haven't heard anything from Keyserling?

MILLER   Yes, I have. But indirectly. During my stay in Greece, I received a letter from a German baroness, Leonie Ungern-Sternberg, Keyserling's sister. The envelope bore a stamp from Manchukuo near Siberia. As a tribute to her brother, who was about to celebrate his sixtieth birthday, she was preparing a volume and asked me to contribute to it. It's the first serious article I wrote in Corfu. Too serious even: my tribute was almost an obituary.

BRASSAÏ   Your early letters were sometimes thirty or forty pages long. Don't you consider letter-writing a huge waste of time?

MILLER   Not at all! Between twenty-five and forty, when I was desperately aspiring to become a writer, letters were for me what shadowboxing is for the pugilist. They served as experiments, training. For example, it was by slipping into my letters all the bizarre, exotic words I wanted to add to my vocabulary that I tried them out. In my "literary" texts at the time, I was a "man of letters" to the bone. A real chameleon, I adopted the tone and style of the writers I admired, and I neglected the essential thing: the *vital* thing. A "literary writer" of the worst kind! That's what I was! And during all that time, until *Tropic of Cancer*, only my letters were *truthful*. It was owing to my correspondence, and not to my exercises in style, that I was able to preserve the speed, the naturalness, and the spontaneity of my style. With *Tropic* I killed the "literary writer" in me and rediscovered the style of my letters: free, open, spontaneous, flexible, alert, living.

BRASSAÏ   What about afterward, when you became a writer?

MILLER   At that time, very often my letters were the first drafts of articles and essays to come. The ones I sent to Anaïs from Dijon were used for the passage on Burgundy in *Tropic of Cancer;* a letter written to Hilaire Hiler, after being reworked and expanded, became the *Letter to the Surrealists.* I could cite many other examples. But my most important correspondence was undoubtedly with my best friend in America, Emile Schnellock: we went to public school together in Brooklyn. As you know, he was a painter and later headed the art department at a university in Virginia. Our relations were as intimate, as warm, as those between Vincent Van Gogh and his brother, Theo. I continued to write him throughout my stay in Paris and it is those letters that became one of the principal sources for my *Tropic of Cancer.*

BRASSAÏ   I myself discovered with surprise that the article devoted to me from *The Eye of Paris* was already drafted in two letters addressed to Frank Dobo.[2]

MILLER I've never kept a journal. My letters took the place of them. It was to others that I communicated my impressions, the fleeting events of my life. And it's in my letters that I clarified my ideas. When I see a beautiful or interesting thing, or when I've just finished reading a book that excites me, what is more natural than to tell someone about it, and then the whole world?

BRASSAÏ All the same, what an expenditure of energy that letter-writing must be! You insisted on replying scrupulously, I recall, to *all* your mail. Durrell used to smile at your grumbling about that chore: "Come on, come on," he wrote you, "you love it. The mere sight of a Chinese postage stamp could impel you to reply to a student."

MILLER It's true! And I wasted precious hours at it. But I felt I was communicating with the whole universe. And that contact excited me. The responses fascinated me, comforted me, stimulated me.

BRASSAÏ In December 1942, from Beverly Glen, you announced: "For two months, I have written *hundreds* of letters. Really! I wore out the typewriter and the pen—both are being repaired!"

MILLER It was only in Big Sur, when I was truly flooded with letters, that I decided to turn a deaf ear.

BRASSAÏ And resist the desire to respond.

MILLER Yes, but unwillingly. Not to reply to the requests causes me remorse even today. I put myself in the place of my correspondents. What are they expecting? Just a little note from Henry Miller, a piece of advice, a word of encouragement, a criticism, a judgment. How can I resist them? Was I myself not thrilled to receive a note from the writers I admired? Certain voices I perceive in their writing excite me. And I'm not the only one to have the letter-writing vice. Did you know Balzac wrote every day to the "Stranger?" And for twenty years? And he also got a letter every day from his beautiful Polish woman.

BRASSAÏ Then there's Juliette Drouet and Victor Hugo.

MILLER But when the count died and Balzac could have finally married Mme Hanska, could have brought her back to Paris, that was also the end. He'd been dealt a mortal blow, was dying; meanwhile, in a room nearby, his beautiful "Stranger" was making love to his doctor.

BRASSAÏ People doubt the veracity of that story.

MILLER Yet it's reported by all Balzac's historiographers. A beautiful epilogue, isn't it, to that great love, that twenty-year love correspondence! I love the description of Balzac's death agony by Victor Hugo in *Things Seen*. He was one of the last witnesses. On his deathbed, the author of *The Human Comedy* stank like a horse. And do you know the blackmail story? One day, in Balzac's house, blackmailers got their hands on a whole bundle of letters from Mme Hanska, proof of adultery. And to keep them from being presented to the husband, Balzac had to pay a very high ransom. But after he'd bought them back, do you think he kept them? Not at all! He said to himself: "If I keep them, sooner or later the same theft, the same blackmail will happen all over again. So into the fire!" And he burned all those cherished letters from his cherished mistress.

BRASSAÏ But you yourself had a very great love correspondence with June.

MILLER Alas! It's lost. A strange story! We had adopted the habit, June and I, of storing our letters in a large paper sack. One day, mysteriously, it disappeared. It took us a week to discover it was our housekeeper who'd thrown it in the garbage. June took the loss to heart. She's superstitious and saw it as a bad omen. I had to make inquiries with the garbagemen. The garbage dump was miles away. A friend of June's accompanied me. [*Miller's marginal note:* "No, it was a friend of mine. H. M."] We set to the task. Armed with canes, at the place likely to contain our letters, we began to poke through that steaming, smelly rot. A senseless task, of course! We discovered all sorts of curious or disgusting things, everything except the letters.

BRASSAÏ Do you keep the letters you receive?

MILLER At first, I had a tendency to keep them all. A weakness! Folly! But the vicissitudes of a life like mine, with the constant changes of domicile and country, made that impossible. I had to find the courage to tear them up. The first big auto-da-fé was at the Villa Seurat. It was even symbolic: it came shortly before the spark setting off the world war. On the eve of my departure for Greece, I burned all the letters that had been piling up, amassing for ten years. In Big Sur, from time to time, I also held days of destruction. I remember a tragicomic auto-da-fé. I had just married the young Janina Lepska, my "Pole." She'd graduated from college and, at the beginning of our marriage in the solitary house in Big Sur, I assigned a few secretarial tasks to her. "Will you sort that pile of letters," I told her one day, "and destroy all those you find without interest?" She set to work. But what a catastrophe! Her criterion of judgment was the opposite of my own. She threw into the fire all the letters that were a little bizarre, funny, weird, all those I might have received from fanatics, nuts, sexual deviants, the only ones that interested me. By contrast, she piously kept and stowed away the letters from snobs, pedants, academics, "thinkers," "philosophers," which I didn't give a damn about! So I was furious, I took all the packets remaining and crammed them into the blazing fire. It was a beautiful funeral pyre! The craziest, the most delirious letters I ever received were annihilated that day!

BRASSAÏ And how did you get the idea to donate your correspondence to the University of California, Los Angeles?

MILLER It wasn't my idea but my friend Lawrence Clark Powell's. And guess where I met him? In Dijon! He was studying at the Lycée Carnot, where I taught English for several weeks. What a surprise to find him again ten years later in Los Angeles! And when Larry Powell became the head librarian of that university, in 1948 or 1949, he suggested I put both my correspondence and my manuscripts in its archives. All my correspondence automatically makes it way there now and it's the librarians, not I, who sort and organize my letters in metal file cabinets. Thousands and thousands of letters are deposited there, stamped, dated, catalogued. As for Larry Powell, he's almost the only man I know who's happy with his work, truly embodying the best American tradition.[3]

BRASSAÏ What about the manuscripts?

MILLER Same thing. Except that six or seven of my major manuscripts, though deposited there, remain my property. If I need a large sum of money some day, I can auction them and get a good price.

BRASSAÏ Is the manuscript of *Tropic of Cancer* there as well?

MILLER Yes, miraculously! For a long time I considered it lost. When I left France for Greece in 1939, I gave a trunk to a friend to keep for me. It contained all my notebooks and manuscripts. Since the war broke out shortly thereafter, I had no further news. It was only after I'd settled in Big Sur many years later that I received my trunk one day. Imagine my joy! I couldn't believe my eyes. Everything was there, just as I'd left it. And all my manuscripts, *Tropic of Cancer* among other, will probably be worth a fortune one day.

BRASSAÏ The original manuscript was more than six hundred pages. And you cut it by half. Aren't you thinking about publishing the original version some day, as Durrell recommended?

MILLER What would be the point? I have a reputation for being incapable of condensing a text. But at that time, I made a considerable effort to prune *Tropic of Cancer*. A miserable task! Those corrections, those cuts gave me more trouble than writing the book.

It is amusing to follow that work of pruning. On January 22, 1933: "good and major changes." May 3: "I'm going over *Tropic of Cancer* with a fine-tooth comb. A little tiresome here and there, but good on the whole. I'll try to pull out the weeds." May 5: "I'm reading and rereading *Tropic of Cancer*. I am now making major changes in it. Especially cuts. I'm cutting everything that's not the right tone, that evokes other times, other moods, other powers" (letters to Anaïs Nin).[4]

BRASSAÏ But let's get back to your correspondence. For you, writing letters was also a way of turning up money, wasn't it?

MILLER Obviously. Since I'd become voluntarily and definitively unemployed, I was obliged to request funds from all the people likely to give them. I sent distress signals out into the world. The SOS of a shipwrecked man.

BRASSAÏ What was the result?

MILLER Nil! Silence and rejection most of the time. I had to write a pile of letters to receive a few rare envelopes containing checks or dollars. Even today, when I receive my mail, the letters that interest me most are those that have checks in them. I spot them immediately and open them first. Sometimes I've also had agreeable surprises: in addition to containing dollars or postage stamps, certain letters offered to house me, pay my rent, my meals. During the war, I dreamed of spending a year writing in Mexico. And to procure money for me, a major New York bookseller was kind enough to post my request. Obviously, I had no illusions about the result. A few weeks later, I received a letter from New York with two hundred and fifty dollars in it and the promise of a small monthly stipend for a year! Mischievously, the anonymous "donor" had signed his message "Harry Cover"—in French, *haricot vert*, string bean.

BRASSAÏ Just last night, I reread our "conversation" in Cannes on May 7, 1960. It was premonitory. We'd had lunch at the harbor with the Japanese woman. Do you remember? And you said: "I've always dreamed of living with a geisha."

MILLER Really, I said that?

Now Hoki, Henry's little Japanese wife, arrives looking smart and smiling. She has come to watch the television program devoted to her. On the little screen she is walking in front of Notre-Dame, la Saint-Chapelle, on the quays of the Seine, then she can be seen at the Closerie des Lilas. There she sings songs in Japanese, French, and English:

> What now my love
> Now that you left me
> How can I live
> For another day.

Henry leans toward his "geisha" and tells her, pointing to my manuscript: "Hoki, it's a prophecy! Seven years ago, I told Brassaï I'd like to marry a geisha. Our marriage was written in the stars."

CHAPTER 23

Wednesday, August 20, 1969

Returned from the Midi to meet Henry. This evening we are having dinner together with him and his son Tony. After more than seven years of vicissitudes, the film project based on *Tropic of Cancer* has finally worked out. In early July Miller came to Paris to participate in the filming. Through his letters, I was able to follow the incredible cinematographic misunderstandings:

SEPTEMBER 18, 1962 "I will surely be in Paris in the spring when the filming of *Tropic of Cancer* begins."

DECEMBER 13, 1962 "I just signed the contract for *Tropic of Cancer*. The independent producers are now trying to raise a million dollars. It will probably be filmed next spring. The producers, having learned of your extraordinary knowledge of Paris, begged me to write and ask if you'd be willing to collaborate on the film as artistic adviser. They'll pay you, naturally. And I'll spend seventeen weeks supervising the filming, for an additional salary. My friend Berine Wolfe will write the screenplay. He used to be Trotsky's bodyguard in Mexico. He also collaborated on the book by Mezzrow: *Really the Blues*. He'll probably go to Paris in February to explore the terrain (streets, brothels, bars, etc.). Can you help him?"

JANUARY 1, 1963 "I don't know yet if they'll begin filming in Paris in April or June."

JANUARY 14, 1963 "The 'producers' are thinking of going to Paris in March, but I'll come later. I hope you'll be there and not in Japan. Perhaps we can go *together* to Japan later."

APRIL 17, 1963 "I hope to come the end of May, but the exact date is not yet certain. I'll come with the 'producers' and my friend Berine Wolfe. I think I'll stay two or three months in Paris."

MAY 13, 1963 "Don't know yet when we'll arrive in Paris. Now the two 'producers' have fallen out. Therefore delays, complications. But I believe you'll see me in June."

JUNE 17, 1963 "A shame, but I'm not coming to Paris for the film before next spring, 1964."

DECEMBER 14, 1963 "The film project of *Cancer* is still paralyzed because of a quarrel between the 'producers.' In spite of everything, I believe it will be filmed in Paris, spring 1964."

SEPTEMBER 14, 1964 "Joseph Levine of Embassy Pictures settled his suit against the 'producers' and the way is now clear for *Cancer.* He's thinking of beginning the filming in *spring 1965* in Paris. I've lost all interest in the project. I know now that an author is at the mercy of those who finance the film. I'll go to Paris all the same, since I'm being paid (a great deal) extra to be an 'adviser.'"

MARCH 6, 1965 "I'm increasingly convinced they're going to massacre my *Cancer.* What can be done? The author counts for nothing."

JULY 31, 1968 (*three years later*) "The film of *Tropic of Cancer* will be definitively produced and directed by Joseph Strick, who made *Ulysses* (by Joyce). He'll do it the same way. No castration, no modification. Bravo for him, I say!"

JULY 9, 1969 "Here I am in Paris—until the end of August. Where are you now?"

JULY 17, 1969 (*letter written by Miller's secretary*) "Miller is participating in the filming of *Tropic of Cancer* until August 10. He ardently hopes you can find a few days in August."

MILLER Do you know Tony has become a photographer? I'm trying to write a book with him on all the Parisian spots I frequented. But what a difficult task! Many have changed, even disappeared. I haven't found the little hotel I lived in for a time near the Folies-Bergère. And I looked in vain for Au Rendez-vous des Machinistes, on rue Saulnier. Chez Paul, a bistro of pimps and whores near the Chicago Tribune, has also disappeared. I still remember the owner well. [*Miller's marginal note:* "His name was Gilotte. H. M."] Along the grands boulevards, we saw a rather erotic Japanese film. It's called *Michino Sex*, I think, which means *Anonymous Sex*, or *Nameless Sex*. It's not very good, but very instructive on Japanese mores. In the cheap housing, the rooms are separated by only a thin wood partition. So you hear all the noises from the neighbors, especially all the odd cries and moans of Japanese women in ecstasy. So one couple's excitement spreads to the adjacent rooms and the men and women can't control themselves. It's a film to see, I assure you. Under the influence of that film, I got up last night and wrote myself a screenplay—erotic and extreme, naturally. Another thing. I always wanted to ask you if you knew Alfred Stieglitz.

BRASSAï Alas, no. But just before the war, in 1939, Stieglitz, after seeing and liking my photographs, proposed an exhibition in his famous "American Place" on Madison Avenue. But he was already very tired and ill. We had to abandon the idea. I found one of his letters—it was rather heartbreaking—in his beautiful, authoritarian handwriting. "I would like to do your exhibition," he wrote me, "but I don't know how. I am literally alone. Alone, and sick at heart. And thus exhibitions have become increasingly exhausting for me."

MILLER I met him two years later, in 1941. He was seventy-seven at the time. His heart had already begun to fail. I sometimes saw him on the seventeenth floor of that commercial building in his little office adjoining the gallery. Mentally, he'd remained very young. What a man! All his life he let himself be guided by his enthusiasm. If he liked someone, he exhibited him for free, even if it meant making other exhibitors pay a great deal. You can't imagine that man's magnetism! He was stimulating. Every time I left his gallery, I felt inspired. I also knew Edward Weston. I spent a whole day with him in California.

But Henry is impatient to know how far I've gotten in my book on Henry Miller.

The birth of this book is closely connected to a few of my writings that had preceded it, and which Miller carefully followed. At the risk of being considered shameless, let me report a few of his judgments here, to show how stimulating he can be. When my *Story of Marie* was published in 1949, it enchanted him, and he insisted on writing the introduction. In 1952, after reading my autobiographical notes in *Brassaï,* he wrote to tell me: "I love your notes and the entire panorama you offer of fin-de-siècle boulevards." In 1959, I sent him my texts on graffiti, announcing at the same time that I was working on my *Conversations with Picasso*. Miller replied: "Impatient to see the book on graffiti. I'm reading the manuscript—it's fascinating, absolutely. And the book: *Conversations with Picasso!* Bravo! Don't delay!" (Big Sur, November 16, 1959). And a week later: "I've just finished reading your manuscript on graffiti and am very impressed. There are many things in this text that strike me—especially the idea of *creative perpetuity,* elaborated toward the end. I am very much in agreement" (November 22, 1959). Henry then offered to write the introduction to that book. "Dear Friend, send me the illustrations of the graffiti. I'll write a short text with pleasure—excerpts from Picasso: fascinating! No time to say more now" (Big Sur, December 9, 1959).

In 1962, after reading my essays on our friend Hans Reichel and the poet Pierre Reverdy, he wrote me: "I've just finished reading your essay on Reichel and I'm dazzled. I feel like you've said *everything*. Especially about his relation with Paul Klee. It's nice to read your allusions to Mozart, Bach, etc. (And Novalis!) Painting and music—everything you write about them is so true and of key importance. And everything you say about the man himself, his guardian angel and his demon—bravo, bravo! Let me shake your hand. No one could have done better. I want to keep the manuscript, reread it several times. There are passages that make me lightheaded!" (Pacific Palisades, June 17, 1962). "Once more, I am dazzled by your text on Reverdy, a poet I have never read, but whom I will now read—it's required. . . . In all sincerity, I want to say that you have a special gift as an interpreter (of painters and poets). I hope that, after my death, you will do for me what you've done for Reichel, Reverdy, Picasso, and who knows who else? It's too bad your writings aren't yet published here in translation. You have the makings of a very fine book" (letter to Brassaï, July 18, 1962).

And here is his first impression of my *Conversations with Picasso:* "There he is, Picasso, alive, naked, revealed—you have a genius for that! Bravo!" (Pacific Palisades, October 28, 1964). "I'm reading the book here and there, grazing like a nanny goat. Picasso is always fascinating, whether he's talking about the clothes he's purchased or whether he's philosophizing. He always hits the bull's eye. *I am sorry now that I didn't seize the opportunity to meet him.* You've certainly rendered him fully—from every angle, inside and out" (Pacific Palisades, November 13, 1964). "Another little note—I've gotten out of bed to write about your *Conversations* and the subject of Picasso. It's extraordinary how you brought him to life. *He's in front of me in the flesh.* He's no longer that 'terrifying monument,' but a man like us, though a very special man, almost unique. An approachable (and often adorable) giant, affectionate, intimate, and—despite his creative temperament—altogether human. I was surprised to discover he has a sense of humor—I sometimes laughed like a fool reading his words. Your book is therefore *priceless*. No one could give us that truth but you. Your ear has become as important as your eye. Bravo! And also your (friendly) writing hand. I hope our American publishers will be interested in doing a translation of it. And quickly. I tell my friends about this book all the time. I've even become Picasso's *Doppelgänger* (double). It happened while reading Thomas Mann's *The Magic Mountain* (thirty-five years ago).—I have not yet finished the book and *I don't want to.* I'll be sad when I find myself on the last page" (Pacific Palisades, November 25, 1964). "I finished your *Picasso* and am filled with admiration. . . . *You've given us a great tome*—Picasso must have danced with joy after reading it" (Pacific Palisades, December 11, 1964).

In 1964 I had informed Miller that I might write a book on him. Henry's response: "I'm delighted and honored that you'd like to write about me. I wrote Dobo the other day and said you were an astonishing writer. Certainly, the two books on Reverdy and Reichel were remarkable. I'm sure the one on Picasso will be likewise. I long to see it." And on the *Miller* I was thinking of writing: "*You are free to write on me as you like.* The only thing I'd like to be sure of is certain *facts*—dates, marriages, houses, etc. As far as your opinions or judgments go, *that's your responsibility.* (Perhaps if you thought of me as dead, it would help you to get everything in focus.) In a sense, I've already left this earth, spiritually speaking. What I hope is that you'll write poetically and with imagination, as you did with Reverdy and Reichel. I must tell you one more time that these two texts were *absolutely masterful.* Perhaps throughout your life the experience with other means of expression—painting-sculpture-photography—led you to this career as a writer" (Pacific Palisades, September 14, 1964).

The years went by. From time to time Henry asked me: "How far have you gotten with my portrait in words? I'm becoming more and more curious" (Pacific Palisades, January 19, 1966). "I'm becoming more and more impatient to see the book on Henry Miller" (Pacific Palisades, November 27, 1966). Then: "When are you thinking of finishing your book on me? I hope I'll be able to read it on this earth and not up in heaven" (Pacific Palisades, May 14, 1968). "Let me know how far you've gotten in the Henry Miller book. Would it be possible for me to read it before I die?" (Pacific Palisades, January 5, 1969). Four months later: "Have you finished the book on me?" (Pacific Palisades, April 26, 1969). And finally: "I'm delighted to know that your book (on me) is approaching its conclusion. I'm so curious to read it" (Pacific Palisades, May 18, 1969).

This time, I could satisfy his desire. My manuscript was completed, I could submit it for him to read.

MILLER I believe you speak in it of the prewar period, of the ten years we spent together in Paris.

BRASSAÏ It's much too well known, through Fred, through Anaïs, through yourself. I don't want to devote more than a *single* chapter to it, the only one still missing. The rest is an account of our many meetings after the war, up to today.

MILLER I'm curious to find out how you see me, how you judge me. And now that you know me *down deep*, what is your dominant impression? Chaos?

BRASSAÏ No, not chaos. *Contradiction!* In all areas without exception, you oscillate between extreme and opposite poles. In my view, you're the very embodiment of contradiction. And not only the contradiction inherent in human nature, half-angel, half-beast, but also that of modern man, of civilized man, split in two, in four, between increasingly irreconcilable, contrary desires. One day you dream of pure and chaste love, and the next you would like to jump the first "vulture" to happen by. Sometimes you desire virgin nature, never trod by man, at other times places that have been teeming with humanity since antiquity. At one time you put the passion to write above all else, another time you execrate "literature" and the only thing that counts for you is *to live*. Like the pendulum of a clock, you oscillate constantly, between the sense of being a genius, a superhuman man, and that of being a poor devil who made a mess of his life. When you're in America, you're homesick for Europe; when you live in the country it pains you not to be a city-dweller. Someone could do an anthology of your likes and dislikes, interchangeable depending on the moment, the mood, the era. In fact, don't you like Dostoyevsky and Powys precisely because they express the profound contradictions you feel within yourself? The Redeemer redeemed all men's sins. You are the Redeemer who took upon yourself all the contradictions that assail twentieth-century man.

A little while later, in an "interview" on French television, Miller said: "Do you know what my dominant characteristic is? Well, it's *contradiction!*—according to Brassaï, who's writing a book about me."

After reading the first version of the manuscript during his stay in Paris in summer 1969, Henry returned it to me, writing: "This part of the book is very interesting. I'm sure you'll make a very fine book out of it. I made a few notes in the margin" (Paris, August 29, 1969). I then began to compose the missing first chapter. But very quickly that text took on scope and a critical and poetic tone, in keeping with Miller's wish. In the end, it reached twenty chapters, the material for the first volume: *Henry Miller: The Paris Years.*

CHAPTER 24

Thursday, June 28, 1973

We are driving along the endless Sunset Boulevard, which goes through Hol-lywood, Beverly Hills, Westwood, and ends at the Pacific Ocean, in Santa Monica. Before us is Henry Miller's beautiful white home in Pacific Palisades. He is waiting for us in the doorway. I was afraid I'd find him a little weakened after his arterial operation. Won't he soon be eighty-two years old? But he is only a little more gaunt and slender. A Ping-Pong table dominates the large living room and the glass walls look out on the blue swimming pool sur-rounded by luxuriant vegetation: banana trees, palm trees, cacti, exotic plants.

BRASSAÏ Henry, I would never have thought that, after Big Sur, you'd settle in Los Angeles. When I look at the map of this city, crisscrossed with high-ways, I get dizzy.

MILLER The American way of life is becoming increasingly absurd. It fills me with horror. Since I wrote *The Air-conditioned Nightmare* thirty years ago, my country has become even more automated. Los Angeles is in fact the last city I would have chosen to live in. But one is not altogether free in one's decisions. Remember when I separated from Eve?

BRASSAÏ In 1961, I believe.

MILLER In the end, she was the one who stayed in Big Sur. I had to move somewhere. Valentine and Tony were studying in Los Angeles, and their mother, Janina Lepska, lived with them. Since I had a little money, I bought this house and moved here in 1962. And I don't regret it at all. The dry cli-mate is good for my rheumatism.

The proximity of Hollywood may have also played a role in Miller's choice. Twenty years earlier, in Beverly Glen, he had suffered so much that now he undoubtedly wanted to take his revenge by moving here as a famous author. For a long time, his house was always full of stars, starlets, and above all, *nisei*, the nickname for Japanese- and Chinese-American women. They exerted a great attraction on Henry: "I have love affairs and passing fancies, yes! with such beautiful young women from every corner of the globe," he wrote me. "It's ridiculous at my age" (letter to Brassaï, March 14, 1964). "I'm annoyed by the visitors. But I find nothing to say when it's a star or starlet who's invading—like Kim Novak, Gia Scala, Diane Baker" (letter to Brassaï, September 22, 1965). One day he announced: "I am thinking of going to Japan next spring. In the meantime, I may very well go to Hong Kong with two pretty Chinese women (one an actress, the other a script writer)" (letter to Brassaï, September 28, 1966). A month later, his secretary informed me that, beginning on December 15, Henry would be in Hong Kong, then, ten days later, that he would not go. "Hong Kong is a long way off now," he wrote me, "as if I'd taken that trip in another incarnation. There are several reasons for this *nonjourney*. First, a voice (like the one that troubled Socrates) that was always telling me: 'Don't go!' Second: the women (three, to be precise). A Japanese, a Chinese, and a Dane. I spare you the details. I'm happy not to have gone. Here there are always unexpected events" (letter to Brassaï, November 18, 1966). Ten days later, he wrote me: "Last night, it was the tenth evening in a row that I came home at three o'clock in the morning. I was at Bunny, the Chinese club in Los Angeles's Chinatown, in the company of a very beautiful Chinese actress—delicious. There is no lack of women here. Every night a different one" (letter to Brassaï, November 27, 1966). Finally, of all these *nisei*, it was Hoki who prevailed.

MILLER Of course, Los Angeles is an inhuman, nightmarish city, but this neighborhood is silent and peaceful, full of greenery. I don't live in the city but in my own house, within a limited circle of friends.

BRASSAÏ And, after twenty years, did you set up house with your ex-wife again?

MILLER Not set up house, we were "cohabiting." After all, she's the mother of my children. So we were living under the same roof. But during a trip to Europe, she met a man and asked me if her lover could live with us. A scabrous situation, don't you think? Even the children were shocked to have a stranger living in the house. I agreed, but it was not without clashes, altercations. And, one day, after a violent quarrel, she left, taking with her not only the children but also all the furniture: chairs, tables, armoires, rugs. They belonged to her. Suddenly, that big house was deserted. In truth, I was rather happy about that emptiness. Happy as well to have regained my solitude.

At the time, Henry informed me, in fact: "Now I live all alone in this big house—and without even a housekeeper. I do everything myself (as at the Villa Seurat). Good for the health!" (letter to Brassaï, November 27, 1966).

MILLER   I had so much space in all those empty rooms that I could roller-skate on the bare floors.

BRASSAÏ   What about Hoki, your Japanese wife?

MILLER   We separated but have remained on good terms. From time to time she comes by to say hello. The other day she prepared us a good dinner. What's she doing? She opened a high fashion boutique.

A pretty, very petite blonde appears, loaded down with Henry's mail. She is going to the post office.

MILLER   That's Conny, my secretary. She's perfect except that I have to type my own letters. I had the same difficulty with my former secretary, Ro-bitaille. He never wanted to write what I dictated to him. He always changed my idea to suit himself. By the way, have you read his book *Papa Miller*? Very nasty, smutty even! Don't you think? Full of lies! And I gave that man my friendship and my full confidence! He was a friend, now he's turned into an "enemy." When he announced that he wanted to leave me, I was in agreement. If I had any scruples, it was about him and Diane. They lived in poverty in Paris. What will become of them? Nothing obliged me to give him any compensation. He left me all of a sudden, of his own will. I offered him a few thousand dollars. And I have to laugh! Because it's with *my* money that he was able to write that nasty book *against* me. Ha-ha-ha! Henry Miller financing *Papa Miller*! What a moron I am! Ha-ha-ha.

The evening of the breakup took place at Stéphaninos, the most high-class restaurant in Hollywood, where the "secretary" had invited his "boss." Henry guessed right away what he was brewing up. "Bravo Gerald!" he told him. "I knew very well you wouldn't want to be someone else's shadow your whole life." And the secretary declares: "He had such affection in his voice, such sincerity, like I had never known." Miller, after questioning him about his plans in Paris, then proposed: "You know, I wanted to offer you a trust fund of ten thousand dollars in case I were to die. Well, I'll give you that amount, it will help you get settled again in Paris."

How to explain that "betrayal"? Robitaille had probably had enough of Los Angeles: "Better to die in Paris like a beggar," he wrote, "than to be force-fed starlets, *nisei*, hippies, Ping-Pong, and Hollywood swimming pools." And he added: "Of course, it's not him I'm abandoning, it's America. I can't go on! His 'air-conditioned nightmare'—let him have it, since he loves it so." But it was also, obviously, the son's revolt against the father, against that "Chinese bonze" who formed him, molded him. What he could not forgive was that he owed him everything. Robitaille felt that, during the four years he spent in his service, his guru had taken hold of his life, that he no longer existed on his own, but only in him, through him, for him. He felt crushed under the weight of that giant, "crushed like a bug!" And it was to liberate himself from him that he had to "kill the father."

Tony, who has become a tall and handsome young man, is preparing dinner for us. He busies himself with an enormous hunk of Charolais beef rib, cooks broccoli and potatoes Lyonnaise. The pretty girl in a bathing suit helping him is Diane, his ex-girlfriend. She is now taking care of Henry's house. Tom, the bearded young man, a filmmaker Miller treats somewhat like his own son, is producing a short film: *Henry Miller Asleep and Awake.* "You'll see him sleeping," he tells me. "He wakes up, goes to the toilet. Because his toilet is also a print room. Do you want to see it?" On all four walls, pressed tight against one another, are drawings, engravings, photographs, evoking all Miller's friends. I am represented by my "Chair at the Tuileries" from 1930, which Henry particularly liked. "So he'll give a tour of the toilet," Tom explains to me, "mentioning the people who played a role in his life." Another regular at the house is the usual Ping-Pong partner, Sava Nepus. A Russian, he speaks French better than a Frenchman, having lived in Paris for eighteen years. Enthusiastic about jazz from the heroic age of the blues and ragtime, he was a friend of Huge Panassié, the "French pope of jazz," founder of the Hot Club, and also a friend of Charles Delaunay, Django Reinhardt, the gypsy guitarist, and Stephane Grappelli, the incomparable jazz violinist.

MILLER So you visited Big Sur. *Finally!*

That "finally" summed up our many empty promises and Henry's impatience to welcome us to his eagle's nest. For years, to attract us, he sent us a mass of illustrated documentation about that wild coast. "Did I send you the Big Sur Guide? The photos will give you an idea of this region. We are situated a little like you in Eze. Alas, we don't have Nietzsche here, but idiots and assholes, of course. Tell me, my dear Brassaï, could you come here some day? We're still expecting you." Fred, who had managed to take a trip to Big Sur, added on the same sheet: "It's as if the Villa Seurat had been transported to the virgin forest! The same atmosphere, the same conversation, the same appetites as in the past. You and Gilberte would like this magnificent region, wild and delicate at once. Is there a chance you'll come? The Millers would welcome you with open arms" (letter from Miller and Perlès, December 11, 1954). "The idea that Gilberte and you might come to our place excites us," Henry wrote us two months later. "*You must come to Big Sur. You'll be enchanted"* (letter to Brassaï, February 1, 1955). And, a year later: "If you and your charming wife come to America next spring, make a big effort to see us here in Big Sur. *We can put you up!* And arrange to see the Grand Canyon in Arizona. Stop at the Bright Angel Lodge. You won't see a thing like that twice in a lifetime!" (letter to Brassaï, September 1, 1956).

BRASSAÏ I was happy to get to know Big Sur. That cliff! That view of the Pacific! And I understand your obstinacy in living there so long.

MILLER And did you meet Valentine, my daughter who lives there now? And Emil White?

BRASSAÏ Valentine was away. We had dinner with Emil White in Carmel.

MILLER Emil was my salvation! Often he collected wood for us in the forest, sawed it, cut it, repaired everything that was loose, leaking, or falling apart. He even built a cart for me to get the mail in. And did you visit the Grand Canyon in the Colorado River? I dreamed of seeing it for thirty years. The most fantastic, the most grandiose thing you can see in the United States, insanely beautiful! Usually, don't you find, one is rather disappointed by the sites from which one expected too much for too long. But the Grand Canyon was truly beyond everything I imagined.

BRASSAÏ We weren't able to see it. Next time. America is so rich in natural beauties.

MILLER Thank God they're not yet spoiled, unlike our cities. But I fear it's only a matter of time. You ought to see Colorado, New Mexico, Utah, Arizona, still wild and almost unexplored regions, the territories of the Indians, the race we massacred, almost exterminated.

BRASSAÏ I too was able to see something I'd been dreaming about for a very long time. At the Jardin des Plantes I often stopped with astonishment in front of the cross-section of a sequoia trunk, *twenty-five hundred years old!* Inlaid on the annual rings, written on small silver plaques, are the historical events of Greece, the Roman Empire, the birth of Christ, and the entire history of the West. A living thing, witness to twenty-five hundred years of history! That's beyond all understanding! If only I could see those millenary trees standing in California some day! And it was everything I could have wished for! We were able to visit both Muir Woods in Mill Valley north of San Francisco and Mariposa in Yosemite National Park. Those giants, twice as tall as Notre-Dame, never lose their leaves, are impervious to the seasons, nothing changes for them! The very picture of duration, if not of eternity, they must possess a mysterious elixir (which no scientist has yet studied) to withstand, for millennia, illnesses, microbes, insects, fungus, storms, lightning. Yes, the extraordinary thing is that they withstand even fire. Sequoias are related to resinous conifers—pines, firs, larches—which easily fall prey to flames; but, unlike them, they must secrete a flame-resistant substance. So the fires that have often ravaged forests at the foot of these giants could only lick and blacken their trunks. I spent unforgettable hours in those sequoia sanctuaries.

MILLER It's odd, I've lived in California for a long time, but I've never visited them. They must be marvelous.

This is especially surprising to me since, in the area of Big Sur itself, there is a small forest of sequoias.

BRASSAÏ Do you work much?

MILLER I've become very lazy. Sometimes I look at my abandoned typewriter with a guilty conscience. Basically, I've said everything. Now I write only when I get a shock, like the tragic and horrible death of Mishima. It affected me more than Hemingway's suicide, especially because I met him once in Germany. You know how Japan excites and intrigues me. Despite my great sympathy, that country remains impenetrable to me, enigmatic. What was Mishima after in killing himself in the flush of youth? Did he want to keep his country from the path of modernization? Remind it of the traditions of ancestral life: *the Samurai spirit?* Wake up his compatriots, force them to change their ways?—Those are questions I ask myself and ponder. That's the article I'm working on at the moment. But basically, I prefer to paint. It gives me more pleasure. And I observe with astonishment that the older I get and the more my body disobeys me, the younger I feel! I'm even becoming more romantic, more anarchical than before, open to every sort of folly.

BRASSAÏ Every sort of folly in love?

MILLER Why, yes! And I'm in love again. In love with a Chinese actress. Beautiful, seductive. Her name is Lisa Lu. Let me show you her photograph. The only thing one never reaches the end of is love! And every woman, every love affair is a new adventure. New suffering as well, since the mind, which has remained young, doesn't want to hear the dictates of age.

What fervor, what youthful enthusiasm, what openness, what curiosity after more than eighty years! It is such youth of mind, I think, that Goethe called *the second puberty.*

MILLER When I fell in love with Hoki, I was tormented by jealousy. She sometimes told me she was going to spend the evening with her sister or a Japanese girlfriend. And she didn't come home. I suffered from insomnia when she was gone. What loneliness! I was down in the dumps, in a rage. What could I do! Scream out my jealousy, my despair? Smear the wall with insults? Yes, I did that. Then, one day, I told myself, why don't I paint, why don't I write those *bad thoughts* that the devil dictates to me? And that is how *Insomnia, or the Devil at Large* was born. My French translator proposed the title: *L'insomnie ou le diable en liberté*. But I was not entirely satisfied. "En liberté" does not adequately convey the wickedness of the devil, capable of evil tricks. Do you have an idea, a title to propose to me?

BRASSAÏ Perhaps *L'insomnie ou le diable qui rôde*, or *L'insomnie ou le diable évadé*,[1] which would indicate he can be dangerous. Do you still suffer from insomnia?

MILLER Every night at about ten o'clock, I retire to my room, look at the late news on TV, go to bed, and fall asleep. But an hour later I wake up and the insomnia keeps me awake till dawn. So I write, paint, or take care of my correspondence. Naturally, I get up late, skim the *Los Angeles Times*, have my cup of coffee and my bowl of corn flakes, then I go swimming for about twenty minutes. Apart from Ping-Pong, that's my only physical exercise. But the swimming pool has to be heated day and night, which causes problems and costs me a great deal.

BRASSAÏ And do you go out much?

MILLER Very rarely. Twice a month—two Tuesdays—I go to my Japanese doctor, Dr. Vatanabe, for my osteoarthritis. The same day I also see my cardiologist. Twice a month—a more agreeable outing—I attend, at the home of the famous pianist Sasha Gimpels, classes with his students. Some already play very well. Sometimes he plays the piano himself. And that's a treat. Otherwise I almost never leave the house. I have too much pain walking and there's even the prospect of another operation.

He speaks of his physical ailments without bitterness and with detachment, as if he were speaking of someone else. In one of his letters he wrote me: "Sometimes I laugh myself. . . . My body is beginning to be 'dilapidated.' When I suffer (from pain), I laugh. It's appalling and loony at the same time. It's idiotic!" (letter to Brassaï, March 6, 1968).

BRASSAÏ Do you still play the piano?

MILLER No. I've completely given it up. I didn't have enough talent. But I adore music! Something loftier than painting or literature. Whether I'm writing or painting, I work better listening to one of my favorite pieces. And even while I'm playing Ping-Pong, music stimulates me. Scriabin's sonata for piano, for example, which I love. It's my favorite piece, in fact.

I look at the walls covered with Miller's gouaches, paintings, photographs, and especially photomontages. But three large collages of fabric in delicate colors are the work of the painter Varda, who died recently in Monterey. It was he who let Henry live in his red barn and led him to discover Big Sur. And here is a portrait of an old Chinese man. I wonder what sage it depicts. "Don't rack your brain!" he tells me. "It's the portrait of an unknown. I found it in a magazine and had it framed. He's my master! That kind face, that benevolent smile, and especially the expression in the eyes profoundly struck me. I would like to be like him, to look at the world with the same detachment, the same love as he does."

The shelves of an entire wall are filled with Henry's books, which, with the countless translations, now number several hundred. A fantastic output when one considers that he only began to publish when he was forty-three. The walls of another room where he paints his watercolors are covered with scrawls, graffiti, and words: swear words, quotations, maxims, proverbs, curses. Since he invites all his visitors to inscribe something on his walls, you find them in every language: German, Russian, French, Japanese, Chinese. Sometimes at night, during the hours of insomnia, he gets up and himself inscribes an extraordinary sentence he has just read or that is going through his brain.

But Henry is impatient to show that, at eighty-two years old, and in spite of his operation for osteoarthritis, he has preserved his physical vigor. After one game of Ping-Pong with me, he plays another with Gilberte.

The dinner is excellent, accompanied by good French wine. And we talk about friends. Perlès has left Greece for Cyprus, and Durrell, who has recently come to Los Angeles, was giving lectures at the university. And what about Anaïs Nin?

MILLER She's left New York and now lives here, in Los Angeles, near Silver Lake in the center of the city, in a very modern building, built by the son of the architect Wright. Did you know she is now in the forefront of "women's liberation," that she has acquired a very great reputation? She gets asked for autographs like Liz Taylor. It's funny, don't you think? Do you remember that puny and timid creature? She now faces crowds with pleasure and authority, gives lectures, participates in political meetings, and gets applause.

I think of that other woman—is she still alive or dead?—who marked Henry's life even more profoundly and of whom he wrote: "In the tomb which is my memory I see her buried now, the one I loved better than all else, better than the world, better than God, better than my own flesh and blood" (*Tropic of Capricorn*, p. 231).

BRASSAÏ What about June? Where is she? Is she still alive?

MILLER Yes, she's alive, but can you still call that *living*? Old, ill, penniless, she's ending her days in a nursing home in New York. I help her out as I can. Sometimes she still sends me little love letters, just to tell me she's still thinking of me, her "dear Val."

BRASSAÏ Have you seen her?

MILLER Yes, and it was awful! She wanted me to stay and have dinner with her. But I was so sad that I ran away crying.

Even ten years ago, Henry wrote me that June "had lost all her beauty."

BRASSAÏ June was an admirable creature. She sensed your gifts, had a blind faith in your vocation as a writer, even though nothing yet justified it. And she did everything to see you'd be a writer, a great writer.

MILLER Yes, June was an exceptional creature, and if I hadn't met her, I might have remained a failure and no one would know my name. She's also the one who provided me with the major subject for my books: Would *Tropic of Capricorn, Sexus, Plexus*, and *Nexus*, exist without her? She's the one who delivered me from the horrible telegram company where I'd been a slave for five years. "Dump that awful job!" she told me. "You must write!" She's the one who took me to Paris, who formed me, who literally transformed me. So I named her MONA, *the only one, the unique!* It's only now, looking back at my life, that I can measure her greatness and devotion.

We have coffee. Tony tells his father: "Dad, don't forget that tomorrow afternoon Barbara is coming to visit you."

Barbara—Barbara? Could that be Henry's daughter, the one he abandoned? For me, that name evokes one of the most poignant scenes Henry wrote, worthy of Dostoyevsky. After he abandoned his wife, the pianist Beatrice Sylvia Wickes, and his little girl for June, he still paid them a few rare and brief visits, then never concerned himself with them again. Feeling as guilty as "hell," he remembered with remorse the last horrible scenes with Barbara. "The child screaming and clinging to me, begging me to stay and sleep with mama." Or his enormous, intolerable sorrow, his tears even, when Barbara put her arms around his neck, kissed him tenderly, and called him "dear daddy" (*Plexus*, p. 69). The desire to see his daughter constantly gnawed at him. One day, he went out to their old house and kept watch. And suddenly, among the children playing in the yard, he caught a glimpse of Barbara. He wanted to rush over, take her in his arms, but his apprehension held him back.

Wouldn't she be afraid of her own father, now a shaggy, ragged stranger? Wouldn't she take him for a sex maniac? "And to think that maybe I would never see her again," he told himself. "Her own father crouching in a doorway, spying on her like a kidnapper. It was like a horrible cheap movie." And Miller adds: "I would pray, yes, pray to God, to give one more chance. I *must* see her and talk to her . . . someday when she would be able to see things in a better light. I begged God not to let her hate me" (*Plexus*, pp. 390–91). He had spoken to me as well of Barbara, forty years ago: "I was so cruel to my little girl. I wonder if I'll ever see her again. I love her. But will Barbara forgive me?"

Could Henry's prayer have been answered, then? Had his daughter forgiven him?

MILLER   Why yes, it's my daughter Barbara. The one I abandoned. I saw her thirty years later, in 1955. She was thirty-six at the time. She's forgotten the past. She loves me. She doesn't reproach me for anything. A very sweet creature, really. No, she never married. She's in real estate. From Pasadena, near Los Angeles, a few miles from here where she lives, she sometimes comes to see us.

While he was talking, Henry lit one cigarette after another.

BRASSAÏ   What, you're smoking? Didn't the doctors absolutely forbid you to use tobacco?

MILLER   Yes, they forbade it. And *absolutely*. But haven't I reached the age of eighty-two while smoking heavily? Not bad, huh? Next December 26, I'll be *eighty-three*, Goethe's age! So why would I deprive myself of the pleasure of smoking?

SPRING 1953

1. [Henry Miller, *Letters to Anaïs Nin,* ed. Gunther Stuhlmann (New York: G. P. Putnam's Sons, 1965), p. 186. Hereafter cited in the text.—trans.]
2. [Henry Miller, *Remember to Remember,* vol. 2 of *The Air-conditioned Nightmare* (New York: New Directions, 1947), p. 306.—trans.]
3. [Henry Miller, *The Air-conditioned Nightmare,* vol. 1 (New York: New Directions, 1945). Hereafter cited in the text. The passage appears not in the chapter entitled "Vive la France" but in the previous chapter, "Good News! God Is Love!"—trans.]
4. [This passage does not appear in *Aller Retour New York.* It is therefore my translation from the French.—trans.]
5. [In *Lawrence Durrell and Henry Miller: A Private Correspondence* (New York: E. P. Dutton, 1963), pp. 288–89.—trans.]
6. [Ibid., p. 289.—trans.]
7. [Ibid., p. 302.—trans.]
8. [*Big Sur* is the title of the French translation of Lillian Bos Ross's *The Stranger.* For this translation Miller wrote an introduction, which is not available in English.—trans.]
9. [Henry Miller, *The Books in My Life* (New York: New Directions, 1969).—trans.]

SUNDAY, APRIL 19, 1959

1. [Henry Miller, *Big Sur and the Oranges of Hieronymus Bosch* (New York: New Directions, 1957). Hereafter cited in the text.—trans.]

THURSDAY, APRIL 30, 1959

1. [Henry Miller, *Tropic of Capricorn* (New York: Grove, 1961). Hereafter cited in the text.—trans.]

APRIL 9, 1960

1. [Henry Miller, *Plexus* (New York: Grove, 1965). Hereafter cited in the text.—trans.]
2. [*Lawrence Durrell and Henry Miller,* p. 73.—trans.]
3. [Ibid., p. 97.—trans.]
4. [Ibid., p. 230.—trans.]

SUNDAY EVENING, MAY 8, 1960

1. [The synopsis to *The Rosy Crucifixion* is apparently not available in English. This is therefore my translation from the French.—trans.]
2. [This passage does not appear in the American edition of *Max and the White Phagocytes*. It is therefore my translation from the French.—trans.]

TUESDAY, MAY 10, 1960

1. *Maurizius Forever* (San Francisco: Colt Press, 1946).

FRIDAY, MAY 13, 1960

1. Miller is right: his very first article published in France was "Cirque Médrano," but it appeared, I think, in Samuel Putnam's *New Review* and not in the *Herald Tribune*.
2. At age seventy, Michel Simon was finally able to return to the Théâtre de l'Ambigu after four years of inactivity. The same year, he began a new career as a music hall singer.
3. [Miller, *Letters to Anaïs Nin*, p. 44.—trans.]
4. [Marcel Proust, *A la recherche du temps perdu*, ed. Pierre Clarac and André Ferré (Paris: Gallimard, "Bibliothèque de la Pléiade," 1954), vol. 3.—trans.].
5. [Ibid., 2:352.—trans.]
6. [Ibid., vol. 3.—trans.]

FRIDAY, MAY 13, 1960 (CONTINUED)

1. Since then, a commemorative plaque has been placed at the entrance to the village.

FRIDAY, MAY 13, 1960 (CONTINUED)

1. Proust, *A la recherche du temps perdu*, 1:221, 362–63.

TUESDAY, MAY 17, 1960

1. [*The Diary of Anaïs Nin*, vol. 1: *1531–1534*, ed. Gunther Stuhlmann (New York: Harcourt, Brace & World, Inc., 1966), p. 8.—trans.]
2. [Henry Miller, *The World of Sex* (New York: Grove, 1965), p. 12.—trans.]

OCTOBER 1960

1. In 1966, at the twentieth Cannes Film Festival, when Antonioni won the Grand Prize for his film *Blowup*, he made a declaration to the press: "I will never forget that horrible evening seven years ago when, in this very room, *L'Avventura* was welcomed with protests and whistles. A disaster. . . . Monica Vitti, my wife, giving in to a fit of nerves, cried all night. I consider this prize, not exactly revenge for *L'Avventura*, but an event that will partly erase my sad and bad memories" (*Nice Matin*, May 15, 1967).

SUMMER 1962

1. [*Lawrence Durrell and Henry Miller: A Private Correspondence*, p. 87.—trans.]
2. *Zéro de conduite* (Zero for conduct) is the title of one of the three films of the French nonconformist filmmaker Jean Vigo, who died at age twenty-nine.
3. Frau Gerhardt wore a "Joan of Arc," close-cropped hairstyle; hence the name I gave her.

TUESDAY, SEPTEMBER 19, 1967

1. But Bibalo wrote: "In Big Sur, California, Miller welcomed me with the grace of his generous heart, with such compassionate, helpful kindness" (*Synthèse*, Brussels, February-March 1967).

2. [Henry Miller, *Nexus* (Secaucus, N.J.: Castle, 1965).—trans.]
3. [This passage does not appear in the American edition of *Tropic of Capricorn*. It is therefore my translation from the French.—trans.]

TUESDAY, OCTOBER 3, 1967

1. In the end, Miller had to abandon his plan to make Giono's acquaintance and to film at his home, and he never did meet him.

FRIDAY, OCTOBER 6, 1967

1. [This passage does not appear in the American edition of *Tropic of Cancer*. Therefore, it is my translation from the French.—trans.]
2. Both versions have been reproduced in *Henry Miller: The Paris Years*, chap. 4.
3. It was Lawrence Clark Powell who, in 1950, had the idea of publishing *Lawrence Durrell and Henry Miller: A Private Correspondence*. By chance, Henry's letters had been preserved in England in the attic of Alan Thomas, one of Durrell's best friends.
4. [These passages do not appear in the published editions of Henry Miller's letters to Anaïs Nin. They are therefore my translation from the French.—trans.]

THURSDAY, JUNE 28, 1973

1. [*Rôder* means "on the prowl," *évadé*, "escaped."—trans.]